AL-QA'IDA'S DOCTRINE FOR INSURGENCY

AL-QA'IDA'S DOCTRINE FOR INSURGENCY

'Abd Al-'Aziz Al-Muqrin's
A Practical Course for Guerrilla War

TRANSLATED AND ANALYZED BY
NORMAN CIGAR

FOREWORD BY JULIAN LEWIS

Potomac Books, Inc.
Washington, D.C.

Library of Congress Cataloging-in-Publication Data
Muqrin, Abd al-Aziz, 1973–2004
    Al-Qaida's doctrine for insurgency : a practical course for guerrilla war / translated and Analyzed by Norman Cigar.
        p. cm.
    Includes bibliographical references and index.
    ISBN 978-1-59797-252-9 (hardcover : alk. paper) — ISBN 978-1-59797-253-6 (pbk. : alk. paper)
    1. Guerrilla warfare—Saudi Arabia. 2. Qaida (Organization)—Handbooks, manuals, etc. I. Cigar, Norman L. II. Title. III. Title: Practical course for guerrilla war.
    U255.S38M87 2008
    355.4'25—dc22

                                                            2008043561

Printed in the United States of America on acid-free paper that meets the American National Standards Institute Z39-48 Standard.

Potomac Books, Inc.
22841 Quicksilver Drive
Dulles, Virginia 20166

First Edition

10 9 8 7 6 5 4 3 2 1

Dedicated to my mother, Amalia, and the memory of my father, Slavko.

CONTENTS

FOREWORD

One of the most striking ideas in the military chapter of Sir Thomas More's *Utopia*, written in 1516, is its emphasis on targeted assassination. Once a war is declared, Utopians "promise great rewards to such as shall kill the prince, and lesser in proportion to such as shall kill . . . those on whom, next to the prince himself, they cast the chief balance of the war." Even in the heat of battle, shock troops "single out the general of their enemies, set on him either openly or by ambuscade, pursue him everywhere . . . so that unless he secures himself by flight, they seldom fail at last to kill or to take him prisoner."

Thus, a technique regarded in this day and age as symptomatic of terrorism was advocated almost five hundred years ago as an entirely ethical course of action. One does not need to be a moral relativist to understand the logic of insurgents who—believing that God is on their side—view Western codes of warfare as murderous and illegitimate, and terrorist techniques as sanctified and just. This book is not about morality but about efficacy.

Norman Cigar has applied his encyclopaedic knowledge of military doctrine and Middle Eastern politics to select and preserve what is in effect the field manual of Al-Qa'ida in Saudi Arabia. It will be of consuming interest, not only to scholars and analysts, but also to those in government involved with the consequences of militancy in parts of the Islamic world. Whilst there is a vast body of work commenting on developments both before and after September 2001, much less attention has been paid to what the militants actually reveal about their own methods. Their exploitation of the Internet as a means of communication and training offers their adversaries a window on their world.

One of the virtues—if such a term may be applied in this deadly context—of 'Abd Al-'Aziz Al-Muqrin's *Guerrilla War* is its utilitarian focus. Only occasionally does ritual obeisance to Al-Muqrin's perceived Holy Cause surface in his text. The practical actions he details and recommends could be transplanted, for the most part, into the context of any other revolutionary movement on the extreme left or extreme right. Extreme political movements—even those which appear directly to contradict one another—have a great deal in common. Their advocates share an absolute certainty that nothing must obstruct the One True Doctrine to which they subscribe. Their opponents can, and must, be pitilessly destroyed. This uncompromising stance has featured in extreme interpretations of religion in previous centuries, and in the secular totalitarianism of Communism and Nazism more recently. Indeed, the threat currently posed by militant distortions of the Islamic faith unhappily combines the worst elements of all three: the theocratic intolerance of the Inquisition, the fifth-column potential of revolutionary Communism, the implacable racialism of the Nazis, and the readiness of each to deny justice, human rights and life itself to any perceived adversary. It is hardly surprising, therefore, that techniques employed in any of these contexts transfer quite easily to them all.

After thirty-eight years punctuated by innumerable sectarian bombings and assassinations, the counterterrorist effort in Northern Ireland was recently declared to be over. Shortly before this, in 2003, when Al-Muqrin was publishing the first installment of his manual, a history of the main Irish terrorist group—the Provisional IRA—was published in the United Kingdom. In reviewing it, I was struck by the extent to which its author, a distinguished professor of politics in Belfast, seemed somewhat in awe of the intellectualism of leading Republicans. In fact, it is a fallacy to believe that people at the head of extremist movements are stupid. History is replete with examples of the Articulate Terrorist—and Al-Muqrin is undoubtedly one of these.

Although he begins by tendentiously defining Just and Unjust Wars respectively as those waged by and against dispossessed Muslims, he sets out four objective classes of conflict. Two are passed over in a couple of sentences: namely, traditional conventional warfare and total war involving the use of weapons of mass destruction. With regard to the latter, it is typical of his rational approach that he states, "This type of war is considered unlikely because it leads to mass destruction, which could spell the end of all of mankind." It is to be hoped that other *jihadists* also share his assessment.

While Al-Muqrin's manual is almost entirely confined to guerrilla warfare, it is intriguing that he regards his third category of conflict—cold wars—as that being waged by "the Zionist-Crusader alliance" against the Muslim world by "spending billions of dollars on the media . . . setting up fifth columns, and sowing the seeds of division and disunity . . . by using the leading Muslim champions of secularism, modernity, and Westernization, who want to spread such abominations among the faithful" and to groom such secular Muslims to govern Islamic states like Afghanistan and Iraq.

What emerges, time and again, from Al-Muqrin's writings is his understanding of the crux of the conflict: *that this is a battle of ideas—with doctrine underpinning the will to win.* The inability to win militarily must be compensated for by the ability to defeat psychologically—to cause the mental collapse and capitulation of the enemy. Assassinations and explosions in cities are described as "diplomatic-military" initiatives, with "a political meaning connected to the nature of the ideological struggle" and designed "to send messages to multiple audiences." For this reason, al-Qa'ida chooses its targets "extremely carefully" and such targets may be ideological, economic or human.

Dealing with the first two categories, at the beginning of chapter 6, Al-Muqrin maintains, for the most part, his objective style. Nor does he entirely forswear it in explaining why human targets should be attacked: it is for the purpose of "making clear what the ideological struggle is about. Thus, when we target the Jews and Christians, we make clear the religious nature of the struggle." Such attacks lift the morale of the Islamic *Ummah*, shatter the prestige of the regime that is attacked—as when "America's nose was ground in the dirt"—and thwart the political plans of one's opponents, such as securing the withdrawal of Spanish troops after the bombings in Madrid.

Yet, one passage above all reveals the depth of hatred and the unappeasable global ambition of al-Qa'ida:

> We must target and kill Jews and Christians. To anyone who is an enemy of God and His Prophet we say, "We have come to slaughter you." In today's circumstances, borders must not separate us nor geography keep us apart, so that every Muslim country is our country and their lands are also our lands. We must turn the idolaters' countries into a living hell just as they have done to the Muslims' countries. . . . All the active cells in every corner of the world must pay no attention to geographic borders that the enemies have drawn. Instead, these cells must make every effort to transform the infidel countries into battlefronts and to force the infidel and collaborationist countries to deal with that. Just as the Muslim countries have been turned into test labs for their weapons and inventions, so also their countries must be turned into hell and destruction. The sons of the Islamic *Ummah* are capable of doing that (God willing).

What also emerges, underneath the ritual denunciation of Christians and Jews, is the reality that most prime targets for assassination are Muslims who do not share the views, values, and objectives of Al-Qa'ida. The detailed exposition of assassination "tradecraft" includes two contrasting accounts of attempts on the life of Muslim presidents. One was made when President Mubarak visited Addis Ababa and reads like a lethal parody of a script for the Keystone Cops: "The owner of the Volvo that had been tasked with blocking the motorcade had turned off the engine and was not able to restart it. . . . The RPG that was to be fired at the car had a faulty trigger mechanism and did not fire, may God help us." The other—the successful assassination of Algerian President Mohamed Boudiaf—was a model of ruthlessly planned infiltration, diversion, and execution, with the assassin standing directly behind the president as he delivered a speech and only a curtain separating them: "The brother threw a hand grenade under the curtain, which rolled before stopping in the middle of those present. When they all turned their attention to that, he fired two shots at [Boudiaf's] head, with all that happening in a matter of only a few seconds." Indeed, of all the examples of past assassination operations listed by Al-Muqrin, only one of the victims was Jewish and none were Christian.

In 2007, in a paper written for the British defence think tank the Royal United Services Institute, I set out a mantra—"Double-I, Double-N"—of four criteria for counterinsurgency. These were Identify, Isolate, Neutralize, and Negotiate. The first deals with intelligence, the second with separation from the community, the third with security measures, and the fourth with striking deals—not from an early position of weakness, but from a later position of strength or at least near-stalemate. Of particular interest to me, therefore, is Al-Muqrin's description of what he expects his enemies to do during the attrition phase of guerrilla warfare. Although he mocks as "preposterous" the idea that such methods would prevail, the terms in which he describes some of them indicate a degree of apprehension on his part: "Continuous fears and frantic campaigns to distort the image of the guerrillas or the *mujahidin* and to mislead the public . . . deceptive propaganda about the guerrillas or the *mujahidin* . . . [the] claim that the *mujahidin* are criminal killers who were failures in life and who have despaired of life." This is a pretty fair description, by Dr. Cigar's account, of Al-Muqrin himself.

Real anxiety is indicated, too, by the reference to the Saudi regime having "even used the leading figures of Islamic movements who until recently have been calling for opposition to the oppressors." This technique he describes as disinformation and diversion employed "to expel the *mujahidin* from the ranks of society and to cut off the logistic and material support that the people provide to the *mujahidin*." Al-Muqrin is also alert to the danger of secret offers to negotiate and throw down one's weapons in exchange for a blanket amnesty or exile from the country: "Negotiations during this phase are prohibited—no negotiations, no military truce, no abandoning your military bases, no dialogue—because the principle of fighting and the appearance of the *jihadi* movement are based on irreconcilable differences, since the conflict is between the Muslims and the Crusaders, and between the *mujahidin* and the apostates, so that there is no room for compromise solutions." For all this bravado, Al-Muqrin is undoubtedly well aware that, when insurgencies are successfully infiltrated, isolated, and contained, their defeat is generally secured via terms negotiated with those leaders who prefer to salvage something from the campaign rather than facing total elimination in the long term.

It can never be repeated too often that propaganda—in the nonpejorative sense of the word—is central to the outcome of ideological conflict. When the Allies were fighting the Second World War—the most extensive high-intensity conflict in history—they still felt it necessary to invest heavily in positive propaganda to boost morale and remind society what was at stake and in negative propaganda to demoralize the enemy. With the absence of open conflict during the Cold War, the battle of ideas became still more important. Military deadlock between East and West encouraged a strategy of containment within which the concepts of freedom and democracy could be promoted against the alternative totalitarian dogma. Al-Muqrin's manual clearly shows how well he understands this dimension in addition to the bloody mechanisms of terror and targeted killings. Norman Cigar has done a great service by applying his linguistic and analytical skills to this deadly document and dissecting it so comprehensively.

Julian Lewis MP
London, August 2008

PREFACE

As the challenge of radical Islamic movements has loomed larger on the national security agenda for both the United States and countries around the world, the importance of having a familiarity with and an understanding of the intellectual underpinnings of such movements has also increased. Initially, my interest in providing an accessible version of the text presented here, 'Abd al-'Aziz al-Muqrin's *A Practical Course for Guerrilla War*, came in response to the frequent request from my students at the Marine Corps Command and Staff College to be able to read—as part of their educational process—the original doctrinal sources related to the adversaries they were likely to face. They often complained that the texts of military thinkers in the curriculum were heavily Western-oriented, unavoidably so because of the lack of the availability of sources from other cultures translated into English. Students in the professional military education system will benefit from an exposure to the original sources produced by military thinkers representing actual and potential adversaries—especially if such works are accompanied by some guiding analysis to provide a cultural and political context. One needs to engage such texts with a professional approach, focusing on the genuine military thought that underlies the political hyperbole or emotion that they also often contain. In fact, anyone interested in radical Islamic movements—and particularly in Al-Qa'ida—whether in academia, think tanks, policy circles, or the media, can profit from direct contact with the original sources, and especially from the work of a systematic and authoritative thinker such as the one presented here. Any additions to the growing library of accessible works that focus on what militants study and how they think can enhance our insights into their planning process, decision-making, and operational art, and thereby make dealing with their challenge more effective. To that extent, I hope that the greater availability of Al-Muqrin's work will illuminate a broader expanse of military and political thinking by radical Islamic movements on an intellectual plane and, at the same time, facilitate the practical side of dealing with these movements.

I would like to express my appreciation to the Smith Richardson Foundation for providing a generous grant, which made the research and writing of this study possible;

the Marine Corps University for sponsoring me as a Research Fellow; and the Marine Corps University Foundation for administering my research grant. The views expressed here are those of the author and do not reflect the official policy or position of the Smith Richardson Foundation, the U.S. Marine Corps, the Marine Corps University, or the Marine Corps University Foundation.

Part 1:

OVERVIEW AND ANALYSIS

OVERVIEW AND ANALYSIS

THE TERMS OF REFERENCE

The ferment in the Islamic world during the past several decades has led to the blossoming of writing in the field of military thought, as well as in the political/religious field.[1] It was Saudi Arabia that, until recently, provided the most fertile ground for this intellectual production. That is not surprising given that country's unique fully articulated religious educational system at all levels, ample private and government financial support, and relatively benign environment reflective of a complacent—and at times supportive—official attitude toward radical Islamists. Even non-Saudis with extremist tendencies benefited from this permissive environment over the years, spending time in Saudi Arabia as students or teachers and participating in this intellectual process.

Usama Bin Ladin, the leader of Al-Qa'ida, is originally from Saudi Arabia, and it is not surprising that he views his native country as a prime theater for Islamic militancy for a combination of emotional, ideological, and pragmatic reasons.[2] In fact, Saudi Arabia has merited its own branch of Al-Qa'ida, one of the largest in the region—Al-Qa'ida of the Arabian Peninsula (QAP). Indicative of its close ties to Bin Ladin, the QAP's origins were unlike those of the better-known Al-Qa'ida branch in Iraq, which developed from a preexisting organization that the Jordanian-born Abu Mus'ab Al-Zarqawi had already established (Al-Tawhid wa-l-jihad, or the Unity and Jihad). Al-Zarqawi, who was already active in Iraq, had then joined his organization to Al-Qa'ida when he presented his oath of allegiance, or *bay'a*, to Bin Ladin in December 2004. Although the move may have been largely symbolic, at least until Al-Zarqawi's death in June 2006, it nevertheless represented a convergence of radical interests in the region. The QAP emerged from a personal initiative by Usama Bin Ladin himself, as will be discussed below, and developed under his tutelage. Although, in a sense, an outlying and subordinate branch of the mother Al-Qa'ida, the QAP has been one of the most active subversive groups in the region in its own right and has been especially notable in intellectual terms, having produced an impressive corpus of writings over the years, including works on military theory.

Since the early 1990s, intellectuals and practitioners in *jihadi* circles have grappled with the problem of establishing a military component to complement their emerging political strategies. This development is not surprising, given the need to prepare for and conduct the military activity that has become increasingly commonplace in the Islamic world. As one could expect, the focus of such writings has been heavily on the lower end of the spectrum of conflict, given the imbalance of power between those in the *jihadi* movements and those they have viewed as their likely local and international adversaries. Whether these writers used terms such as asymmetric war, fourth-generation war, or guerrilla war, the thrust was similar in that they recognized that conventional wars against such potent enemies were not realistic and that new approaches had to be developed.[3] Although few of the Muslim writers who have addressed the issue have had formal traditional military training, they have often acquired considerable practical experience through years of combat, tactical training, and personal study.

One of these writers, 'Abd Al-'Aziz Al-Muqrin, stands out for the systematic and analytical approach with which he thought about warfare. Although 'Abd Al-'Aziz Al-Muqrin may not be a household name in the West, this revolutionary from Saudi Arabia deserves recognition as an innovative military thinker who produced a professional study that should be of interest to anyone dealing with Al-Qa'ida and insurgency within the Islamic world in general. A definition of doctrine by one of today's leading writers on the subject not only reiterates the importance of doctrine in preparing for and fighting a war, but also highlights the fact that Al-Muqrin's work fulfills all the main requirements of sound doctrine: "In generic terms, a doctrine can be defined as a set of commonly held, concisely stated, and authoritatively expressed beliefs, fundamental principles, organizational tenets, and methods of combat force employment intended to guide the planning, preparation, and execution of one's forces to accomplish given military objectives."[4] Al-Muqrin's ideas are of particular interest given his leading role within the QAP, the branch of the mother Al-Qa'ida that has operated in Saudi Arabia. Saudi Arabia is a pivotal country for the United States given its vast oil reserves, its unique role in the Islamic world as the focus of religious observance, its potential impact on regional stability, and the significant in-country presence of American nationals engaged in economic, military, and diplomatic activities. The QAP, while now apparently under control, may yet prove to be a significant long-term threat to Saudi Arabia and major U.S. interests, and requires a thorough understanding of how its leadership thinks and operates.

Access to Al-Qa'ida's doctrinal literature can provide valuable insights into the latter organization's planning, training, and operational thinking—insights that can help policymakers shape a more realistic profile of its leaders and of its strategy, which can be key in developing effective counterterrorism and counterinsurgency policies. In particular, Al-Muqrin provides in his doctrinal manual, *A Practical Course for*

Guerrilla War [*Dawrat al-tanfidh wa-harb al-'asabat*], a unique window to understanding the intellectual underpinnings of what has been Saudi Arabia's most serious security concern in recent years and, specifically, of the military dimension of that threat.

The present study provides a translation of this work and an analytical introduction intended to highlight specific aspects of Al-Muqrin's thinking and place his work within the context of his times and religious-political environment. The principal intent of making this text available to an English-speaking audience is to facilitate an understanding of how an adversary thinks, something that can be helpful in devising more effective methods in dealing with what has emerged as one of the most significant threats to U.S. interests and to governments in the Middle East in the contemporary world. It is beyond the scope of this present study to provide a history and analysis of the internal situation in Saudi Arabia, or even of the QAP insurgency as a movement, which bound Al-Muqrin's thinking and action, since those are considerably broader topics deserving complete studies of their own. However, some details of the political and social environment will be addressed that will provide the necessary context to the practical application of Al-Muqrin's ideas and contribute to amplifying or clarifying his theoretical work.[5] The focus here will be on Al-Muqrin's book itself, although his other writings and those by his comrades can also provide insights that will elucidate certain points of Al-Muqrin's thinking.

What is striking in terms of military thinking is the variety of approach and coverage in the radical Islamic military literature despite the fact that the focus for all is similar: how to solve the problem of dealing with a technologically advanced, powerful foe from a position of relative weakness. Perhaps one of the earliest such contemporary *jihadi* military manuals is the one available on the U.S. Department of Justice website. This work, dating from the Afghanistan War period, was found as a computer file by the Manchester Metropolitan Police (Great Britain) during a search of an Al-Qa'ida member's house.[6] Although a valuable document, judging from the excerpts in the public domain, its focus is largely on tactics, techniques, and procedures (TTPs), often in pithy bullet format. Other recent military writings range in length from two- to three-page think pieces to encyclopedic reference works over fifteen hundred pages in length. Al-Muqrin's book stands out among these works for its blend of a theoretical and practical approach and for providing a cohesive analysis in a work only seventy-eight pages long, making it suitable as a doctrinal publication that a military organization could use in the real world. Purists usually distinguish between the terms "insurgency" and "guerrilla war," the latter being a subset of the former more inclusive term or a type of operational art. However, this is not the case for Al-Muqrin, who conflates and interchanges the two terms. For Al-Muqrin, unconventional war *is* specifically guerrilla war. Mao also called the phenomenon "guerrilla warfare," as reflected in the title of his masterpiece, although the reach of the latter's treatise went far beyond just military technique.[7]

THE MAN BEHIND THE TEXT

The author of the text presented here, Abu Hajir 'Abd Al-'Aziz bin 'Isa bin 'Abd Al-Muhsin Al-Muqrin (locally often pronounced Al-Mugrin, or Al-Migrin, and occasionally known as Abu Hajir Al-Najdi), was a longtime *jihadi* militant and one of the founding members of the QAP, which has been essentially a Saudi organization.[8]

He became the QAP's leader for a short time until his death at the hands of Saudi security forces in June 2004. There are gaps and questions about some of the details and dates of his life. Often, the early lives of those militants who appear suddenly and who had not been in the limelight of the front ranks are not well documented, and moreover, there is often the influence of either mythologizing by his admirers or of attempts at vilification by Saudi government sources. Nevertheless, one can ascertain at least the general lines of his biography.

Al-Muqrin was born into a pious family in Riyadh (some sources say Dar'iyya) in 1973 and lived his early life in Al-Suwaydi, a conservative working-class neighborhood in Riyadh inhabited heavily by recent immigrants from the countryside. Al-Muqrin displayed his religiosity early. According to his fellow students in middle school, he exhibited signs of piety such as sporting sideburns and avoiding frivolous activities common to others his age. The only exception was his love for soccer, which he indulged as goalkeeper for his middle school team, but even then he insisted on not wearing shorts out of modesty. While in school, he joined a religious youth group, the "Islamic Awareness," and reportedly also established contacts with even more radical groups.[9] Because of his religious scruples, he would not have his picture taken and did not get an ID card. There are only two extant photos of Al-Muqrin from his entire life. He left school at age seventeen without finishing, apparently dissatisfied with the lack of religiosity in the program, as was true of many Saudi *jihadis*, who felt the education system was becoming too secularized.

With some bitterness, Al-Muqrin noted years later that in the early days the mosques and local media had promoted the *jihad* in Afghanistan constantly, with government approval and even reduced-fare tickets from the latter to travel there. He relates that he also felt the impulse to embark on the *jihad* from a very young age. His strict interpretation of religious law, however, proved to be an obstacle, as most *'ulama'* did not interpret the situation in Afghanistan by 1990 as a defensive *jihad*, so that anyone wishing to go could do so only with his parents' consent. This presented a problem for the youthful Al-Muqrin, since his parents were apparently opposed to his going. It was not until he found an *'alim* who was willing to give him a *fatwa*, or religious opinion, to the effect that going to prepare for the *jihad* was a personal duty characteristic of a defensive *jihad* (as opposed to a communal one)—and therefore did not require parental consent—that he was able to travel to Afghanistan in 1990 for the first time.[10] He soon experienced his first combat near the Jihad Wali training camp near Khost, repelling a night attack by forces of the post-Soviet Afghan government.

He underwent extensive training at that camp and Al-Faruq camp, noting that his fellow Saudis there were not predisposed to military affairs or to discipline, and that it took some skill by the instructors to get them to learn to adapt to military education.[11]

After returning home, he went to work selling dates on the street in front of the Sheraton Hotel in Riyadh in 1993. Later, he would speak of this with pride, given the fact that Muhammad had also been a merchant and that he was able to avoid working for the "apostate" Saudi government.[12]

As part of his business, he reportedly traveled frequently to the Qasim region, known for its date production and its conservative reputation. Municipal authorities tried to close his small business, and he reportedly reacted by attacking local officials with an iron bar before taking off in his Mitsubishi Galant.[13]

Over the next few years, Al-Muqrin gained experience in a variety of theaters and in various capacities outside the country. In the mid-1990s he went to North Africa, where he helped smuggle arms from Spain to Morocco. From there he went to the Islamist insurgency in Algeria, which ended when most of the members of his cell were arrested. He returned home and went back and forth between Saudi Arabia and Afghanistan, after which he went to Bosnia-Herzegovina, where he served as a trainer and took part in combat in support of the local Muslims. Once again back in Saudi Arabia, he crossed the border into Yemen and from there went on to Somalia, where he fought with local elements in Ethiopia's ethnic-Somali province of Ogaden. Ethiopian forces captured him, and he was held in prison for two years and seven months, after which he was extradited to Saudi Arabia, where he received a four-year prison sentence. However, he was released from Al-Hayir prison after only two years, thanks to his good conduct and his having memorized the Qur'an but, as one journalist concluded, he left prison with ideas that were even more extreme than those he had when he entered.[14] He again returned to Afghanistan by way of Yemen after 9/11 in time to take part in the fighting against the American forces in 2001.[15] During this stay in Afghanistan he met Bin Ladin and apparently was very impressed with him.[16]

In 2002 Al-Muqrin returned to Saudi Arabia as part of Bin Laden's initiative to establish a distinct Al-Qa'ida organization presence in Arabia. He moved into his family house in the Al-Suwaydi neighborhood of Riyadh, where he stayed until 2003, at which time he cut off his ties to his family, perhaps out of concern for potential consequences to them stemming from his clandestine work. After returning home, he had plunged into activism, devoting his time and energy to field training, classroom instruction, and writing for the QAP media. His expertise in all areas of weaponry and explosives and extensive practical experience were assets that would make him not only a formidable field commander but also an educator and thinker. He said in an interview that when the Saudi government put him on a wanted list he did not hear of it immediately because he was busy in a training session in a secluded *wadi*—or valley—specifically instructing on military operations in urban terrain.[17]

Within a short time Al-Muqrin emerged as the QAP's leader as the government eliminated more senior militants. Given the QAP's horizontal cell structure, it was sometimes difficult to determine who, if anyone, was in charge overall. Even Saudi security seemed to be divided as to Al-Muqrin's position within the QAP. Some security sources saw him as the QAP's de facto leader as early as 2003, after the death of Al-'Ayyiri, who, as the organization's founder and intellectual luminary, had been its undisputed leader.[18] By then, Al-Muqrin, the head of one of the QAP's five cells, had become the most wanted man in Saudi Arabia.[19] Others in Saudi security believed that Al-Muqrin lacked the necessary leadership and organizational skills and that he was actually a front man for the real leader, the Jeddah-born Yemeni Khalid Al-Hajj (nom de guerre Abu Hazim Al-Sha'ir), and that it was only when the latter was killed by Saudi security forces on March 16, 2004, that Al-Muqrin became the QAP's leader in the full sense of the term.[20] The QAP media referred to him as "the overall commander of the *mujahidin* in the Arabian Peninsula."[21]

Al-Muqrin was totally committed to the idea of *jihad*, spending sixteen of his thirty years associated with Al-Qa'ida in one capacity or another. For him, the *jihad* was one of the greatest duties required by Islam (*awjab al-wajibat*), outranked as an obligation only by the basic proclamation of faith in the oneness of God.[22] Al-Muqrin was prepared to sacrifice everything for the sake of fighting the *jihad*. One of his comrades who knew him in Bosnia-Herzegovina and later in Somalia, the Yemeni Nasir Al-Bahri (nom de guerre Abu Jandal), remembers that when he had talked of settling down and getting married after returning home, Al-Muqrin had rebuked him: "You're crazy. Are you going to abandon the afterlife, the *huris*, the *jihad*, and martyrdom, just to get married?!?"[23] According to the same source, Al-Muqrin believed that marriage was a burden entailing onerous obligations that interfered with the freedom necessary to pursue the *jihad*.[24] Al-Muqrin had married when he was only nineteen years old and had fathered a child but had divorced very soon thereafter, and his daughter lived with his former wife, who had later married a judge. Still, he had apparently remarried recently, and he acknowledged that he had fathered another daughter.[25]

A number of sources, mostly hostile ones, have stressed Al-Muqrin's limited formal education. One of his contemporaries remembers that Al-Muqrin "did not know how to read the Qur'an correctly without committing basic errors."[26] Supporters emphasized that Al-Muqrin was a diligent student who had attended courses taught by Islamic scholars, but that his preoccupation with the *jihad* everywhere had taken him away from his studies.[27] However, there is a consensus that he was not much of a reader, preferring instead to listen to religious tapes. Nevertheless, as shown by his work, he was a straightforward, clear, and disciplined thinker and writer. People who knew him characterized Al-Muqrin as high-strung and suffering from migraines, but as someone who was brave.[28]

Al-Muqrin, more a man of action than of subtle thought, was intellectually unambiguous in his positions and remarkably consistent over the years, and he was anything but reticent in expressing his views. His uncompromising belief in a cataclysmic global struggle between good and evil, between Islam and infidelity, motivated his every action and sustained a life committed to the *jihad*. As he told his audience in one of the tapes he made, "Let the world, America, and America's allies know that we are coming (may God grant us power, and we ask for God's help, and it is not us who shoot when we shoot, but it is God who is shooting), in order to fulfill the mission which the prophet of God (may God bless him and grant him peace) and his Companions began when they conquered the world and liberated it from the worship of man to that of the Lord of men."[29]

Al-Muqrin expressed his motivation for the *jihad* in no uncertain terms, reacting to what he saw as unwelcome changes in his local society and to aggression from the West. As far as the United States was concerned, he was particularly incensed by the fact the U.S. forces had had the audacity (*jur'a*), as he termed it, to establish military bases in "Muhammad's Peninsula," a place especially holy to Muslims, which they then had used to attack Muslims in Afghanistan and Iraq. In addition, he accused Americans of plundering the country's wealth and of setting their agents in place.[30] At the same time, Al-Muqrin was also reacting to what he perceived as a secularization of life in his country, which he blamed on U.S. pressure, and to the greater acceptance of the Shi'a. Labeling the Saudi government as "the most glaring of these apostate agent governments," he accused it of having given "power to other than the *shari'a*" (Islamic law), of having "opened the country to the Crusaders," and of having "made the Arabian Peninsula and its riches subservient to the international Crusader-Jewish project to set up foreign military bases and to provide America with oil at the lowest prices, as their masters desire, so that the latter's economy does not collapse."[31] In an impassioned letter intended to mobilize former *mujahidin*, he catalogued his concrete and emotional grievances in detail:

> What benefit do we get from having that which belongs to God the Almighty insulted by some secularists and atheists (*zanadiqa*), without anyone reproving them or taking revenge against them? What possible good can we wish for after the Crusaders invaded Muslim lands [setting out] from our country and bombing them while flying over our heads? What benefit do we hope for when the *mujahidin* around us are kidnapped and are treated like criminals, in order to please America and its helpers? What benefit do we look for while Islamic doctrine is being butchered every day, and its traces are erased from our society, the secularists consolidate themselves, religion is mocked, there is a rapprochement with the Refusers [i.e., the Shi'a] and the secularists, the religious curricula are changed, polytheism and polytheists are protected, and the Shi'a— who practice the rituals of their religion [openly]—are under the protection of the forces of the tyrants and the Crusaders' servants?[32]

What concerned Al-Muqrin most were grievances that were heavily weighted to the religious-cultural arena, and he seemed to avoid even alluding to such potential socioeconomic issues as the country's closed and arbitrary political system, unemployment, or government corruption, although others in the QAP and the mother Al-Qa'ida were more apt to exploit such problems in their appeals to the public.[33] In general, however, it was left to individuals with more worldly grievances to make the direct linkage between such concerns and the QAP movement's calls for radical change in the governing system.

The perceived situation of subservience and abandonment of traditional values, however, were sufficient to engender a feeling of humiliation in Al-Muqrin—a theme that recurs repeatedly in his discourse—and he stressed that those who had been victorious in the early Islamic battles of Qadisiya and Yarmuk, or in the anti-Crusader battle of Hittin, would not accept such humiliation.[34] He added that those who, more recently, had expelled the United States from Somalia and had fought against it in Afghanistan and Iraq would not allow the United States to occupy the Land of the Two Holy Shrines. In an emotional video where, wearing a mask and an explosives vest and standing in front of a wall message that read "Expel the Infidels from the Arabian Peninsula," he delivered a warning to Americans that there could be nothing but combat against them in his country.[35] It was difficult for Al-Muqrin to accept that anyone, much less former *mujahidin* who had returned to Saudi Arabia, would decline to fight in such a vital war as the *jihad* at home.[36]

Al-Muqrin understood the value of ideas and of the information effort and was an active contributor to the QAP's Internet effort. He helped to establish the QAP's online military journal, *Mu'askar Al-Battar*, and eventually become the editor of it and of its sister political publication, *Sawt al-jihad*. Later, when he became head of the QAP, Al-Muqrin took a particular interest in the media. One press source estimated that under Al-Muqrin, half of the QAP's effort was devoted to media operations.[37] Direction of the internal media was a powerful lever of control over the organization, and Al-Muqrin's writing of the lead article in each issue was a clear indication of his authority and of QAP priorities.

The details, if not general outline, of his death are still unclear. According to the official police version, the security forces received intelligence about the movement of three cars from one of Al-Muqrin's hideouts in Al-Mu'nisiyya, a neighborhood in Riyadh.[38] Police cars began to tail Al-Muqrin's party along the Riyadh streets as he left the house. When Al-Muqrin stopped to fill up at a gas station in Al-Malazz, the undercover police demanded he surrender. However, one of Al-Muqrin's followers had already gotten out of the car to make a purchase. Police quickly surrounded the gas station, and Al-Muqrin's men barricaded themselves in the convenience store. A shootout ensued. It is not clear who opened fire first, but apparently both sides were equipped with automatic weapons and the whole area was soon engulfed in a hail of bullets. A second version had Al-Muqrin rushing to help his beleaguered comrades in the gas station shop, whereupon he was hit in the leg. As he tried to jump over a wall, he was shot fatally. One of the men in his party managed to flee into a nearby building, but a local resident pointed him out to the police. Another car with QAP reinforcement arrived, and the occupants began to fire in order to draw attention away from Al-Muqrin's party. In the shootout, which lasted between sixty and ninety minutes, all four in Al-Muqrin's party were killed while twelve more of his followers were arrested, all with the reported loss of just one policeman. Yet another version of these events claims that the police discovered by chance a green Nissan Patrol booby-trapped to explode, sparking their surveillance of the surrounding area. When Al-Muqrin's men arrived in a GMC vehicle, the latter apparently realized immediately that they were being ambushed and got out of their vehicle, abandoning it in front of the gas station and firing as they ran. According to one of the gas station attendants, the resulting gun battle lasted thirty minutes. Al-Muqrin had taken refuge in the gas station's shop, from where he continued firing until he was shot and killed by a policeman. According to yet another version, the videotape that the QAP had broadcast on the Internet of their killing of Paul Marshall Johnson, whom they had kidnapped, had provided clues as to the location of their hideout, which was then tracked down.[39]

Others in the QAP, not unexpectedly, portrayed Al-Muqrin's death as an act of martyrdom, and all the characteristics of a *shahid*, or martyr, were attributed to him, including claims that he had died with a smile on his face.[40] Admirers eulogized him as a "bright star" and claimed he had "shaken the White House and made the leading Crusaders tremble and foam with rage."[41] He is still spoken of with continued respect in *jihadi* circles and is often referred to as "the leader" (*al-qa'id*) or "the general" (*al-janaral*). He is also remembered as a teacher. *Mu'askar Al-Battar* has praised him for having "shown the *Ummah* the path to save itself from the enemy" before his death and has reminded readers that he left behind as his heritage "knowledge from which one can benefit by means of his military courses and his golden advice" and that he had "trained huge numbers of Muslim youths."[42]

Al-Muqrin even seems to have become something of a cult hero within *mujahidin* ranks in Saudi Arabia after his death. In January 2007, for example, QAP activists reputed to be his followers were trying to recruit youths in Al-Zilfi and Riyadh using CDs praising Al-Muqrin.[43] Ultimately, his legacy will rest on his doctrinal writings, whose influence may outlast his accomplishments in training or in the operations he oversaw during his brief tenure as head of the QAP.

DEVELOPING A DOCTRINE

Al-Muqrin's *Guerrilla War* is a document benefiting from multiple influences, with the author drawing on ideas from various foreign sources, from lessons learned from past *mujahidin* operations, and from his own personal experience and that of his immediate colleagues. Clearly, the element of Al-Muqrin's experience in the field is reflected in many of the TTPs, and especially so in those dealing with mountain warfare. Al-Muqrin was exposed to both the theory and practice of warfighting during his many years in the field. He trained, and later became a trainer, in *mujahidin* camps in Pakistan. We know not only that were the lessons learned of past and current operations taught in such camps, but also that foreign doctrinal material, including U.S. Army field manuals, were readily available there.[44] As it emerges from his text, Al-Muqrin also absorbed the teachings of Clausewitz and Mao Tse-tung, whether directly or indirectly.[45] The concept of the phasing of insurgencies is clearly Mao's, and Mao may be the single greatest outside theoretical impact overall on Al-Muqrin's doctrine. Moreover, Al-Muqrin was a veteran of several wars that spanned a variety of physical and sociopolitical environments, which no doubt provided firsthand lessons to him and his fellow *mujahidin*. In addition to drawing on past theorists, Al-Muqrin reworked their ideas into what is an original synthesis designed to address the needs, as he sees them, of the Islamic community and, in particular, of the inhabitants of Saudi Arabia.

In many ways, Al-Muqrin's *Guerrilla War* reflects a general consensus on doctrine present within the QAP leadership, arguably the product of shared experiences and discussions over the years, which he codified. From that perspective, it is not possible to delineate the origin of all the ideas the text contains, that is, whether an idea originated with Al-Muqrin, whether it is one he absorbed from one of his colleagues, or whether it is part of a shared outlook within the QAP. Al-Muqrin had apparently long pondered the issues involved in the text and had already taught the "Practical Course" in Afghanistan. The QAP's teaching of basic military and political concepts reflects the dissemination of a collective outlook, based on shared experiences and extreme commitment to transcendental goals, which created an atmosphere where ideas ceased to be proprietary and became part of the movement's accepted canon of operational art. From that perspective, it is often difficult to separate strands of thought on the basis of individual originator, although the process nevertheless still requires specific individuals to synthesize and package the ideas into a coherent whole. On the other hand, several audiotapes on the QAP website of lectures by his colleague Yusuf Al-'Ayyiri essentially reproduce material found in *Guerrilla War*. In the case of the section on urban operations (pp. 171–175), we know that the material in Al-Muqrin's work is taken largely from Al-'Ayyiri's teachings, as Al-Muqrin acknowledges this. However, he adds important structure and detail to Al-'Ayyiri's teaching with his accompanying commentary. Since one cannot establish a solid date for the works of either of these two thinkers, all one can say is that they coexisted and were probably the product of mutual influence as the doctrine crystallized over time.

Al-'Ayyiri has been perhaps QAP's most impressive figure so far in terms of intellect and organizational skills. A graduate in religious-legal studies, he was widely read and had broader intellectual horizons than did most of his comrades. And, he was a prolific writer in his own right, as attested by his numerous books, articles, *fatwas*, and instructional videos, which are still available and apparently are still being used after his death. Al-'Ayyiri had also read widely in military theory, as he notes on his tapes, and shows a broad familiarity with Western and Eastern military thinkers. For example, we know for certain that Al-'Ayyiri had read Clausewitz (even though he may have called him a Frenchman in his taped lectures) and Mao, and that he was familiar with other figures in the field of insurgency, such as Ho Chi Minh, Che Guevara, and Fidel Castro.[46]

It is reasonable to assume that some of the literary knowledge that Al-'Ayyiri had absorbed was transferred through his personal filter in aural form to others during discussions within the organization, including to Al-Muqrin as the latter prepared his own work. Conversely, there does not appear to be any real influence—either in approach, substance, or language—from the military literature that other radical Islamist thinkers have produced. Even when similar topics are addressed, there seems to be no crossover, suggesting a lack of familiarity or interest on Al-Muqrin's part with the other writers.

Al-Muqrin's text should be viewed as the capstone document within QAP's overall doctrinal architecture. That is, Al-Muqrin's work was the summary overview, while he and the QAP as a whole provided an elaboration of many of the concepts found in his document with complementary texts and training videos. For example, the QAP's *Mu'askar Al-Battar* contained detailed presentations of specific facets, particularly TTPs, which expanded on what Al-Muqrin had said. Thus, there were articles and videotapes on the handling and maintenance of small arms, techniques of tactical intelligence, physical conditioning, navigation, operational security, planning, survival techniques, etc. Often, this technical information in the QAP's complementary instructional material was drawn directly from U.S. or Soviet service field manuals.

In addition, other works written by QAP activists, such as Muhammad b. Ahmad Al-Salim's *39 wasila li-khidmat al-jihad wa-l-mujahidin fi sabil allah [39 Ways to Serve the Jihad and the Mujahidin Fighting for God's Cause]*, at least in part, deal with military matters and contain ideas borrowed freely from Al-Muqrin's text.[47] Likewise, there was a book by another QAP figure, Faris b. Ahmad Al Shuwayl Al-Zahrani, *Kharrabat Amrika jazirat al-'arab [America Has Laid Waste to the Arabian Peninsula]*.[48] In addition, a specialized study by a QAP leader on targeting the oil sector justified this action on legal grounds and stressed its desirability in political and economic terms.[49]

In addition, the QAP produced audiotapes and videos, often a mixture of instructional material and outright propaganda. The QAP projected the publication of other scattered texts by topic into stand-alone books such as *Guerrilla War*, but this project was halted by the severe government crackdown, which paralyzed virtually all QAP media activity for almost two years thereafter.

The process by which *Guerrilla War* came into its final form is not clear. Specifically, one cannot know whether the text was written originally as individual pieces (as they appeared originally in successive issues of *Mu'askar Al-Battar*) and then combined posthumously into a book by unnamed editors, or whether it was written as a complete piece and then serialized, to be then recombined and published as a book. The latter method seems more likely, as the work exhibits an overall cohesiveness and forethought, proceeding from the strategic to the tactical level, which would have been difficult to achieve if the book were the result simply of scattered texts stitched together by another hand at a later time. In any event, after Al-Muqrin's death it was the QAP's shadowy "Military Committee" that undertook the editing and republishing of his work. According to the QAP, the committee considered how best to republish in a new series various texts that had been serialized in previous issues of *Mu'askar Al-Battar*. The QAP claimed that readers, communicating either directly by e-mail or in online forums, had expressed a preference for the scattered installments to be grouped and republished by topic in stand-alone format, and this led to the publication of Al-Muqrin's *Guerrilla War* as a unified text as part of that effort.[50] The online publication has high-quality graphics (as do all the QAP products) and is laid out in a visually appealing mode, although the edition contains some deficiencies, such as textual repetitions and gaps.

THINKING ABOUT WAR

A military publication can only be as good as the ideas it contains and the degree to which it is relevant to the problems at hand. This section will examine some of the key concepts in *Guerrilla War* and assess the doctrine within the context of the QAP as an organization and the operational environment with which its author had to inter-act. From a professional point of view, Al-Muqrin's *Guerrilla War* deserves high marks as doctrine. It is not just a checklist of tasks, but relies both on a descriptive approach, when it deals with strategic and operational issues, and a more prescriptive one, when it deals with detailed TTPs. It does not provide answers as much as it asks the right questions, guiding the reader to make his own decisions in order to solve a problem rather than imposing ready-made formulas. The sample planning problem included in *Guerrilla War* (which, according to the text, was sent in by readers relying on the earlier installments of the book that had appeared in *Mu'askar Al-Battar*) is for an assassination operation against Prince Nayif bin 'Abd Al-'Aziz Al Sa'ud, the Saudi minister of the interior, and is in itself a psychological operations message. The editorial staff (possibly Al-Muqrin) evaluated the proposed plan and provided a critique, pointing out gaps and potential improvements without, however, imposing a "school solution," a single answer. Rather, the magazine suggested questions intended to stimu-late the students to further thought, based on the material contained in *Guerrilla War*. In fact, Al-Muqrin reminds readers that they must adapt the concepts he presents to specific conditions rather trying to apply them uncritically: "One must be careful that these characteristics not become a rigid template or a 'school solution' but, rather, that they remain adaptable to developments in the region" (pp. 97–98, footnote vii). Al-Muqrin also encourages the questioning of everything, apart from the basic ideological/religious premises, which must be accepted.

THE STRATEGIC LEVEL OF WAR

Al-Muqrin proceeds from the strategic level, defining what war is, using a basic definition of war that is very much in the traditional Clausewitzian vein as "a state of conflict . . . between two armed camps" (p. 89). For Al-Muqrin, however, the conflict may be a situation in which the adversaries are not necessarily nation-states. They could be communities or factions as well.[51] What is clearly key for Al-Muqrin is that conflicts have a strategic objective, whether it be political, economic, or ideological (p. 89). Al-Muqrin's strategic level of analysis encompasses not only military considerations, but also all the elements of power, including the political (domestic and international), economic, and informational. Al-Muqrin's holistic approach to understanding wars is reminiscent of the Soviet framework of analyzing two interactive spheres—the political-military and military-technical.[52] Al-Muqrin's work distinguishes these two aspects, even if he does not explicitly identify them as such, analyzing at each stage the situation with respect to each of these two spheres, both for the enemy and the friendly side. At the same time, he also classifies wars using a taxonomy reminiscent of the Marxist one in which wars are divided into just and unjust conflicts according to class criteria, with those waged by the proletariat (or in their name) as just and those waged by the bourgeoisie as automatically unjust. Not surprisingly, Al-Muqrin adapts his perspective explicitly to an Islamic framework, identifying the criterion for just or unjust wars as whether the wars are fought by virtuous Muslims or by infidels—including those who are outwardly Muslims but who have lost their way and are "apostates" (p. 89). In Al-Muqrin's words, just wars are those fought by "a party or peoples deprived of power, who are oppressed and wronged . . . against an oppressive aggressor or tyrannical ruler." Conversely, Al-Muqrin categorizes unjust wars as "those wars that unjust powers wage against the dispossessed. The objective of such wars is to dominate other belief systems, to replace the prescriptions of religious law, to seize territory, and to plunder [others'] riches" (p. 89). Consistent with his Islamic frame of reference, his examples of just wars are those in which Muslims have been engaged against a non-Muslim foe—such as in Palestine, Afghanistan, Chechnya, Kashmir, and the Philippines—or wars fought against those he would define as apostate Muslims, such as the QAP insurgency in Saudi Arabia (p. 89). As he saw it, there is now a global war, with the battle line drawn clearly. On one side is the United States, "a spiteful infidel Crusader state which kills Muslims in Afghanistan, Iraq, Palestine, and Chechnya, and whose forces are concentrated in bases in the Gulf, in Central and South Asia, and elsewhere in the Islamic countries." On the other side, stand the *mujahidin*.[53]

From another perspective, within the Islamic world itself, Al-Muqrin also saw a more abstract ideological total war pitting two contrasting visions of the world. On one side, there is "a dark black image, filled with idolatry, infidelity, hypocrisy, sedition, injustice, outrage, and immorality, which covers most of the world. Muslims there live a marginal life full of submissiveness and subordination. . . . The other image is a bright one, radiant with rays of light, faith, true religion, piety, and virtue, under whose protection the unitarian *mujahid* youth—who have not become accustomed to a life of humiliation and submissiveness—are prominent." While still a minority, the latter, virtuous party was said to be growing in strength day by day.[54]

The essence of the guerrilla war that Al-Muqrin proposes is a revolutionary one whose objective is to destroy the old system and replace it with "a pure Islamic system" based on the Qur'an and the *Sunnah* (p. 92). Al-Muqrin thus envisages a total war, and he speaks of "irreconcilable differences" and of "no room for compromise solutions" (p. 97). As for war termination, there can be no alternative to victory, as Muhammad's march will be completed only when the *mujahidin* "conquer the world and liberate it from worshipping the worshippers and [change it to] worshipping the worshippers' maker."[55] The focus of Al-Muqrin's doctrine is the seizure of power, not how power will be wielded and made secure once the *mujahidin* take control. Accordingly, the discussion of the future government system is minimal and vague. Ultimately, for Al-Muqrin, the strategic goal of any just war has to be an eschatological and ethereal—albeit distant—one of promoting Islam's ultimate global victory or, as he puts it, "to fight for the sake of God to make the *shari'a* the law of the land and for the word of God to become supreme" (p. 89). A religiously based state—an Islamic Caliphate—would be established as the institutional framework for these changes (pp. 97–98).[56] Although it may only occur in the distant future, he projects light overtaking the present darkness, when "the sun of the truth, Islam, and the *Sunnah* will shine." This may occur slowly, but it will occur, until one day God establishes the rightly guided Caliphate, which will fill the world with righteousness and justice.[57] The *jihad* will continue until final victory: "Let all know that our *jihad* will continue until God curbs the power of the infidels . . . and until there is no more discord and God's religion prevails."[58]

In fact, Al-Muqrin believed that the *jihad* would be a permanent condition, ending only on Judgment Day (*qiyam al-sa'a*).[59] Al-Muqrin was certain that the outcomes of all events were in God's hands, as he suggests again and again in his text, and he is confident that the final outcome of the struggle pitting the *mujahidin* against the United States and the Al Sa'ud is inevitable, with God having preordained victory for the *mujahidin* fifty thousand years before He had even created Heaven and Earth, as he puts it.[60]

At the same time, however, Al-Muqrin proposes a more tangible—although still revolutionary—intermediate goal of achieving "the liberation of the downtrodden Muslim population" and an accompanying "new social system" drawing "its legitimacy from the light of the Book and the *Sunnah*" (p. 92). This intermediate objective, as he proposed elsewhere, would be reached when the *mujahidin* "expel all the infidel armies from the Land of Muhammad (may God bless him and grant him peace), cleanse Al-Aqsa Mosque from the impurity of the Jews, and liberate all the occupied Muslim lands."[61]

In particular, the near-term goals were focused on Saudi Arabia. The first goal, as Al-Muqrin expressed it, was that "the enemies of God—the Jews and Crusaders—be expelled from the Land of the Two Shrines."[62] As for the Saudi regime, once the confrontation had escalated into violence between the latter and the QAP, Al-Muqrin concluded that the Saudi state was now at war with the *mujahidin*, and the implicit end-state of this confrontation was the overthrow of the Saudi system.[63] Indeed, the essential purpose of *Guerrilla War* is to provide a blueprint for accomplishing the overthrow of an existing regime, which is perhaps stated most clearly in the discussion of Phase Three of an insurgency (pp. 100–102). Repeating Bin Ladin's fulminations, Al-Muqrin was explicit in his rejection of the legitimacy of the Saudi political system and hierarchy, accusing the current rulers of being "agents . . . volunteering their army and money to be a shield for the armies of the Cross" and, in his view, all the regimes in the Gulf were "apostate and traitorous," and no more than "apostate tails of the Crusaders."[64] The Saudi rulers had also disqualified themselves because of their domestic policies, and Al-Muqrin called the National Dialogue, an initiative by the Saudi government to give other religious currents in the Kingdom a voice, "the *jahili* gathering under the banner of pagan nationalism," organized by "the apostate rulers."[65] Even when not made explicit, simply the determination that a regime is apostate would automatically entail its rejection and replacement.

In his writings and speeches, Al-Muqrin avoids using the term "Saudi" when mentioning the country's name. This in itself is indicative of how completely he and his comrades had become alienated from the Saudi regime, refusing to use the country's very name because it is drawn from that of the royal family. Instead, various circumlocutions appear in the QAP's discourse, such the Arabian Peninsula, the Land of the Two Shrines (i.e., Mecca and Medina), the Islamic Peninsula, or the Land of Muhammad.

Al-Muqrin's rejection or bypassing of the traditional religious hierarchy also carried clear undertones of an upheaval, given the important role of the religious establishment in sanctioning religious and political legitimacy in Saudi Arabia.[66] Typically, he condemned the fact that Saudi *'ulama'* participated with those Al-Muqrin termed hypocrites, secularists, polytheist spokesmen from the *sufis*, and Refusers (i.e., Shi'a) in the country's National Dialogue in order to promote "a culture of tolerance which America likes and to abolish the principles of 'supporting what God loves and avoiding what God hates' (*al-wala' wa-l-bara'*), which is what America hates."[67] Other spokesmen for the QAP dwelled at even greater length on their rejection of the traditional Saudi *'ulama'*, presenting extensive and often personal condemnations crafted in legal arguments. Given the symbiotic relationship between the conventional religious hierarchy and the Saudi state, any attack on one automatically also implies a rejection of the other and of the system as a whole.

Implicitly, even at the individual level, revolutionary changes would likely occur in a genuine *jihad*, with the loosening of traditional social restrictions. Simply declaring and promoting a defensive *jihad* implies an obligation on the part of every individual to become involved, even without obtaining permission from one's parents or guardians.[68] What is more, even women will take part in this process, as they can go to fight without the need to get permission from their husbands, fathers, or other male guardians.[69] In a traditional society, the implications of such a development for family relationships—if applied—can be far-reaching and unsettling. The potentially revolutionary impact also applies to the appeal the cause of *jihad* has at a level above that of narrower tribal loyalties.[70]

To be sure, Al-Muqrin, like all his fellow *jihadis*, had distinctive measures of success, which did not always stem from a conventional interpretation of victory. Al-Muqrin's emphasis was often on personal spiritual victory, thereby shaping goals that are unconventional. Ultimately, according to Al-Muqrin, an individual's objective in participating in the *jihad* must be martyrdom, entailing the attainment of "the great victory and the highest levels of Heaven," thereby achieving a fusion of the communal and personal *jihad*.[71] Perhaps Al-Muqrin's greatest wish was for martyrdom, a wish he repeated often, matter-of-factly, and in no uncertain terms.[72] Al-Muqrin often extolled martyrdom as something to be sought out eagerly. As he waxed lyrically, "Happy are those whom God has taken as martyrs, those who feel no pain when they die except that of a slight pinch. . . . After death, they will enjoy a delightful life, eternal bliss. . . . Please, God, grant us martyrdom fighting for Your cause."[73]

From another perspective, Al-Muqrin also classifies wars according to four categories, based on their level in the spectrum of conflict, although he does not actually place them in the order of ascending violence on his list. The four categories encompass conventional wars, wars of mass destruction, cold wars, and unconventional wars, each of which he defines in terms of their level of violence and the weapons used (pp. 90–91). In this manual the author's focus is on unconventional war and, specifically, on what he terms "guerrilla war." For him, echoing a Maoist view, an asymmetric war is one of necessity, as it is the only means available to the weak and the poor to deal with the strong, given the imbalance of power, until symmetric forces can be developed (pp. 92, 93).[74] This is the method that Al-Muqrin has selected as the most appropriate for "fighting, defeating, and humiliating the infidel" (p. 119).

For Al-Muqrin, war is always primarily a political phenomenon, and military operations "are conducted in order to attain specific objectives, whether political or economic" (p. 109). Military operations, "the language of blood and fire," in his words, should be used to send "diplomatic messages," for example, to foreign governments to convince them to stop supporting a local regime (p. 98). In this context, describing this type of diplomacy as "normally written in blood, decorated with corpses, and perfumed with gunpowder," he stresses the political meaning of such operations (p. 127). Later he singles out hostage-taking operations as an example that, although a "military" operation, is intended primarily as a means to attain political or economic objectives, as well as sending "diplomatic messages" (p. 109). He considers attacks in cities, in particular, given the high visibility of operations in the latter, as "diplomatic-military" actions.

Al-Muqrin is closer to Clausewitz in terms of believing that victory will necessitate violence—as he notes, "there is no *jihad* without force" (p. 105)—rather than to Sun Tzu, who believed that the ideal was to win without having to fight, with victory possibly achieved through successful preliminary shaping using all the other elements of power to render an adversary impotent to resist.[75] Al-Muqrin accepts the nature of war as a violent, even brutal, phenomenon (p. 127). This was standard QAP thinking, repeated by one of its ideologues, Luways 'Atiyat Allah, who notes that "the *jihad* is a battlefield filled with blood and corpses, fear that strikes the heart, and heads, hands, and legs that are cut off, and bones broken. . . . The *jihad* is not a pleasant picnic."[76]

The Decision to Start a War

Al-Muqrin recognizes that one of the most critical decisions for any policymaker is that of when to initiate a war, a decision that cannot be made without due deliberation given the high stakes involved. In effect, according to Al-Muqrin, in making such a decision, the *mujahidin* must remember that they are fighting for the *Ummah* as a whole (p. 104). Before initiating a war—specifically, a guerrilla war in this case—Al-Muqrin stresses the need to take a hard look at the actual situation and develop a candid net assessment, looking at all the relevant positive and negative aspects (p. 104). He urges patience rather than rushing into a war before the conditions are ripe, stressing that there is nothing wrong with waiting until the time is right to launch an insurgency (p. 105). Developing the correct assessment, moreover, is not a formulaic process with quantifiable inputs, but rather a subjective one, requiring judgment on the part of the leadership. The latter must evaluate changing qualitative trends and assess both domestic and external conditions (pp. 103–105, 108). Al-Muqrin identifies two principal preconditions before a successful insurgency can be launched. First, there must be a cadre that has the equivalent of unity of purpose, sharing an ideology and commitment, with a leadership that is up to the task being a key part of that requirement. Second, conditions on the ground must be suitable, and he offers the example of the widespread popular outrage against the government in Algeria for invalidating the elections of 1990 as providing the suitable environment for initiating an insurgency (pp. 103–104).

If conditions are not yet suitable to launch an insurgency, that does not mean that the *mujahidin* should remain passive and simply wait for conditions to mature. According to Al-Muqrin, it is the *mujahidin*'s task to shape the situation by creating the conditions necessary to launch a successful insurgency (pp. 104–105). That entails mobilizing popular support, very much in the vein of Mao, but not something about which Clausewitz or Sun Tzu would be concerned (p. 105). Al-Muqrin specifically directs the *mujahidin* not to retaliate against the population for remaining passive, placing the responsibility, instead, on the *mujahidin* to mobilize the population (p. 104).

One way for the insurgent organization to do so is by spectacular attacks (the 9/11 attacks are provided as an example), which will attract popular attention and highlight the issues at stake.

THE OPERATIONAL LEVEL OF WAR

At the operational level, Al-Muqrin envisages a protracted war (p. 93). In fact, he assessed specifically that the ongoing insurgency in Saudi Arabia would last twenty to thirty years.[77] Al-Muqrin begins with the basic premise that "Leaders must know the enemy whom they are fighting" (p. 109), and he sets the QAP's operational design within the framework of the global *jihad*.[78] Specifically, that meant that "in our *jihad* in the Arabian Peninsula, we target the Crusader forces and the latter's military, intelligence, and political centers, as well as anyone who supports them and wields weapons in their defense, since anyone who does so is the same as they, even if we do not target him primarily."[79] He borrowed heavily from Mao in his understanding of the nature of the three phases into which he organizes the war, with the general lines, detail, and terminology all drawn from Mao. Al-Muqrin presents a methodical exposition of political and military factors in each phase for both the enemy and the *mujahidin*. Within each phase, individual engagements are to be linked together in order to achieve greater objectives and make it possible to move up to a higher phase until victory is achieved. In certain cases, according to Al-Muqrin, the enemy may be defeated during the first or second phase, obviating the need for all three phases, which is a Vietnamese concept that runs counter to Mao's own thinking (p. 94).[80] However, as he cautions, the transition from one phase to the next is always event-driven, and one must be careful not to rush this transition before the conditions are appropriate. Urging instead patience and careful analysis, he presents the cautionary case of the ongoing Islamic insurgency in Algeria as an example where the leadership proceeded too quickly to Phase Two, suffering a defeat and being forced to retrench to phase one again (p. 94).

Phase One
Al-Muqrin labels Phase One the "Strategic Defense." This phase is characterized by protracted combat intended to exhaust the enemy, which he refers to as the war of the flea and the dog, borrowing the classical image of guerrilla operations (p. 111). During this time, the insurgents become combat proficient, build up their force structure, and lay the groundwork for developing a conventional force in the future. During this phase guerrillas are to refuse major battles against government forces, which the latter will try to engineer. Instead, the focus should be on numerous small hit-and-run attacks, with the military objective being to induce enemy forces to overextend themselves. The author notes that he specifically wants to bring about the classic dilemma in guerrilla warfare of obliging a conventional force to either mass and limit its

territorial control or disperse and become vulnerable in detail (pp. 96, 118). During this phase, the *mujahidin* will not establish fixed bases, but will move them as needed (p. 96). While the *mujahidin* will focus on the classic hit-and-and-run tactics, they may also mount "spectacular operations" for the benefit of media attention, to mobilize the population, and to complicate the government's foreign relations (p. 96). The political objective of this phase will be to expose the government's weakness and mobilize the population and—specific to the Middle East—expose the presence of "Crusaders and Jews" in Muslim countries and the local governments' collaboration with these foreign elements. On the international front, the *mujahidin* are to develop links with their counterparts abroad and ensure that potential foreign supporters of the government remain neutral (p. 95). The guerrillas' success and ability to survive will also encourage people to join (p. 93).

Phase Two

Phase Two is the "Strategic Balance" or "The Policy of a Thousand Cuts," and can begin once there has been a mobilization of popular support. In liberated areas, where the *mujahidin* can take control, they can establish bases and media centers. They can also build their own conventional forces and begin conventional operations against the adversary. At this time, appeals should be made to foreign publics to pressure their governments to cut ties with the adversary government and to remain neutral (p. 98). Paradoxically, Al-Muqrin refers to Bin Ladin's heavy-handed messages to various countries as a successful example of such diplomacy. The *mujahidin*'s military objective is to paralyze the government by creating strategic friction, splitting elements within the government, and rendering it unable to make decisions and to take effective measures. Intensified *mujahidin* attacks against government positions will draw attention to the presence of foreigners and serve to further alienate the population from the government. At the operational level, government forces will be obliged to retrench to secure areas and seek to use political means to neutralize the *mujahidin* and will cut back its operations in areas that the *mujahidin* control, limiting government operations to the use of airpower or long-range artillery (p. 98). At this time, the *mujahidin* can set up permanent bases and establish what is, in effect, a parallel government, with hospitals, *shari'a* courts, and broadcasting stations (p. 99). The intent of the *mujahidin* is to translate military success in the field into a political advantage at the negotiating table. Negotiations are acceptable, but only as a stalling tactic or if dealing with the enemy's surrender, not as a means to arrive at any power-sharing agreement (p. 99).

Phase Three

Phase Three in Al-Muqrin's book is called the "Decisive Phase." In this final phase—marked by internal divisions in the government, which requires massive foreign aid—the *mujahidin* achieve victory with the government's political and economic collapse.

The government's presence in the countryside will shrink, government officials and military personnel will defect, and the remnants will be compelled to retreat to the larger cities for security. Unlike Mao's strictly sequential schema, in which conventional forces will replace the guerrillas, Al-Muqrin is closer to the Vietnamese concept of the functional coexistence of conventional and unconventional forces, implying an interpenetration of phases.[81] Al-Muqrin stresses that a guerrilla capability must be retained even after a conventional capability has been developed (pp. 94, 101). The *mujahidin* seize the rest of the country progressively in a process accompanied by a propaganda campaign. Al-Muqrin's model is that of the Taliban's victory over the post-Soviet government in Afghanistan. The will of the government can then be expected to break, resulting in the *mujahidin's* final victory.[82] There are to be no negotiations with the government even in this phase, given the latter's impending defeat, and religious courts are to be set up to try the "apostates" (p. 102).

Unlike Clausewitz, Al-Muqrin does not envision major engagements, at least at first, and does not suggest that there will necessarily be a decisive engagement at all, even as an ideal toward which to strive, however rare a decisive engagement may be in the real world.[83] Rather, Al-Muqrin suggests the accumulation of many small engagements, as in his metaphor of the fleas who resume biting the dog again and again (p. 92). Likewise, in Phase Two, that of the relative strategic balance, Al-Muqrin posits that the government will halt, or at least reduce, its military actions and will take a defensive posture (pp. 95–99). For the insurgents, in this phase the "strategy of a thousand cuts" is still the rule (p. 97). This ethos is closest to that of Mao, who is categorical in his opinion that in guerrilla warfare there is "no such thing as a decisive battle."[84] Even after the insurgents have formed conventional units and can match the government forces in Phase Three of the insurgency, there is no suggestion of a decisive engagement, with the model given being that of Afghanistan, with the end result coming about as a result of the accumulation of engagements (pp. 100–101). Significantly, Al-Muqrin focuses on government defections (pp. 100) with the government on the defensive and not engaging in any major ground operations (pp. 100–101). The *mujahidin* are depicted as engaged in capturing small cities in a serial manner, accumulating the results until the collapse of the enemy's will (p. 101). Whatever method is used, the intent is to break the enemy's morale or will (pp. 99, 101, 118, 131).

Tactical Considerations
The Guerrilla Force: Rural Environment

Moving into the tactical realm, Al-Muqrin lays out his conception of the desired guerrilla force, no doubt relying on his personal experience. He posits two different types of forces based on the area of operations: those for urban operations and those for mountains, although this latter force structure is also applicable to rugged rural environments in general.[85]

The "mountain forces" conform to the popular image of classical guerrilla units: they are small (squads, companies, and battalions), light, and constantly on the move. In terms of sustainment, guerrillas will carry all the supplies they need for at least forty-eight hours. Camouflaged caches will furnish additional supplies, and in some circumstances guerrillas may also establish permanent bases in the rear or in neighboring countries (pp. 106, 108, 111, 117). Al-Muqrin reminds the planner to consider the use of various beasts of burden and motor vehicles for transport (p. 117). He has some unorthodox suggestions for this function, including making use of those who have experience evading the law, such as smugglers and criminals (p. 123). Each cell is to be autonomous in terms of its own sustainment (p. 106). The guerrilla's fires consist of personal weapons and light crew-served weapons—with the weapons of preference the Kalashnikov and other Soviet-era equipment, apart from Western GPS devices. Al-Muqrin provides a Table of Organization and Equipment for these guerrilla squads, and although the personnel have functional specialties, they are first of all combat infantrymen. As for command and control, squads will be in wireless contact directly with the company commander (p. 113). Force protection is ensured by their mobility (including marches of eighteen to twenty hours per day), their use of the cover of rugged terrain, deception against the enemy, operational security measures (including information released on a strict need-to-know basis), and an understanding of the terrain in order to facilitate escape and evasion. In addition, the guerrillas must be able to blend in with the local population (pp. 111, 117, 118).

The guerrillas' maneuver consists of conducting ambushes and raids, leveraging surprise, speed, determination, patience, and the initiative to keep the enemy off balance (pp. 31–33, 139). Al-Muqrin's guidance for ambushes and raids is traditional and could be drawn from any relevant military manual in the West.

The Guerrilla Force: Urban Environment

In an urban area of operations, many of the aspects Al-Muqrin identified for rural guerrillas also apply, but there are significant modifications owing to the differences in the environment. Although Al-Muqrin recognizes the benefits of mounting operations in a city, in terms of the value of potential targets, as noted below, he also weighs the difficulties. He stresses that the urban combat environment is very demanding, requiring the guerrillas' best personnel in terms of education, sophistication, and training (p. 120). Noting that "cities burn up money," he also reminds readers that urban operations are expensive, given the high cost of safe houses and even cars that are needed if operatives are to blend in and not draw attention to themselves (p. 120). Indeed, operatives are advised not to base themselves in cheaper working-class neighborhoods, where everyone knows everyone else and outsiders stand out (p. 162). On an individual level, operatives are to lead an outwardly normal life and avoid locations where clerics preach the *jihad* in order not to arouse suspicion (pp. 134, 140). Forging documents, procuring vehicles legally and illegally, acquiring arms, and establishing safe houses are the most common logistics tasks in Al-Muqrin's schema (pp. 120, 123–124).

The force structure is different for cities, with small functional cells (four to six men) so as to minimize compromise and damage and to ensure flexibility (pp. 106, 120–123). Command and control over the various cells can be exercised by the field command element over the other functional elements either within a pyramid structure or in a chain-like configuration (p. 121). Communications between the leadership and the rank-and-file are key and special care must be taken to ensure a solid communications plan that integrates the latest technology (p. 123). Urban cells should communicate only with the leadership directly and not with each other, making for a flat organization rather than a hierarchical one, thus limiting damage in case of penetration (p. 140). If cells do communicate with each other, they should do so only indirectly, using the "dead drop" (p. 121). Command and control for Al-Muqrin is intelligence-driven in the sense that the intelligence collected on the ground is submitted through the field command to higher headquarters, which then issues orders to the field command based on these reports (pp. 124–125). Preferably, personnel operating in cities should be locals, since they can operate more effectively in that environment (p. 120).

Assassinations

Al-Muqrin devotes special attention to human targets. What one can justifiably classify as terrorist techniques—assassinations and kidnapping/hostage-taking—are a normal and integral part of everyday operations to Al-Muqrin.[86] To be sure, there is still some ambiguity as to what is to be considered terrorism, as opposed to legitimate resistance actions. The defining criterion for the U.S. government since 1983 has been that of the targets, namely when "noncombatants" are targeted.[87] "Noncombatant" in the U.S. government's working definition, however, "is interpreted to mean, in addition to civilians, military personnel (whether or not armed or on duty) who are not deployed in a war zone or a war-like setting."[88] The QAP, while in principle operating with a much broader legitimate target set than that of the international community, has also been sensitive to public opinion on this score. Thus, when the QAP kidnapped and later murdered Paul Marshall Johnson (a U.S. contractor helicopter engineer working in Saudi Arabia) in June 2004, Al-Muqrin was anxious to prove that Johnson was a legitimate target. As Al-Muqrin argued, Johnson worked on military helicopters, and, even if he was not in uniform, he was said to be still involved in supporting combat operations against Muslims, and therefore an infidel and outlaw (*kafir muharab*), that is, a legitimate target.[89] Ultimately, in the case of targeting military personnel or government officials, the criteria for qualifying such attacks as terrorism or something else may revolve around the legitimacy of a conflict and the authority to declare and conduct a war, which in the case of the *jihadis* is a controversy at the heart of their cause. Although such assassination attempts may be limited to one person and can be considered a tactical attack, the impact may be considerably greater, especially given the conflating of levels of war in low-intensity conflicts, with the inherent nonlinearity of a tactical action that can have a strategic impact. Al-Muqrin stresses the concept of nonlinearity in his section on "The Objective in Attacking Human Targets," noting that the effect of such attacks can be far out of proportion to their size (pp. 130–131).

Al-Muqrin's guidance in his text that "We must target and kill Jews and Christians" is chilling (p. 129). There is no differentiation between civilians and military targets for Al-Muqrin. If anything, as the official *Sawt al-jihad* stressed during the period when Al-Muqrin was in charge of the QAP, killing civilians would be preferable to killing military personnel because that would be more painful for the United States.[90] One is also struck by Al-Muqrin's cold and detached attitude in relation to the assassination of public figures (pp. 141–148). He stresses that assassination operations are legitimate and seeks religious sanction from the *hadith*. At the same time, he acknowledges that there has to be an effort to ensure that the members of hit squads are also convinced of the legitimacy of such actions, and he notes that some are happy to accept this mission, suggesting that that may not be true for all (p. 142). However, he believes that characterizing the intended target as an enemy of Islam would be a sufficiently compelling argument for the *mujahidin* (p. 142).

He creates a target list for foreigners, with a hierarchy based on nationality and his evaluation of their relative importance. Christians and Jews holding official positions in Muslim countries or supporting local regimes have the top priority, and Al-Muqrin advises that, at least at first, those who are easy prey be targeted first (p. 129). He then formulates a matrix, with Americans usually at the top, although the priority may vary in a specific country, for example the French in Algeria or Australians in Indonesia. Jews are also further subdivided by country of residence, with those from the United States and Israel having the highest priority. Again, these targets are further classified by function, with those involved in the economy at the top, "given the importance of money in our age," and tourists the least valuable (p. 130). Local "apostates" merit a separate category, headed by rulers who are close to the West and Israel (in his schema especially the "rulers on the Arabian Peninsula"), but also secularists and alleged agents of foreign governments (p. 130). He specifies numerous objectives in conducting assassinations: to influence policy, deter would-be collaborators, boost morale, or undermine a government's prestige, as he concludes occurred in the wake of the 9/11 attacks when "America's nose was ground in the dirt" (pp. 130–131). Al-Muqrin examines some high-profile acts of assassination, successful and unsuccessful, to draw out positive and negative lessons learned. In particular, Al-Muqrin provides detailed techniques for the assassination of targets traveling on the road, complete with diagrams and alternate techniques. When dealing with the planning process, he spends the most time applying that to preparing for assassinations.

Kidnapping and Hostage-Taking

Al-Muqrin also devotes considerable attention to kidnapping and hostage-taking (pp. 156–164). Disagreeing with those who claim that such operations never succeed in the end, he believes they can (p. 157). There must be a rational, concrete, objective for undertaking a kidnapping, but that can include embarrassing the local government and its allies, obtaining information, ransom money, or generating publicity for the insurgency (p. 156). As with the assassination operations, he places considerable emphasis on setting objectives, target selection, planning, intelligence, rehearsals, and operational security, but also adds a section on negotiations and handover operations for hostage situations. Again, Al-Muqrin provides extensive TTP material, but often in the form of questions to ask in order to facilitate decision-making.

General Considerations
Leadership

Al-Muqrin places considerable emphasis on leadership and the human element in general, suggesting that it is the leader who makes of any doctrine a success or failure and who translates a doctrine into plans and operations (p. 103). Al-Muqrin, in fact, asserts that it is this human element, these moral factors, that outweigh the material factors, such as weaponry, in contributing to success (p. 106). Noting the many failed revolts throughout history, he identifies the cause of their failure as "a lack of leaders who know the art of conventional and unconventional warfare and [because of] leaders who are incapable of organizing and building cohesion" (p. 107). Al-Muqrin wants a leader who demonstrates high religious standards and commitment to the cause. But, he must also have well-developed professional qualities such as experience, boldness, courage, expertise, and situational awareness (*diraya*), characteristics that might easily qualify for Clausewitz's desired military genius (p. 103). Leaders must be masters of their profession on the battlefield—both conventional and unconventional—where they must be creative and innovative and display "moral preparation for the worst," that is flexibility and moral courage (p. 107).

In addition, leaders must be motivators for their subordinates, especially when difficulties are encountered, since Al-Muqrin, ever the realist, recognizes that "the fortunes of war fluctuate and one cannot win every time" (p. 132). At the same time, a leader must not be indifferent to the outcome of engagements and should avoid defeat either by winning or by refusing battle if the probability is against him in order to prevent "a weakening of confidence among some of the people and within the organization if there are repeated instances of failure" (p. 132).[91]

According to Al-Muqrin, a leader must have organizational skills, including the ability to acquire military equipment, organize the force structure effectively, and allocate personnel appropriately. He should have an understanding of logistics, establish a flexible system of caches and depots related to the cell structure of the force (pp. 108–109), serve as an active teacher (p. 110), and be an effective planner (p. 108). Being adept at collecting and administering money, which Al-Muqrin calls "the nervous system of the *jihad*," is especially important (p. 108). A leader must also be a motivator and preacher, someone who can instill in his subordinates the "*jihadi* idea" and who is able to build a force that has commitment and cohesion, ensuring continuity in case he is killed or captured (p. 106). A leader's propaganda work must reach out to the general population as a form of political action, using *'ulama'* as key trusted communicators. As part of this outreach effort, leaders must also be good recruiters of both combatants and auxiliaries (p. 108). In the characteristic Red vs. Expert dilemma characteristic of most ideological movements, Al-Muqrin recognizes the importance of professional competence. As he notes with respect to field commanders, "Those who are the most knowledgeable and have the greatest familiarity with military science will be promoted over those who are better in the field of religious learning" (p. 121). However, perhaps not surprisingly given his ideological orientation, Al-Muqrin proposes three Muslim figures as embodiments of the ideal leader: Muhammad, Usama Bin Ladin, and Ayman Al-Zawahiri (p. 93).

The Role of the People

Al-Muqrin underscores that the people are a crucial factor, or a critical requirement, for both the government and the insurgents to succeed. For Al-Muqrin, that means that the people must be mobilized so that they accept the *jihad* and are willing to participate in the effort by at least providing material support. Al-Muqrin emphasizes the key role that auxiliaries play in insurgencies, calling them "the winning card" (p. 126), and appreciates their vital role in providing money, intelligence, shelter, and food to the *mujahidin*, as well as their role as potential recruits (p. 105). At the same time, Al-Muqrin is a realist and recognizes that most people will not be interested in taking part in an insurgency because they are preoccupied with their daily lives and are held back by fear and a reluctance to bear the burdens that being involved in an insurgency entails (p. 105). He warns that people, therefore, will be unlikely to join the *jihadi* organization unless the latter proves it is successful by demonstrating "its ability to manage and control matters effectively" (p. 105). He recognizes that victories are a valuable recruitment tool since there is an upsurge in support "after every successful operation by the *mujahidin*" (p. 105). In practice, Al-Muqrin was disappointed that few people became *mujahidin* and that the public attitude was often one of criticizing or pitying those who did.[92]

He admonishes his readers that they must pay attention to the people by understanding what their grievances are and that they will have to live among the people in order to gain their acceptance (p. 104). Knowing the people (the "human terrain" as it is often called nowadays) is a key part of the intelligence preparation of the battlespace, including for the process of selecting where to locate a base. One should know not only the population's socioeconomic profile but also where their loyalties lie (p. 115). The people are also to serve an important force protection function for the *mujahidin*, who are to hide and blend in with the local population when the enemy attacks (pp. 118, 175).

The concept of a people in arms was an accepted axiom within the QAP. Spokesmen urged ordinary people in Saudi Arabia to acquire arms in order to prepare to repel an expected U.S. invasion, arguing that among the arms "which should be in every Muslim home" were Kalashnikovs, handguns, RPGs, anti-tank weapons, and SA-7s, and opposing the Saudi government's campaign of gun control.[93]

Command Relationships

The question of command relationships (and command and control) for the QAP and higher authority presents some peculiarities, specifically in its relationships with the leadership of the mother Al-Qa'ida and with the latter's leader, Usama Bin Ladin.

The QAP is like a task force of the mother Al-Qa'ida, operating with guidance from the latter. Bin Ladin apparently provided general direction, legitimacy, and inspiration, but not detailed instructions or direct command and control, at least during the early period. According to former CIA Director George Tenet, terrorist mastermind Khalid Shaykh Mohammed, after his arrest told the CIA—albeit allegedly under torture—that Al-Qa'ida's operatives on the ground in Saudi Arabia had "blanket autonomy to conduct attacks on their own."[94]

The chain of command has been highly personalized, with QAP leaders having developed a direct relationship with Bin Ladin over the years. As a result, the latter probably was able to exert his influence more out of personal than official authority, relying on his charisma rather than on any office he held. Al-Muqrin, for his part, gave Bin Ladin the *bay'a*, or personal oath of fealty, as his *amir*, or leader, when he was in Afghanistan. And, asked later how he felt about Bin Ladin, Al-Muqrin unhesitatingly likened his relationship to him as that of "a son to a father."[95] Al-Muqrin stresses that without Bin Ladin "we would not have learned of many issues . . . or have taken the path we did."[96] He called Bin Ladin our *shaykh* and the *imam* of the *mujahidin*, highlighting Bin Ladin's missives, which he claimed would "refresh our resolve, remind us of our goals, and direct the Muslims and the *mujahidin* in many parts of the world." Al-Muqrin also called Bin Ladin and his associates the "leaders of the *jihad* . . . who are in the front lines thwarting the infidels' efforts which aim to conquer the Islamic countries, and especially the Gulf region and the Land of the Two Holy Shrines."[97] Al-Muqrin also referred to Bin Ladin as validation for his and the QAP's policies. Al-Muqrin, as leader of the QAP, was seen as the link between the QAP and Bin Ladin. For example, as one of the QAP commanders, Turki Al-Mutayri, was preparing to carry out an operation, he asked Al-Muqrin to deliver a farewell letter to Bin Ladin for him.[98] As late as 2007, QAP sources were still addressing Bin Ladin as the *amir* of the QAP and informing him of "your armies on the Arabian Peninsula."[99]

The overwhelming government crackdown that culminated in the death of Al-Muqrin and most of its experienced cadres seems to have thrown the QAP into disarray, and it appears that for a time at least the organization had to rely on more direct command and control from Bin Ladin.[100] When the QAP mounted the operation against the refinery at Abqaiq in February 2006—by the "Shaykh Usama Bin Ladin Squad"— the QAP claimed that it had done so "based on the guidance which our *amir*, Shaykh Usama Bin Ladin (may God preserve him) gave to target oil assets."[101] To be sure, this aside may have referred to general guidance, as Bin Ladin had often publicly given his encouragement to do so in general terms. However, it reportedly was not unknown for Bin Ladin to intervene directly to issue orders to the QAP's Internet staff, along with orders from local QAP leaders.[102] These days, however, communications between the QAP and Bin Ladin appear more tenuous. According to the confessions of a QAP cell commander, 'Abd Allah Al-Muqrin, who was arrested in 2007, had wanted to obtain Bin Ladin's approval—in the form of a *fatwa*—before mounting an attack on Saudi oil facilities, but was told it would now take six to eight months to do so, given the Saudi government's continuing security crackdown and Bin Ladin's isolation.[103]

Internally, organization appears to have been modeled on the "worry bead" schema, characterized by a direct relationship with the overall QAP commander by each of the constituent cells rather than the latter with each other, as Al-Muqrin mentions in his text. He inherited this flat organizational structure from his predecessor Al-'Ayyiri, who had concentrated direct links with the individual cells to himself personally.[104] Significantly, Al-Muqrin relied on personal ties and loyalties for support. For example, he appealed directly to those individuals he had trained, calling on them to join the *jihad*, no doubt feeling that such an approach would carry the greatest weight.[105] Marc Sageman identifies as a distinctive organizational aspect of Al-Qa'ida what he called the "small-world networks," where followers cluster around individual leaders (which he terms "hubs" or "nodes") based on personal loyalty.[106] In many ways, however, this type of organizational structure is very much in the traditional pattern of "patrimonialism" in the Middle East. This pattern is characterized by personalized patron-client power relationships and loyalties at all levels and is so well-established in Middle East society that it has proved resistant to its replacement by alternative patterns of organization despite frequent attempts by various local political and military organizations.[107] The centrality of personal ties—in practice even if not in doctrine—would do much to overcome the dysfunctional command and control aspects of allowing so much autonomy and neglecting a systematic command and control architecture.[108] In the case of the QAP, the cells into which the operating forces were organized probably acted very much as autonomous units, with perhaps overall guidance from and coordination with the top QAP leadership (who interpreted Bin Ladin's mission-type orders), but with detailed guidance coming only from the internal leadership of each cell. After Al-Muqrin's death there reportedly was no longer a single overall QAP leader, with a split into East and West coast cells.[109]

The history of the QAP's initial establishment would also have favored broad local cell autonomy. Although the details of the founding of the QAP remain murky and probably are completely known only to the top leadership of the mother Al-Qa'ida and the original leaders of the QAP—with most of the latter dead by now—there are enough bits of information to reveal at least the general lines. Although as a functioning organization one can trace the QAP back only after the events of 9/11, it appears that Bin Ladin had taken preliminary steps to set up such an organization a few years earlier. Saudi press reports indicate that by 1998 he had singled out Al-'Ayyiri—who had just been released from a Saudi jail—as a potential leader for such an entity and had tasked him with recruiting additional cadres and *jihad* veterans within Saudi Arabia.[110] And, at least by 1998, there were attempts to conduct terrorist attacks within the Kingdom.[111] However, it was only after 9/11 that Bin Ladin sought to actually put a new distinct organization in the field in Saudi Arabia.[112] The first cell of the nascent QAP was reportedly set up in Afghanistan and then transferred to Saudi Arabia while the rest of the cells were to be generated locally.[113]

Simultaneously, at least several returning *mujahidin* had also set up operational cells in Saudi Arabia on their own, apparently independently of Bin Ladin. For example, when Faysal bin 'Abd Al-Rahman Al-Dakhil, a veteran of the war in Afghanistan, returned home to Saudi Arabia, he began to recruit, arm, and train men, as well as collect money. He had prepared a plan and was set to carry out an attack when he happened to meet another militant, Turki Al-Dandani, who asked him to wait since the establishment of the new *jihadi* organization—the QAP—was being planned in conjunction with Al-Muqrin, who later also met Al-Dakhil and suggested that they coordinate their efforts, whereupon their two forces were amalgamated.[114] Likewise, when Turki Al-Mutayri returned to Saudi Arabia after the Taliban's defeat in Afghanistan, he intended to strike at U.S. bases in his home country and began with his own cell to scout out a target. However, one of his men happened to run into Al-Muqrin, with whom Al-Mutayri had lost contact, and they subsequently also joined forces.[115]

Based on the confessions extracted by the Saudi police from the QAP members they arrested, it appears that individual QAP cells did not hold meetings with other cells and that they had no direct organizational link to each other.[116] The Internet was used to transmit orders to the scattered cells.[117] Today, there is probably even less centralized command and control given the difficulties of the operational environment, and autonomous cells are often bound more by unity of purpose than by unity of command. As Al-Muqrin noted in reference to the situation in Saudi Arabia when he was in charge of the QAP: "It is no secret that the Al-Qa'ida organization depends on a cell structure, in which each cell depends on its own leader and on its own autonomous capabilities, and that it usually does not seek to establish a traditional organizational structure." He added that this autonomy guaranteed "greater survival and effectiveness," giving as an example the recent success of the Yanbu' cell as proof of the desirability of this organizational mode.[118] Perhaps out of necessity, a good dosage of delegated authority and mission-type orders seems to have been common, rather than attempts at micromanagement. Al-Muqrin praised the QAP cell based in Yanbu' and its leader, who had contacted Al-Muqrin and had promised in general terms to do something significant. According to Al-Muqrin, that cell leader had fulfilled his promise by hitting a Saudi-U.S. oil refinery and killing Western personnel and it seems that the initiative had come from the local cell.[119] Significantly, Al-Muqrin urged would-be *mujahidin* not to wait for "orders from anyone to engage in the *jihad* in the Arabian Peninsula."[120]

To a certain extent, the shared outlook and training acquired in past *jihadi* action facilitated delegating authority. In fact, as Al-Muqrin highlighted repeatedly, one of the most important aspects of his experience in all the foreign theaters where he had fought was his meeting and forging personal relationships with other like-minded militants, with whom he would collaborate in the future. No doubt, the personal bonds and mutual trust established were all that much stronger given the origin of these relationships that were based on a shared experience in the crucible of combat and danger. In fact, Al-Muqrin tried to use that personal bond as a means to motivate those *mujahidin* who had withdrawn from militancy after their return to Saudi Arabia, stressing to them the fact that he had trained many of them.[121]

Civil-Military Relations

To a great extent, Al-Qa'ida combines the functions of a traditional military and political leadership even more completely than was true of the Maoist movement, where the Party and the military were intimately joined and even interpenetrated, but still distinct entities, with the military at all times subordinate to the Party. To be sure, in the case of the QAP there was a "Military Committee" (*al-lajna al-'askariyya*) and a "political" side encompassing both a "Legal Committee" (*al-lajna al-shar'iyya*) and an "Islamic Committee" (*al-lajna al-islamiya*), but there is no visible political organization. While individuals certainly might have political or military functional specialties based on their experience, talents, and operational needs, in organizational terms the distinction between the two functional realms has been less clear-cut than it was even for the mother Al-Qa'ida. The leader would combine political-military authority and be untrammeled in his ability to fight the war by a separate local political leadership, although rivalries with other cell leaders could serve to limit the QAP leader's real authority, as could guidance from the mother Al-Qa'ida. However, Al-Qa'ida in itself can be said to constitute both the vanguard party (the role traditionally played by a Marxist-Leninist party) as well as the military component, and all the more so in a flat organization such as the QAP branch of Al-Qa'ida. Al-Muqrin's insistence on ideological conformity, which he repeats several times in his text, could serve the functional role of providing the basis for a parallel "party" or ideological influence or chain of command, ensuring unity of purpose and command outside the traditional "military" chain of command. Although Al-Qa'ida might act as the surrogate and equivalent of the vanguard party, in the QAP there is little indication that there was a distinction made within its membership, as individuals, between a "party" and a "military" role, and it is not surprising that Al-Muqrin makes little, if any, civilian-military distinction in *Guerrilla War* among the *mujahidin* when he discusses preparing the conditions to launch the insurgency.[122]

Intelligence

Al-Muqrin places considerable emphasis on intelligence (and counterintelligence) throughout his book. When discussing the process by which to select the location of a base, he provides an Intelligence Preparation of the Battle outline in all but name, orienting on the enemy and how the latter's forces are organized and equipped, how they fight, the terrain, the local population, etc., always in relation to the mission (pp. 115–116). He emphasizes field reconnaissance (p. 115) and has a solid understanding of key terrain, identifying it as "locations which when controlled or occupied give one side an advantage over the other . . . in relation to carrying out a mission," and avoiding the pitfall common even in professional circles of equating it to a center of gravity (p. 116). He also suggests including a topography expert in each squad (p. 112).

Intelligence collection can be highly specialized—especially so in an urban environment, according to Al-Muqrin—and the intelligence collection element must be able to collect, organize, process, and disseminate intelligence, which will require expertise with computers, photography, and communications (pp. 122–123). Maneuver may consist of operations such as assassinations and hostage-taking—something Al-Muqrin deals with at length—as well as with explosions and infiltration (p. 124). Force protection is especially difficult in a city where the presence of government personnel and spies is pervasive (p. 120). Operational security has to be enforced by compartmentalizing information rather than allowing free access to all personnel, especially in the case of operational intelligence (pp. 117–118, 120). Conversely, Al-Muqrin promotes leveraging deception into surprise. As he puts it, one should deceive the enemy into thinking "that the attack is in the West, while the main attack is really in the East, so that the enemy is kept busy with a supporting attack from one direction and is surprised from another direction" (p. 117).[123]

The Planning Process

Al-Muqrin's preparation for operations involves a sophisticated deliberate planning process. While it may not follow the same steps and terminology as doctrine in the U.S. armed forces, in functional terms there is a rough equivalence, and Al-Muqrin approaches the problems in a professional manner. He has a firm understanding of what a plan is meant to accomplish (p. 165–166) and of its criticality, alerting the reader that "this is very important," and calling it "the heart of the subject" and "exactly what a brother should take away from this course" (p. 165). Al-Muqrin's *Guerrilla War* envisions a virtual audience using his book as the basis for crafting planning problems of their own and encourages readers to send in the resulting plans so that they can be shared with everyone else. This concern with sound detailed planning as the basis for operations has continued to be stressed in the advice that the QAP's military magazine has offered, with Al-Muqrin's book as the basic reference for this process, even after his death.[124] Overall, his text is also a useful planning tool, as it provides questions to ask and a guide to decision-making on significant issues.

In the sample planning problem for an assassination operation that Al-Muqrin includes in *Guerrilla War*, one can recognize the equivalent of mission analysis, course of action development (including the mode of killing), orders development, and transition to execution, while other steps may be inchoate (pp. 165–166). He also calls for realistic rehearsals (pp. 144, 145, 166, 170). He emphasizes the important role of intelligence in this process and provides a detailed sample collection plan with a list of essential elements of intelligence needed to support planning (pp. 142–144). He also recognizes the need for flexibility in a plan, recommending alternative getaway plans and the preparation of alternative weapons to be ready for any contingency (pp. 147, 169). In practice, according to captured QAP operatives, the QAP's "Legal Committee" would propose targets to be attacked, and an operative might then offer a plan to his local commander, who would pass on it.[125]

Targeting

Al-Muqrin emphasizes that selecting the appropriate targets is a significant decision with more than tactical implications. Targets have to be selected not just on the basis of purely "military" considerations, but also in relation to the objective that one intends to achieve. For example, Al-Muqrin is adamant that local targets be avoided because that could alienate the population who may not understand ("owing to the public's unclear picture of the struggle and of the truth about the struggle," p. 109). In particular, targeting religious figures—that is, Muslim ones—should be avoided when a *jihad* is in its early stages, out of recognition that the potential negative reaction that such attacks could engender from the Muslim population. However, targeting religious figures of other faiths is permissible, especially missionaries or those who might be considered to be acting against Islam (p. 128). "Jews and Crusaders" living in the Muslim world are preferable targets to local religious figures. The intent of hitting such targets is to show that such people are present and to embarrass the host government, and Al-Muqrin contends that attacking foreigners will surely unite the Muslim world against the foreigner (pp. 95, 109, 130–131).

He also points out that the most lucrative targets are in the cities because that is where one finds government officials, businessmen, wealthy individuals, and foreigners (p. 120). Also, targets struck in a city are more visible than those elsewhere and will thus have a greater impact (p. 131). Urban targets will usually also have the greatest effect on the government because, according to Al-Muqrin, cities represent a state's prestige, and such attacks can also have a significant economic impact (pp. 120, 131). Al-Muqrin sees as the objective of striking economic targets the undermining of the sense of stability that any economy requires, whether in a Muslim country or abroad. For the Middle East the primary target in this category will be the oil industry. This

may take the form of attacking the infrastructure itself or personnel, especially foreigners, working in that sector (p. 128). Not surprisingly, Bin Ladin has repeatedly
given public guidance to target the oil sector in Saudi Arabia.[126]

Technology

Although wary of the potentially corrupting influence of some technology such as
television, the QAP, unlike the Taliban, overall has been technology-friendly in a utilitarian sense.[127] Al-Muqrin embraces and seeks to integrate the latest technology into his
doctrine, adapting to its impact and using it as a tool while not allowing it to drive his
thinking. He recognizes the utility of all areas of technology, such as cell phones for communications, digital photography, and the use of computer programs and simulators
to learn flying. However, he highlights in particular the role of computers and wants to
ensure that the *mujahidin* exploit that capability. This emphasis on computers is hardly
surprising as the QAP has mounted a sophisticated effort on the worldwide web, both
on its own homepage and by participating in the global network of *jihadi* forums,
websites, and media, including films geared especially for use on cell phones. Its
products have a polished, professional look, and at the time there had been no other
Al-Qa'ida-affiliated organization that had produced so much material specifically for
an electronic audience. In a way, the QAP was able to create a virtual liberated zone
on the Internet, an area that it could control and in which it could conduct some forms
of training, recruitment, propaganda, and intelligence collection in relative security.[128]
The QAP has used computers as a form of nonlethal fires, a veritable combat arm,
targeting the government's legitimacy. Significantly, the Internet has enabled a number of women to become participants in the *jihad* by not requiring their physical presence and has included them in what one can term as a genuine combat support arm by
working on both the technical and conceptual aspects of the QAP's electronic effort.[129]

Issues Ignored

What Al-Muqrin does not address or even allude to in his text is also interesting,
although his motive in not doing so is not always clear. He does not include suicide
attacks as a technique, despite the widespread use of this technique by Al-Qa'ida
around the world—although considerably less so in Saudi Arabia. On the contrary, he
emphasizes the withdrawal phase in every operation as a force protection measure
and stresses that provision be made for a successful getaway, including determining
escape routes beforehand, assigning personnel to delay pursuers, and preparing suitable hideouts (pp. 119, 144, 145, 161, 166).

Nor does he discuss weapons of mass destruction (WMD), although the latter could
conceivably be used in guerrilla wars. If anything, he segregates WMD use in a special category in his schema of wars, viewing this as a distinguishing feature of total
war whose probability he calculates as low (p. 90). This is all the more surprising
given the reported attempts by the mother Al-Qa'ida to acquire such weapons and the

explicit legitimacy of their use that is current in extremist Islamist circles. On the other hand, Al-Muqrin does not address in detail even attacks using conventional explosives, which many of the QAP actions in Saudi Arabia have involved.

ISLAM, CULTURE, AND MORALITY: KNOWING ONE'S AUDIENCE

Despite its reliance on preceding thinkers, Al-Muqrin's work nevertheless represents an original synthesis, innovating primarily by casting the theory for insurgency within an Islamic framework. Although guerrilla war doctrine may have universal applicability, Al-Muqrin's adaptation and reliance on Islamic terminology, such as referring to guerrillas by the term *mujahid*, can be expected to limit the appeal of his book to within the Islamic community, but at the same time facilitates its adoption within that community. Becoming a practitioner of *jihad* or a sympathizer of the ideas found in *Guerrilla War* does not contradict one's Muslim identity. Clearly, the language and imagery used are designed to be familiar to an Arabic-reading audience. Casting an argument in an Arabic/Islamic mold makes the content more accessible in cultural terms to a Muslim audience than if it were seen as an alien concept imposed from the outside. Even using culturally accepted formats—such as the frequent poetry in the QAP's military journal—facilitates the transfer of information.

However, the Islamic framework used in this book is not just a cosmetic or marketing factor.[130] The Islamic basis for legitimacy is embedded throughout the text, with recourse to the Qur'an, Sunna, and religious scholars, as one might expect for a text originating from an organization that views itself as the champion of genuine Islam. This preoccupation with Islamic legitimacy goes beyond mere phraseology and impinges on key concepts in Al-Muqrin's thinking. For example, in the latter's vision, among the essential moral qualities required of the commander and the *mujahidin* in general is the "fear of God" (p. 103). The rank-and-file *mujahid* must be a model for the rest of society, embodying faith, good behavior, loyalty, and lofty morals, and must serve as "a beacon showing the path to the people" (p. 107). Indeed, for Al-Muqrin, "*Mujahidin* who do not possess a knowledge of the *shari'a* will end up being nothing but bandits" (p. 106). Islamic principles, however controversial the Islamists' interpretation of these may be, provide the moral compass for Al-Muqrin and inform his view of *jihad*, or the equivalent of basic just war considerations. Although the QAP's interpretation of Islamic tenets may be extremist, its views are still within a broader spectrum encompassing contemporary Islamic thought in Saudi Arabia—albeit at its edge.[131] In Islamic intellectual circles, the concept of *jihad* has been undergoing a rethinking involving an expansion of limits in the past two decades or so—very much as has been the case with just war thinking in the West. The focus of this rethinking has been in terms of who can declare a *jihad* and under what circumstances, what constitutes valid targets, combatant status, and proportionality.

Al-Muqrin's evident religious vision and frame of reference notwithstanding, this does not cloud his practical approach to preparing for and fighting a war. However inevitable Al-Muqrin may have believed that ultimate victory would be in the long run, this outcome belonged to an indeterminate future and this clearly did not obviate the need for doctrine, planning, training, and expert execution of operations in the real world, as seen from the meticulous care he devotes to such mundane concerns and the implicit recognition that a human agent is necessary. Balancing God's power and the need for human activity, for example, he noted, "We never tire of repeating the warning to the military and police officers who sell their religion for small earthly honors, and we warn them of God's punishments and wrath, which He will administer *by our hands and the hands of other believers* and in any way He wills [emphasis added]."[132] Moreover, rather than returning to traditional Islamic military foundations, Al-Muqrin was steeped in Western and East Asian military thought, beginning with his basic premises, analytical taxonomy, and reliance on foreign material technology, and he was more than willing to assimilate any foreign aspect of warfighting that might be of use. This conforms to what some analysts had observed as "a marked 'Westernization' of anti-imperialist revolutionary thinking" that had been a trend for many years already.[133] Al-Muqrin remained a pragmatist at the tactical and operational levels, though his strategic objectives may have been strongly colored by ideological-religious considerations.[134] Ultimately, Al-Muqrin was an idealist in strategic terms, driven by an ideological vision, but very much a realist at other levels.

Paradoxically, Al-Muqrin is insistent that moral principles be obeyed, such as always following the *shari'a* in kidnappings or not looking at women hostages (p. 162). He also notes, "It is necessary to keep your promises, as our pure religion demands of us. I do not kill hostages once the enemy has accepted my demands and has fulfilled them" (p. 161). On the other hand, one is also struck by his hard, calculating attitude. For example, he coolly advises kidnappers "not to have pity" for hostages and not to pay attention to their sighs and tears, to kill the security personnel immediately (as a deterrent to the other hostages), and to execute hostages in order to gain credibility and send a message if the negotiations drag on (p. 161). At the strategic level, his ultimate objective, once victory has been achieved, is a draconic one as he expressed elsewhere: to present non-Muslims with a choice "of either accepting the religion of God [i.e., Islam] . . . or we kill every last one of them."[135]

APPLYING AL-MUQRIN'S IDEAS

There seems to have been broad-based acceptance of Al-Muqrin's doctrine within the QAP, and there were no real disagreements spilling out into the public domain over basic concepts or even techniques. This unanimity is not surprising, given the fact that his doctrine appears to have been the distillation of existing common practices and represented a consensus hammered out over the years in the mountains of Afghanistan and other *jihad* battlefields. The disagreements—some of them apparently quite bitter—that did occur within the QAP were over the doctrine's application. The internal debates in the QAP are often hard to follow, given the closed nature of any clandestine organization. According to a former QAP Internet technical worker, leaders would often engage in debates with each other using pseudonyms in the shadowy world of online forums, which unfortunately are almost impossible to track down retroactively.[136] However, even if the partisans of only one side of any argument were dominant and controlled the internal open media, one can still identify the basic issues of contention from the arguments presented by one of the parties.

To Launch or Not to Launch the Insurgency

As noted, whether or not and when to go to war constitutes a key decision for any political-military system, and there are indications that this was a thorny issue for the QAP. Apparently, the leadership of the mother Al-Qa'ida had pressed the QAP to begin attacks in Saudi Arabia, perhaps as a way to retrieve momentum for Al-Qa'ida after the U.S. campaign had dealt it and its Taliban allies a serious setback in Afghanistan.[137] According to George Tenet, the Agency's information was that debates with the mother Al-Qa'ida over initiating attacks within Saudi Arabia started in the fall of 2002.[138] Reportedly, Bin Ladin wanted the QAP to begin operations immediately. According to information available to the CIA, Bin Ladin at that time "urged a key Saudi operative . . . to move forward with the attacks at any price."[139] However, some in the top leadership of the recently established QAP were reluctant to launch an insurgency at that time, fearing that it was too early to do so since its organization was incomplete and that it could therefore collapse in the expected government reaction.[140] In the end, it was apparently the Egyptian leaders around Bin Ladin, including Al-Zawahiri, who convinced Bin Ladin to override the QAP's objections and give the order to in effect launch the insurgency.[141]

This decision was a serious miscalculation by the senior leadership of the mother Al-Qa'ida, and this was all the more surprising given the caution and need for careful preparation before launching an insurgency that Al-Zawahiri had emphasized in his own earlier writings.[142] In a way, the situation was reminiscent of the classical dilemma of the divergence of perspectives and interests between a central organization and a local affiliate, not unlike the situation that sometimes happened between the Communist Party of the Soviet Union and local parties where the interests of the latter might be sacrificed for the benefit of the greater entity.[143] In this case, perhaps the need of the mother Al-Qa'ida to relieve the pressure on itself by engaging the United States elsewhere outweighed other local considerations.

There was also an internal debate within the QAP on this issue, and Al-Muqrin reveals the two positions on this question in a surprisingly candid manner. There were those who were adamant in wanting to strike at "those aggressor forces who were polluting the Land of the Two Shrines," and to keep them from using their country to attack other Muslims one country at a time. Those holding the opposing position argued, however, that it was necessary to maintain the QAP's base, Saudi Arabia, secure so that the *mujahidin* could raise forces and other support there. Al-Muqrin was one of the QAP leaders who opposed launching the war within Saudi Arabia at the time, but he took an intermediate position, wanting at least to wait a while longer. One can imagine his net assessment and methodical exposition of the pros and cons in the internal debates, reflecting the principles found in his doctrine. As he was to recount later, he appreciated the necessity of exploiting the country in safety, since it was the principal source of funding for most *jihadi* movements and provided relative security and freedom of movement. However, Al-Muqrin also cited the need to balance that with the fact that the United States had invaded the Islamic world and that there was already pressure on the *jihadi* movement in Saudi Arabia by the local government. The situation in Saudi Arabia was deteriorating from day to day insofar as the conditions for the *mujahidin* and their funding were concerned, quite apart from the increasing secularization allegedly owing to orders from the White House. He added that it was advisable to engage U.S. forces in the Kingdom because otherwise those forces would have a secure rear, making it easier for them to strike Muslims elsewhere with impunity. At the same time, his decision was tempered because he realized that "it was necessary for us to prepare the necessary arms for this undertaking and prepare ourselves as completely as possible for this enormous task. I used to tell them 'Wait. Let us make preparations, and then we'll strike the Americans.'"[144]

In the event, it does appear that the recently established QAP was still in the organizational stage with limited numbers and capabilities and a fragile structure, and that it was not prepared to absorb the massive security countermeasures the Saudi government was able to unleash. Moreover, once the mother Al-Qa'ida had made a decision, Al-Muqrin seems to have felt it his duty to support it wholeheartedly, and we find him arguing in its support in order to deflect continuing criticism by many for having launched the insurgency at all. Logically, a psychological campaign and the completion of training would have preceded the beginning of operations. However, indicative of the unexpected requirement to launch the insurgency at the time, the QAP had not yet activated its media campaign or even its media infrastructure, nor had Al-Muqrin's *Guerrilla War* been published yet (and perhaps had not even been fully written yet). Al-Muqrin published the first installment of *Guerrilla War* in the first issue of *Mu'askar Al-Battar* in December 2003 after the insurgency was already in progress and, therefore, asserts in his work that conditions in the Kingdom had become "thoroughly ready" for the *jihad* there, in what may have been an ex post facto justificatory argument (p. 104).

Al-Muqrin later also claimed that the Saudi state had already declared war on the *mujahidin* and women in general and that the government had left the QAP no choice but to defend itself. He felt that if he did nothing, God's enemies would just escalate their attacks, killing the organization's leaders and jailing *'ulama'*, *mujahidin*, and sympathizers. Critics would no doubt have asked why nothing was being done, or would have gone to other theaters to fight. Rhetorically, he asks "How long should we have waited?" He added that the *mujahidin*'s honor and families had been violated, that Crusaders and Jews were being elevated in their home country, and that one could not remain passive as U.S. aircraft flew over their heads, aiming to destroy their brothers' houses in Afghanistan and Iraq. He notes that it is easy to criticize someone for not doing anything but that it is not easy to determine when to do something, and specifically when to launch an insurgency. It is one thing to speak theoretically, but one also needs to be practical. Having embarked on the war, Al-Muqrin exuded unbounded confidence publicly, threatening the United States would suffer so much that "your battles with the sons of the Two Holy Shrines in the Hijaz and Najd will make you forget . . . [even] the horrors of Vietnam."[145] This notwithstanding, Al-Muqrin later was still to express his disappointment—albeit indirectly—with this premature start of hostilities, when he noted that it was wrong to compare the progress made by the *mujahidin* in Saudi Arabia with the relatively greater success in Iraq, since in the latter there had been a long period of shaping, with the *mujahidin* being able to prepare for years in secure bases in Kurdistan.[146]

From another perspective, the QAP's official position on the *jihad* in the Arabian Peninsula also reflected Al-Muqrin's distinction between strategic decisions, which are not open to debate, and tactical points, which can be discussed. Countering the excuse by some that to fight a *jihad* in the Arabian Peninsula would lead only to defeat, the QAP argued, "One has the right to critique military plans, the means by which the battle was conducted, etc. which falls in the realm of application. However, to oppose in principle to fight in a specific *jihad* based on this fallacious premise [i.e., that the result would be defeat] is not allowed."[147]

Bounding the Area of Operations

Another of the issues that the QAP apparently debated was how to define the area of operations. To a large extent, that question was linked to the internal debate on whether or not to mount an insurgency in Saudi Arabia in the first place and the issue of target selection.

Realistically, Al-Muqrin's is a "defensive" doctrine and does not purport to provide a blueprint for out-of-area operations. In theoretical terms, although Al-Muqrin sees the possibility of eventually waging *jihad al-talab*, or preemptive war against non-Muslim countries with the goal of expansion, this lies in the distant indeterminate future after the liberation of all Muslim countries (p. 100). QAP leaders have not devoted any attention to the desirability of striking directly at the U.S. heartland, where the conditions are not present to wage a guerrilla war, which relies on a friendly population, even in the minimal form of a large resident Arab or Muslim community. It seems unlikely that the QAP—as an organization—would launch such attacks, although individuals who have passed through the latter may be recruited for such operations within the organizational framework of the mother Al-Qa'ida. In the case of an American citizen, Ahmed Omar Abu Ali, who was accused of plotting to assassinate President George W. Bush after coordinating with the QAP while he was studying in Saudi Arabia, this may have been a target of opportunity for the QAP or the information, which was allegedly obtained by means of torture while Abu Ali was in detention in the Kingdom, could lack credibility.[148]

Al-Muqrin may have believed that his doctrine had universal applicability, but his focus was the Islamic world and, in particular, his native country of Saudi Arabia.[149] The doctrine is sufficiently flexible in its concepts to be applicable in a generic manner to other similar problems, but it is apparent from Al-Muqrin's other writings and his own activity at the time his book appeared that he was consumed with events in his homeland. Indeed *Guerrilla War* is an attempt to address and solve an immediate concrete problem of waging an insurgency that had already begun in Saudi Arabia. But for the spiraling events in the latter and the need for a practical guide, Al-Muqrin—more a man of action than reflection—might never have penned his work at all.

Al-Muqrin viewed the QAP's area of operations in Saudi Arabia as a theater within a broader war that extended around the globe, underlining Bin Ladin's assessment that the Arabian Peninsula was "a link in the chain of the Christian Crusade which is being fought around the world."[150] Al-Muqrin claimed that by keeping the Americans busy defending their bases in Saudi Arabia and frustrating their plans, "with our *jihad* in the Arabian Peninsula, we are contributing to the Iraqi case and are helping the *mujahidin* who are there, with whom we are in close contact and with whom there is mutual support."[151]

However, the competing demands of other theaters—principally Iraq next door—confronted the QAP and its Saudi supporters with the very real dilemma of whether to contribute to the regional effort or to concentrate exclusively at home. Specifically, the recurring question was whether Saudis should go to fight the *jihad* in Iraq or remain to fight in Saudi Arabia. While Al-Muqrin was in charge, the QAP's policy was that the local theater would have priority, not Iraq. *Sawt al-jihad* presented the QAP's case in Realpolitik terms, arguing that it was best to strike the enemy in the rear, where it was less secure, where it felt safe, and where it least expected an attack. This official QAP source also claimed that "targeting the Americans in the Land of the Two Shrines will have a clear and powerful effect," would cause dissension between the United States and Saudi Arabia, and would energize the *Ummah*.[152] As further justification for this strategy, *Sawt al-jihad* argued that it was in effect supporting the mother Al-Qa'ida's effort. The QAP also maintained that the reason some questioned the latter's prioritization of theaters was that "until now Al-Qa'ida's tactic [*sic*] has not been understood in its great war against America, which seeks to extend the enemy and to strike the latter everywhere and in every country, which will terrorize and exhaust him . . . and the morale of its military personnel and of the civilians will collapse."[153]

Al-Muqrin himself declined to go to Iraq, citing an oath that he had allegedly taken to "cleanse the Arabian Peninsula of idolaters." Whatever the truth of this claim and of the inherent religious importance of the Arabian Peninsula, a sense of patriotism may have been at work as well. Al-Muqrin also gave priority to the argument that "we were conceived, born, and saw the light in this country. So, we will fight the Crusaders and Jews here until we expel them." He also justified his stand based on a statement by Bin Ladin to the effect that "They will not taste security, but we will expel them from the Lands of the Two Shrines, and we will expel them from the land of Palestine, and from the seized, plundered Muslim lands everywhere."[154] However, it is likely that other personal reasons also influenced his stand. As he noted, he had had many offers from clerics and from some of the "leading brothers" to go to Iraq, but he believed that "unfortunately, they wanted to get me out of the Arabian Peninsula," although he concludes that they may just have wanted to get him to a safer place. However, he assured his followers that he intended to stay.[155] Al-Muqrin placed his focus on fighting the *jihad* in Saudi Arabia within the context of the latter as a theater in a broader—global—war, and continued to portray the effort in Saudi Arabia as a contributing parallel war.

Nevertheless, a significant number of Saudis did go to Iraq for the *jihad*, and they no doubt would have been welcome in the QAP, especially as the government's crackdown depleted its ranks.[156] At the time, the QAP leadership itself expressed surprise that so many Saudis preferred to fight in other theaters rather than in "this wonderful theater" and, as it called Saudi Arabia, "the land most worthy of a *jihad*," and attributed that to the fact that activity in the latter was not yet well organized and that the local media and *'ulama'* were not supportive.[157] However, even some prominent figures in the QAP reportedly facilitated the deployment of Saudis to Iraq and went in person to fight there.[158] A later leader of the QAP, Salih Al-'Awfi, in fact, offered to send Saudi *mujahidin* to fight with Abu Mus'ab Al-Zarqawi in Iraq.[159] With the development of relatively greater success of the *mujahidin* operations in Iraq in comparison with those in Saudi Arabia, there was a shift in outlook among at least some of those who had favored an Arabia-first *jihad* policy. Significantly, QAP spokesmen addressed sarcastically those who had changed their minds, noting that they had earlier opposed allowing Saudi youths to go to Iraq, but were now shamelessly promoting precisely that, and accused them of having switched positions merely to win popularity and followers.[160]

Targeting

Another basic issue of internal debate was that of targeting, that is, what or whom the QAP should target once the war had been unleashed. The principal point of contention in this sphere was whether to strike local (i.e., Saudi) personnel and facilities or focus the effort on foreigners within the QAP's immediate area of operations. The conventional dichotomy often seen within radical Islamic movements is that of whether to focus on the "near" enemy, that is, against targets belonging to the local regime, or on the "far" enemy, that is, international targets and, above all, the United States.[161] In Al-Muqrin's thinking, the main enemy and main effort, at least in the early stages, was to be the United States, based on the emphasis in his writing, which focused on the U.S. threat and on the need to counter it. In the QAP's case, however, the issue has not been one so much of whether or not to reach U.S. interests out of area, but whether to strike U.S. (and other Western) targets located in Saudi Arabia or focus on local targets related to the regime. In effect, as an area of operations, Saudi Arabia has presented the advantage of being a target-rich environment of U.S. interests without the need for the QAP to go abroad, given the large U.S. military footprint (initially) and the large American economic and military advisory presence in the country.

Al-Muqrin's *Guerrilla War* focuses on what he calls "clean" targets, which he specifies as Christians and Jews (p. 95). Foreigners were also seen as softer targets, both physically and politically, than locals, and the preference for such softer targets also conformed to what one can call an accepted principle within the QAP to bypass enemy strengths and target the enemy's critical vulnerabilities in an indirect approach. As a leading QAP figure, 'Abd Al-'Aziz Al-'Anazi, advised explicitly, "If the enemy has—as is true of everyone—weak points and strong points, we must avoid the strong points and strike the weak points, which will cause the strong [point] to also collapse."[162] The view that foreigners should have precedence over local targets apparently gained the ascendancy early within the QAP. As one of the first QAP leaders argued, while invoking Bin Ladin's own guidance, "the main enemy are the Jews and the Christians," adding that to transfer the focus to the "slaves" serving the "occupying enemy" was a trap to divert the *jihad*. Moreover, killing one American or Westerner would hurt the local "tyrants" more than killing one hundred of the latter's own soldiers.[163] To avoid such potential traps, he urged his followers to desist from clashing with the local military and police as much as possible except in self-defense and to convince the security personnel to either join in the fight against the Americans or be neutral.

Al-Muqrin also believed, at least initially, that the QAP should avoid targeting Saudi military and security personnel, noting "the brothers are doing everything in their power to avoid confronting the Army and the security forces."[164] However, accusing the government of "escalation" and of wanting to "extirpate me, you, and all the Islamists," Al-Muqrin later suggested that that policy might have to change.[165] As he reiterated in clarifying the QAP's targeting philosophy, "To target the Crusaders and Jews and, reluctantly, apostate agents. That does not in any sense mean that we will stand with our arms crossed with respect to the latter and to their hostility toward us if they oppose us or violate the sanctity of our homes or terrorize our women and children, whereupon we will make them sorry."[166] Eventually, he warned security personnel to stop protecting the Americans or suffer their fate, telling the *mujahidin* to "Fight anyone who stands between you and the Americans and who fights against the *mujahidin* in defense of the Crusaders and clear them out of the way."[167] However, Al-Muqrin remained sensitive to the potential negative reaction from the Saudi public to local casualties, and he categorically denied that the QAP had been responsible for the suicide car bombing at the Emergency Services (and Traffic Police) Headquarters in Riyadh on 2 Rabi' I 1425/April 22, 2004, which had been criticized by Saudi public opinion and would lead to a further escalation in the confrontation between the QAP and the Saudi government.[168] In retrospect, that attack was almost assuredly carried out by the QAP, but probably by a cell not acting on Al-Muqrin's orders, highlighting the command and control challenges the QAP faced with its autonomous cell structure.

However, clashing with the country's security apparatus clearly became unavoidable, given the armed reaction one could expect from the government to the QAP's violent activities. In the event, the confrontations with Saudi security have usually been initiated by the latter, and by and large the QAP continued to avoid Saudi personnel as a principal target, at least as long as Al-Muqrin was in charge. The Saudi government, not surprisingly, accused the QAP of killing fellow Muslims, prompting Al-Muqrin to protest that the *mujahidin* respected the lives of Muslims. He claimed that the public understood "our combat policy, which is to focus on fighting the Crusaders, even though fighting the apostates [*i.e.*, the Saudi government] is easier and targeting the latter is simpler, since the latter have more positions, which are also more visible."[169]

Other leading figures in the QAP, however, were more aggressive in this respect. One, Abu Jandal Al-Azadi, even wrote a book justifying the killing of security personnel, arguing that the Saudi government recruited irreligious individuals for its security forces in any case, so that they—and their Christian advisers—were to be considered "infidels, apostates, and atheistic Zindiq-s," who then could be dealt with accordingly.[170]

Al-Muqrin was also aware that in an urban environment it may be difficult to strike targets without causing collateral damage, specifically causing civilian casualties whose deaths might provide the government with propaganda material and provoke a popular backlash. Noting this constraint, Al-Muqrin claimed that the QAP had been forced to postpone some operations to avoid causing collateral civilian Muslim casualties.[171] On the other hand, the QAP's official *Sawt al-jihad* journal, apparently in response to internal debates on collateral damage, concluded in its February–March 2004 issue that this was unavoidable: "Those innocent Muslims who accidentally pass by the place [of the attack] . . . well, the enemy in the Muslim countries is like a nasty cancer which cannot be excised without removing some of the surrounding tissue."[172]

Subsequently, as a result of the propaganda value to the government of the death of Muslim civilians, QAP became considerably more sensitive in its targeting guidelines with respect to collateral damage. Advice appearing in the October–November 2004 issue of its military magazine cautioned its readers in bold lettering that when developing targets "the most important thing to consider in relation to this is to avoid causing harm to the Muslims who might be in the vicinity of or within the target." The example provided was that if an American officer was targeted, he should not be attacked in the middle of a market as passersby might be hit.[173]

FIGHTING A WAR

As one would expect, an application of the principles that this, or any flexible, doctrine contains is an art form rather than a formulaic process and, ultimately, a test of the quality of the leadership. Al-Muqrin stresses that leaders must analyze qualitative factors before making a decision based on their judgment (pp. 104–105). As was seen earlier, he uses the case of Algeria as a cautionary note about the possible negative consequences of bad decision making.

A logical question is the extent to which Al-Muqrin's doctrine has been implemented and what impact it has had on the operations the QAP has mounted in Saudi Arabia—especially during Al-Muqrin's period of leadership of that organization—and its impact on achieving the QAP's objectives. As Mao stressed, praxis (application of a theory) is all-important. For Mao it is not theory alone that is important but the fact that he "assigns equal or greater intellectual effort to the application of theory."[174] No matter how proficient an organization might be at the tactical and operational levels, if the strategic decisions made by the leadership, or imposed by the political higher command, are faulty, it may be almost impossible to overcome such a handicap.

What Went Wrong?

In a way, the QAP has been successful in achieving at least one objective—that of removing much of the U.S. military presence from Saudi Arabia. The QAP's activity and the Saudi government's concern not to provide its adversaries with a potential issue to exploit at its expense probably contributed to the Saudi government's request to the United States to reduce its operational military footprint, although the U.S. advisory role—especially civilian contractors—remains a mainstay of the Saudi defense system. This was a popular issue throughout Saudi society, but even its elimination did not reduce the QAP's belligerence.[175] However, progress in overthrowing the Saudi regime and opening the way for a "true" Islamic system has been minimal, and the cost the QAP has paid in terms of its own personnel losses and organizational structure have been disproportionate to its achievements. To try to understand why the QAP has not met with greater success so far in the insurgency it has waged, one can modify the traditional question about the relationship between plan and execution for military ventures that have not been successful and ask here if in this instance it was a case of bad doctrine or bad execution. Of course, it is not possible to evaluate the validity or effectiveness of Al-Muqrin's doctrine based solely on its application by the QAP, as one must keep in mind that success or failure is often attributable more to the quality of the leadership and the latter's proficiency in application, as well as to what the enemy does, rather than only to the theoretical principles themselves contained in such a document.[176] What is key is the human element and doctrine and concepts can only be guides to action, but are no substitute for decision making, planning, and skill in execution.

As noted earlier, Al-Muqrin and the QAP's main target at this juncture was the United States, with the QAP's specific short-term objective being that of ending the American presence in Saudi Arabia (and on the Arabian Peninsula as a whole) and, in the process, inflicting as much pain as possible on the United States in order to contribute to Al-Qa'ida's broader global *jihad*. Al-Muqrin's strategy was encapsulated in his guidance to "fight the Americans everywhere . . . terrorize them as they terrorized your brothers . . . make them weep as they made the widows and orphans weep."[177]

When there was a possibility of choosing between an urban or a rural focus of effort, the QAP had deliberately selected an urban war and Al-Muqrin assessed that the QAP was now engaged in the attrition phase of a guerrilla war against the Saudi government.[178] This decision may have been influenced by the presence of most high-value targets in the cities. Fighting in cities would have the highest visibility and greatest immediate impact, as his doctrine suggests. In addition, there may have been an assessment that it might be easiest to neutralize the government's military advantages in an urban environment. Although admitting that an urban environment is difficult to operate in, Al-'Ayyiri suggests that in military operations in urban terrain, one could neutralize the government's air and vehicle advantage, something that could be done only in part in the mountains (where airpower could still function) or forests (where vehicles could still function), or the desert (where both could function).[179] Also, at first, cities may have looked as more suitable than the often bare countryside in Saudi Arabia to provide force protection for the *mujahidin*. Initially, the QAP had conducted its training mostly in rural settings, in places such as *wadis* protected from prying eyes. However, in at least one government raid on a rural training site in 2003, over twenty militants were captured. The risk of discovery and losing so many personnel in one place may have been the catalyst to a change in training venues, because shortly thereafter QAP personnel began to move to cities in order not to draw attention. The training became more theoretical and focused on military operations in urban terrain.[180] The fact that the global *jihad* has had an urban orientation may also have influenced the decision by the QAP to do so.

However, the QAP seems to have underestimated the Saudi government's ability to wield military and other forms of power, and the QAP was clearly overmatched— in particular—in its ability to generate force. Saudi Arabia, in effect, is one of the most militarized societies in the world in functional terms.[181] In addition to the conventional armed forces, which have a domestic as well as foreign defense mission, the government also has at its disposal additional layers of domestic security.[182] There is the Saudi Arabian National Guard, which has primarily a domestic security mission, and which today arguably is more combat effective than the Royal Saudi Land Forces.

There is also the Ministry of the Interior and other security-related institutions, such as the border guards, customs officials, and significant numbers of private sector security personnel. For example, a full 40 percent of the fifty-thousand-plus employees of Saudi ARAMCO (the government-owned national oil company) are security personnel.[183] Even the "morals police" (the *mutawwi'a*), with their ubiquitous presence in the cities, have acquired antiterrorism as an additional mission, ensuring one more set of intrusive watchful eyes on behalf of the government.[184] What is lost in a frequently intentional discouragement of jointness among these various security agencies and institutions is probably more than made up for by their sheer numbers and their redundant, overlapping, capabilities. As Al-Muqrin had recognized, the operational environment in Saudi Arabia for an insurgency is difficult. In his view, fighting against the Saudi government was even harder than it was for the Palestinians against the Israelis, because the QAP was fighting someone from the same nation who spoke the same language.[185]

In addition, the Saudi government can count on a degree of unity of command at the national level that most other countries would envy. Many institutions that would be found in the private sector in other societies have the characteristics and functions of paragovernmental agencies in Saudi Arabia. The official religious establishment, while requiring careful management, is little more than a government institution, bound by interest to the royal family. Likewise, the bulk of the economy—and a significant portion of people's jobs—is controlled by the government, and even more so if one takes into consideration the often blurred distinction between the public and private spheres, with the private assets of those belonging to the ruling elite for all intents and purposes also being at the disposal of the government.[186] The government also tightly controls education at all levels. That is also true for transportation, communications, medical infrastructure, and the media (at least in functional terms, as censorship is still the norm).[187] The government's control of the religious establishment and media, in particular, has been key in the war of ideas waged against the QAP, although the long-term impact of the two contending sides' message on the country's youth is hard to gauge. The Saudi government can also pressure the tribes, as semi-official administrative entities, to distance themselves from any QAP member who belongs to that tribe.[188] The absence in Saudi Arabia of countervailing institutions, such as political parties, labor unions, a free media, an independent judiciary, or civil society organizations that could place limits on government powers, facilitates a decisive and rapid response to a security threat. The Saudi government very skillfully mobilized all the elements of power at its disposal to deal with the QAP threat, even if to use them only as part of a security effort rather than to address basic social, political, or economic issues.[189] The overwhelming government presence created an environment that left little room for neutrality, and even family members of QAP militants found it prudent to distance themselves from their stigmatized relatives and declare their support for the government. Those taking such precautions included Al-Muqrin's father, who dismissed his son's death with the laconic phrase "My son went to his fate," assuring reporters that he had not been in touch with his son and that he had made pleas for him to surrender. Al-Muqrin's mother likewise was careful to tell the local press that she prayed for the country's rulers, for peace, and for stability in the country.[190]

The individual operations—one can think of each QAP attack as a battle or engagement—that the QAP conducted bore the hallmarks of Al-Muqrin's principles, at least at the tactical level. Most of the operations were planned meticulously with attention devoted to intelligence collection and rehearsals, as suggested by the videos the QAP filmed for propaganda purposes. The QAP was innovative, using deception such as wearing police uniforms and driving a police car when they attacked the Al-Muhayya housing compound in November 2003. While the execution at times did not achieve the desired objectives even at the tactical level, it was really at the strategic level that the QAP's effort suffered decisive failure.

Chance, present in any war, also appears to have played a part in the Saudi government's favor, which made possible the equivalent of spoiling attacks by the government at the strategic and tactical levels. As seen, the QAP leadership was skeptical about initiating an insurgency as many believed that was premature, but were induced to do so anyhow by higher authority. As things turned out, the cost of doing so at that time may have been prohibitive. At the tactical level, chance intervened in the form of an accidental explosion in a QAP bomb maker's apartment in Riyadh on March 18, 2003. This alerted the authorities, who were able to track down several QAP operatives based on information found in the apartment, which led to interrogations and arrests.[191] The intelligence collected greatly facilitated the government's response to the QAP challenge and contributed considerably to limiting the QAP's effectiveness and to the eventual tracking down and elimination of most of the QAP's original leadership by the summer of 2004. Unknown numbers of other QAP members and sympathizers were imprisoned as well.[192] Despite the massive government crackdown, Al-Muqrin asserted he was satisfied with the results of the initial period of the insurgency, using as his modest measures of success the fact that the QAP had been able to affirm its presence and to survive. He saw survival as "the basis for success in the attrition phase of a guerrilla war."[193]

Rather than pursuing a policy of low-level attacks while building up an organization, the "flea bites" called for in Al-Muqrin's doctrine, the QAP undertook the equivalent of major engagements against the government. Even if not in terms of numbers employed, the effect of striking major targets—some of which had high visibility and were well protected—all but ensured a massive government response. While avoiding attacks on the Saudi government's operational center of gravity—its military and security forces—the QAP chose to target critical vulnerabilities such as the country's sense of security and stability, without which the presence of foreign personnel and the smooth running of the economy might be put in jeopardy.[194] Thus, the QAP focused much of its effort against targets that struck at the heart of the government's critical requirements, such as the oil sector, which is by far the major source of the government's income. The endangerment of this sector would mean the loss of the government's critical capability of having the money needed to satisfy key constituents, whether in the military, religious establishment, bureaucracy, or the public at large, with potentially serious repercussions for its legitimacy and power. The attacks that the QAP mounted against the oil sector included not only direct attacks on the infrastructure, such as the raid on the Yanbu' refinery in May 2004, but the equally threatening attacks against foreign personnel working in the oil industry, such as the attack against the Halliburton office in Khobar that same month. Likewise, the attacks against the residential compounds where foreign expatriates lived struck at the heart of the capability of having foreign experts to help run critical sectors of the Saudi economy. As it turned out, the QAP had ended up fighting wars simultaneously both against the Saudi regime and against the United States, even though it apparently had not intended to engage the Saudi regime fully at first and was apparently surprised by the massive government offensive. As seen, many in the QAP—notably Al-Muqrin—had sought to avoid striking Saudi targets for practical purposes initially. However, it was unrealistic to think that that the Saudi government would not react forcefully to the attacks planned by the QAP, even if these attacks were focused on foreigners.

In addition, the launching of the insurgency, which many within the QAP had felt was rushed, had forced the QAP's hand before the political organization for an insurgency had really been created. Given the premature start of the insurgency, in many ways the QAP acted in a manner reminiscent of what Bard O'Neill calls a "military-focus strategy." That is, primacy is given to the military aspect of the insurgency over that of traditional political mobilization, as the movement's leaders "believe that popular support either is already sufficient or will be a by-product of military victories."[195] In the QAP's case, the result was probably closer to a hybrid phenomenon, given that the mother Al-Qa'ida had already been carrying out general political mobilization over the years, although not specifically in Saudi Arabia and not with the intent of creating a mass political organization.

The QAP, by mounting large-scale attacks, believed it could mobilize public opinion in its favor as well as undermine the government's credibility and legitimacy. As Al-Muqrin saw it, "spectacular operations," in particular, "motivate the public" and "mobilized the *Ummah*" (p. 96). And, he noted that members and supporters will join the cause "after every successful operation by the *mujahidin*" (p. 105). In fact, he assessed with satisfaction that "the series of attacks against the Crusaders [i.e., Westerners in Saudi Arabia] has shown the power of the *mujahidin* and revealed that the efforts of the collaborationist Saudi regime cannot protect the interests of the Crusaders in the country."[196] Elsewhere, he concluded that the recent QAP attacks were forcing people to take a stand or, as he put it, these attacks were "a purification plant and a sorting out of people."[197] Instead, the attacks seem to have had a negative overall effect. While there is no reliable means to gauge public opinion in Saudi Arabia, the available indications suggest that there was genuine revulsion about the casualties—especially those who were non-Western—resulting from the QAP attacks. Anecdotal evidence in the form of apparently spontaneous opinions expressed to the press to that effect is corroborated by the QAP's attempts at damage control.[198]

Presumably reacting to what it believed public opinion felt, the QAP found itself forced to divert much of its attention and media effort to defending its actions after several of the attacks, no doubt aware that this competition between the Saudi government and the QAP for legitimacy and for the sympathies of the Saudi population was the crucial battleground. For example, following the QAP suicide bomb attacks on the Al-Muhayya housing compound in Riyadh, the QAP was at pains to counter the government version, which focused on the fact that Arab residents, not Westerners, had been killed. A QAP communique stressed that the residents were all "Crusaders," including the non-Saudi Christian Arabs living there, making them licit targets, accused the government of protecting non-Muslims, warned Saudis to stay away from the Crusaders and their dens of depravity where drinking occurs, and claimed that the Saudi government was being hypocritical for regretting the death of a few Christians while having killed many more Muslims in its prisons.[199] QAP ideologue Luways 'Atiyat Allah bluntly concluded that the Saudi government was able to turn the attack on Al-Muhayya compound into a media success by claiming that Muslims were killed, thus "inciting some against the *mujahidin*," although he believed that that result was reversible if the United States were hit again.[200] Similarly, with the kidnapping of an American contract employee, Paul Marshall Johnson, in June 2004, the QAP found itself on the defensive after they killed him, cut off his head, and posted a gory video showing the execution on the Web. The fact that his severed head was found in the freezer of the home of one of the QAP leaders only added to the general public condemnation. The QAP again had to engage in damage control. Al-Muqrin argued that Johnson was equivalent to a military target because he worked on helicopters, that he was an infidel and a criminal because those helicopters were used against Muslims, and that pragmatism allowed even the killing of prisoners of war. He also claimed that war justified any such measure in order to protect the Muslim army and the Muslims' honor.[201]

The media battle was uphill for the QAP with only the Internet to counter the electronic and print media, which the government controlled. Whatever the effectiveness and credibility of the Saudi media, the fact that the government could count on it for a virtual monopoly on information was a significant factor. Unlike some issues, such as the Arab-Israel dispute, where the Saudi government finds it difficult to compete with the more agile satellite networks based abroad, there was not likely to be competition or a different message on the terrorism issue from such sources. Not surprisingly, the government focused its information campaign on the civilian casualties, especially in the housing compounds, and the fact that most were not even Americans, as well as the fact that the QAP was also targeting Saudis. Whatever negative information about the *mujahidin*'s private lives that could be marshaled was also used to undercut the QAP's legitimacy.[202] The QAP's inability to access the mass media, and even its own media assets once many of the QAP's senior leaders and cadres had been eliminated, made it very difficult for the QAP to respond effectively. With the country's official religious establishment joining in the condemnation of the QAP, establishing legitimacy by the latter became even more difficult.[203]

The government was able to force the QAP to fight costly battles. Even when the QAP performed well tactically in these engagements, such as breaking out of encirclements set by considerably larger numbers of Saudi security or holding off superior forces for days before succumbing, the result was still an operational defeat for the QAP. Thus at Al-Rass in the Qasim region, a relatively large QAP force was surprised but still held off vastly superior Saudi forces for two days (the QAP and the Saudi Arabian National Guard claimed it was three) in April 2005. The QAP claimed the government had to bring in artillery and "thousands" of personnel, and that the QAP had all fought to the death in bitter combat among the city's houses. Although at least 105 Saudi security personnel were wounded in the action, according to an official tally, what mattered in the end was that the QAP was defeated, in this case with nineteen killed and three members captured, which included the QAP's top leadership.[204]

Al-Muqrin's death marked the end of a chapter in the QAP's insurgency, coinciding with an accompanying decimation of the QAP's personnel, especially its senior leadership, and experienced cadres. While there was no single decisive engagement, the constant grinding away at the small QAP forces had a toll on the organization. Eventually, virtually all the individuals on the government's wanted lists were killed or captured, including most of the QAP's top leaders. These individuals included most of the early organizers of the movement and represented a fund of shared experience and a web of personal relationships that would be difficult to replace immediately. As a result, the QAP retreated into a period of rebuilding and low visibility. By 2005 many in the Saudi establishment had concluded that the QAP had been defeated.[205] As even the mother Al-Qa'ida's official journal termed it, in the post-Al-Muqrin period the QAP was experiencing "an astonishing quietness."[206]

PROSPECTS AND IMPLICATIONS

Despite the serious losses it incurred, the QAP has apparently retained some capabilities and continued to mount attacks ranging from assassinations to strikes on the oil facilities at Abqaiq, and many more arrests have occurred by the government forces, preempting additional attacks. In 2007 the Saudi government twice announced large-scale arrests. In April they arrested seventy-two individuals from seven cells, and in November they arrested 208 more individuals in six cells, although the actual arrests may have been spread over a period of time and did not include additional individuals arrested or killed.[207] After a hiatus of almost two years, *Sawt al-jihad* also reappeared in 2007. What is significant is that although the Saudi government made use of all the elements of power at its disposal, the framework for that was one focused on security with a goal of repressing the insurgents rather than really addressing the insurgency. The challenge of the socioeconomic grievances and opening up the system to greater participation, which might appeal to the pool of potential QAP sympathizers, remains to be dealt with, and that alone can ensure victory in the long term over the QAP.

All indications are that the QAP still accepts Al-Muqrin's doctrine as valid. However, there may be a rethinking of how to apply the doctrine and, in particular, of the urban-centric approach that dominated in the initial period of the insurgency. It is not clear whether a new approach may emerge or whether the prevailing opinion may result in a continuation of the previous urban-centric approach, but there are hints that there are discussions on that score. It seems there may be some within the QAP who believe that focusing on cities was a mistake at the current time. Not unlike what happened to Mao when the urban-focused Autumn Harvest Insurrection of 1927 resulted in a stinging defeat and obliged the Chinese Communist Party to try a rural-based movement instead, a similar suggestion has been floating on the Internet in relation to the QAP.[208] An anonymous militant (apparently, according to internal evidence, a member of the QAP) proposed that the QAP change its focus following what he termed had been its "military failure." Instead of focusing on the big cities, which he called a mistake, the QAP should focus instead on the countryside. What the QAP should do is establish a liberated area, specifically in the Yemen-Saudi Arabia border area, because the terrain there is rugged, the Saudi government presence there is weak, the situation is marked by "chaos," and the local society is still tribally based, more pious, and more conservative. In addition, neighboring Yemen could be used as strategic depth for the QAP. The writer draws on an analogy in the relationship between Pakistan and Afghanistan.[209] This does not mean a rejection of Al-Muqrin's ideas. The anonymous author emphasizes many of the same principles, such as speed, shock, intelligence, targeting the enemy's will, planning, and operations, such as assassinations and blowing up of government buildings, but seeks to apply such principles to another environment.

However, it is difficult to judge whether such a refocusing to the rural sector has been occurring in operational terms. Recent QAP operations do not indicate clearly whether or not such an approach has become dominant in thinking and whether or not there is a corresponding shift at the operational level. Arrests by Saudi security have preempted most attacks and not all the details have been made public, but it is interesting that some of the more recent arrests have been carried out in the countryside.[210] Other fugitives have also taken refuge in the countryside.[211] Moreover, according to press reports, the fact that on later wanted lists individuals from smaller cities have predominated may indicate a shift to areas with less dense government security and media access.[212] Also, based on the information released by the Saudi government about those arrested in the seven separate cells, it appears that the QAP wanted to send recruits to foreign countries for training. One Saudi-owned newspaper speculated this referred specifically to Yemen.[213] In addition, there has also been a continuing focus on earlier target sets and, in particular, the oil sector, as indicated both by the afore-mentioned February 2006 attack against the oil facilities at Abqaiq and by the alleged plans for even broader attacks on oil facilities preempted by arrests in late 2007.[214] And, echoing the past, there has been at least one prominent attack on foreigners—French expatriates in this case—in 2007. Although this latter attack occurred in the desert, the location may have been more a factor of convenience—while the intended victims were traveling—rather than implying a shift in the area of operations.[215] Those arrested in the past two years have been engaged not only in planning high-visibility attacks but, more frequently, in organizational activities such as training, fund-raising, and recruitment.

THE TEXT AS A TEACHING TOOL

The QAP was particularly committed to making the tools available for professional military education, as attested by the sheer quantity of materials it produced and the emphasis it placed on this aspect of its outreach effort, and *Guerrilla War* was a key component of that curriculum. As one would expect, the QAP provided direct classroom instruction and field training in Saudi Arabia, and made videos of some of the instruction, for both instructional and propaganda purposes. Al-Muqrin personally trained a number of prominent militants in Afghanistan and in Saudi Arabia, as was the case with Turki Al-Mutayri, later commander of the QAP's Al-Quds cell, who took the "Practical Course" from Al-Muqrin in Saudi Arabia.[216]

However, this hands-on training could benefit only a relatively small number of individuals, especially once the government crackdown had begun and the QAP was preoccupied with its operations and its own survival. The QAP's parallel intent, which perhaps could have a greater and longer-term impact, was to provide for distance education, relying on the Internet as a vehicle to disseminate its instruction. Readers were told in an early issue of *Mu'askar Al-Battar* that the magazine was to be "the beginning of a road toward preparing the people of the Peninsula and others. . . . We will facilitate this process of preparation and will teach the *Ummah* to bear and use arms to oppose the invasion by the West."[217] The QAP leadership was frustrated by the what it saw as "a void" in military knowledge, noting that "many Muslim youths even today do not know how to handle weapons, much less how to use them, since the Crusaders' agents have repressed the Muslims and prevented them from preparing [to fight] for the sake of God." In particular, the QAP's intent in using a Web-based capability was to provide the would-be *mujahid* "in his isolation" the exercises and military science he would not have otherwise, and encouraged individuals to apply what they learned when they found themselves outside of built-up areas.[218]

Other military organizations, including the U.S. armed forces, also make use of correspondence courses as a training tool. Although this vehicle is usually a pallid substitute for a residence course, it is nevertheless better than nothing and it can be particularly useful as a socializing tool for newcomers or part-time participants, such as reservists.[219] To be sure, QAP leaders recognized the limitations of such training, for example cautioning readers eager to undertake attacks on their own to be extremely careful about using explosives based on online instruction, since "the first mistake is the last mistake," and suggesting that a "brother go along who has had previous practical, not just theoretical, experience with such things."[220]

Given the QAP's physical limitations, such long-distance education may have been the only realistic means of reaching beyond a narrow circle, especially after the tightened government controls put it on the defensive. Moreover, this was a way to reach far beyond Saudi Arabia, making information accessible to Arabic-speakers anywhere in the region and around the world. The QAP has continued to promote Al-Muqrin's work on its website. There is no way of knowing how many have read Al-Muqrin's manual or other elements of QAP's military writings online, or how many may have downloaded and reproduced any of these, much less determining their instructional effectiveness for their audience. The only quantitative indication of the use made of the QAP's publications is the counter on the QAP homepage. That can provide only a very crude order of magnitude, as it does not indicate which specific readings may have been accessed or downloaded.[221]

As is common with such products, Al-Muqrin's text has also been reproduced on numerous extremist forums and websites and can be tracked down with a bit of effort in multiple locations and formats. Individuals as well as other organizations can have recourse to the text for their own use, whether in toto or as a source of specific information at the touch of a keystroke. Even Arabic-language websites hostile to Al-Muqrin and those of his ilk unwittingly may have given the document additional publicity by repeating some of its key concepts in an attempt to discredit him.[222] Ideas found in Al-Muqrin's work have also been incorporated into other Al-Qa'ida products without attribution.

As for Al-Muqrin's direct impact in other theaters—and specifically on Iraq—that is difficult to measure with assurance. Just as the Iraqi regime was disintegrating during the U.S. invasion in 2003, one or more Al-Qa'ida or QAP personnel wrote a book that was published online, calling on the Iraqis to wage a guerrilla war to liberate Iraq. The analytical portion of the work, dealing with the nature of war and the characteristics of guerrilla war, as well as sections on urban combat skills and guerrilla force structure and organization had Al-Muqrin's ideas embedded in the text.[223] One cannot assess how influential that specific work may have been in contributing to the launching of the insurgency or on the operations of the widely disparate insurgent groups in Iraq. Although many of the suggestions in that work appeared in some form subsequently, there is no way to tell whether that occurred because of the book or simply as a result of conventional wisdom and trial-and-error in the field.[224] Al-Muqrin's ideas have appeared elsewhere in Iraq, as in a summarized version of *Guerrilla War* found in 2005 in *Al-Fursan*, the journal of one of the Iraqi insurgent groups, the Islamic Army in Iraq (*Al-Jaysh al-islami fi Al-'Iraq*).[225]

The availability of Al-Muqrin's text online facilitates its distribution and the propagation of its ideas in a way that earlier technologies, such as the traditional printed book or even the audio or videocassettes, could not. The manufacture and distribution of physical intellectual products has not always been easy in the Middle East because of the tight government censorship that often stifles political writings of any sort— much less anything associated with a banned organization—and because of a lack of an effective marketing infrastructure. With the Internet, however, government controls can be bypassed in part without compromising directly the security of the originating organization or of the consumer. Saudi officials have recognized the challenge that the availability of such virtual training represents as it facilitates recruitment and the acquisition of lethal skills for an exponentially larger audience than could be reached in the traditional training camps in remote parts of the world, even if the product now might be considerably inferior to that resulting from traditional means.[226] As one could expect, governments, including that of Saudi Arabia, have cracked down on Internet cafes and have acted to block unwelcome websites, and a number of the QAP's redundant sites have become inaccessible over time.[227] This probably has limited most a Saudi audience, although Saudis going abroad for study and tourism would have untrammeled access. Moreover, the switching to new sites on the Web and the reproduction of material on the literally thousands of forums and websites with *jihadi* proclivities makes it very difficult to suppress undesirable material permanently. Some organizations even make freeware programs available to defeat the blocking mechanisms, while there are also websites that to the casual observer may seem innocuous, such as an Egyptian-based automobile marketing site, yet carry *jihadi* material in a subcategory. Moreover, the existence of Web servers based around the world—many with services available at no cost—facilitates the permanent posting of many of these products in multiple locations. In fact, some of the QAP's materials have been available even on "The Internet Archive," a 501(c) (3) nonprofit organization based in the United States.

Al-Muqrin's text is written using direct and elegant language, although that may be the result of editing by another hand. At times, Al-Muqrin appears to be struggling in juggling neologisms for military terminology for concepts that are relatively unfamiliar in Arabic-language discourses, and indeed there is sometimes a lack of standardization and of precise terminology even within the conventional military lexicon in the Arab world.

In terms of presentation, Al-Muqrin's style is reminiscent of both Clausewitz and Sun Tzu. That is, Al-Muqrin at times reveals his reasoning process at length, in a sort of dialectic, openly weighing the pros and cons, as did Clausewitz. At other times, Al-

Muqrin offers pithy conclusions with no clarification, in a manner reminiscent of Sun Tzu's presentation of conclusions unsupported by the process by which he had arrived at such conclusions, although in Al-Muqrin's case this is usually done when dealing with TTPs. The style of terse bullet-form phrases sometimes found in the original is typical of a briefing or doctrinal publication, and this aspect has been retained in the translation. The text has a flavor reminiscent of military manuals anywhere, with its repetition of learning points and the use of the "this is what I just finished telling you" approach to promote retention. The current translation retains the original highlighting to show what Al-Muqrin thought was important. The footnotes in the translation are Al-Muqrin's own, while the endnotes have been added. The diacritic "'" designating the Arabic letter *'ayn* has been used in the text, but other letters have not been transliterated.

CONCLUSION

First, Al-Muqrin's doctrine presents a complex challenge that is more than just in the terrorist—or even just in the military—realm, given his parallel emphasis on politics, economics, and religion. We cannot dismiss such adversaries as simply terrorists and believe that such delegitimation provides insights into how to counter them or solve the problem. To be sure, many of Al-Muqrin's positions and actions cannot be described as anything but terrorism by most standards. Nevertheless, that is just one of several tactics he envisioned in his doctrine, and his thinking goes far beyond that single aspect and represents a genuine insurgency, which requires a different, more comprehensive approach than when dealing with a simple terrorist movement.[228]

Responding to such a doctrine and its application is done most effectively by the local government rather than by an outside entity. A local government's understanding of the local language, culture, and society is an indispensable asset. Moreover, the local entity does not operate with the stigma of being alien and is thus better positioned to establish the legitimacy that is essential for success. In particular, in the arena of a war of ideas, outside players have little to contribute. However, the war of ideas itself is far from clear-cut and easy in Saudi Arabia, given the internal ideological contradictions and the shared pool of numerous basic beliefs between outright militants and many in the religious establishment, the governing elite, and the population at large and the linkage of some of these beliefs with the regime's very legitimacy.[229] To be effective in the long term, the response must be as complex as the challenge, with the military component playing only a supporting role, providing a shield of time and security for the "sword" of socioeconomic, political, and ideological response to occur and win the war.

However, conversely, local authorities may find it especially difficult to institute the structural political, social, and economic changes necessary to address popular grievances as a way to reduce the potential appeal of those likely to apply doctrines such as Al-Muqrin's to lead an insurgency. In Saudi Arabia's case, balancing the domestic social, ideological, and economic contradictions makes the issue of change especially complex and the very existence of the insurgency may make the regime even more wary of systemic reforms out of heightened concerns for stability.[230] The country's current economic windfall stemming from high oil prices may be a palliative and allow the regime to feel it can postpone major changes.[231] Admittedly, the core members of an organization such as the QAP may not be amenable to the appeals of even basic change. However, the wider popular pool of potential recruits and sympathizers on which an insurgent leadership relies is more likely to be responsive to such initiatives, which would undercut the insurgency's potential.[232]

Second, Al-Muqrin's work also reminds us that we have to accept the enemy as he is, not as we would like to see him in conformance with some theoretical constructs, and that we cannot impose our vision on how an enemy should think or act.[233] That is, Al-Muqrin's thought in many ways is quite traditional, rather than conforming to notions some may have of threats becoming fourth-generation war, that is, a way of war that some have posited as being completely different from earlier manifestations of low intensity conflict.

Al-Muqrin and the QAP framework within which he wrote and worked do not support the fourth-generation theorists' premises of novelty.[234] Most of the perceived novelty posited by partisans of this theory are actually traditional aspects of insurgency warfare, and where there are new points, such as the perceived appearance of a "non-trinitarian" war and the dominance of a non-state approach to war, there is nothing in Al-Muqrin's work or in the nature of the QAP to support that.[235] In effect, rather than limiting the conceptualization of war to institutions characteristic to a specific time and place, as some interpreters of the concept of the trinity do, both Clausewitz and Al-Muqrin see an enduring universality of forces as part of the common nature of the phenomenon of war itself.[236] Al-Muqrin operates very much within a trinitarian framework, devoting ample attention to the basic elements of Clausewitz's trinity—the rational, irrational, and nonrational forces in war—although he may be doing so in an internalized mode without being explicit about it. Al-Muqrin addresses other traditional analytical Clausewitzian categories and retains very much a traditional approach to war, albeit his focus is at the lower end of the spectrum of conflict.

As far as thinking in terms of states or abandoning that as a frame of reference, although the QAP is a subnational clandestine organization fighting, as it sees it, within a global conflict, its frame of reference has still been that of the existing state structure and state system. Al-Muqrin's work, while it has in many ways a broader applicability and scope, reflects the author's primary concern with addressing the situation in his home country. To be sure, the QAP also has wider pretensions, purporting to speak for all of the Arabian Peninsula. In operational matters, Al-Muqrin notes, "In today's circumstances, borders must not separate us nor geography keep us apart, so that every Muslim country is our country and their lands are also our lands" (p. 129).[237]

However, in reality—despite coordination and linkages with Al-Qa'ida organizations in neighboring countries and the potential supranational appeal of a religiously based ideology—the QAP's actual focus and area of operations has largely followed existing state boundaries, recognizing states as a key reference point, even when not feeling bound to respect state boundaries in operational matters. Significantly, the QAP's official organ, *Sawt al-jihad*, in promoting attacks on Americans, urged the people of the Arabian Peninsula to fight them each in his own country, with the Yemenis to do so in Yemen, Kuwaitis in Kuwait, and the people of the UAE, Qatar, and Bahrain all in their own respective countries.[238] Indicative of the factor of local national pride that underlay the thinking of local *mujahidin*, was an incident in a training camp in Afghanistan. According to a Saudi militant, when a Yemeni there suggested, "We will enter Riyadh as conquerors," the Saudi bristled with indignation and retorted, "Why should you enter as conquerors in Riyadh, since we have our own families, brothers, and sisters there?"[239]

Insurgencies by their very nature usually are not waged by states because such wars most often represent an effort to overthrow the existing system or expel an invader, which almost always consists of a state or are the default choice in the absence of other options. What an insurgent movement envisions as its final objective is perhaps more significant in this respect in determining its relationship to the state concept. That is, Al-Muqrin's long-term goal was to set up an Islamic state on the Arabian Peninsula as a prelude to a revived mega-state, the Caliphate. Rather than representing a new theory of war, Al-Muqrin's doctrine is novel more for its refashioning of operational art in the service of new concrete goals, for its Islamic ideology, and for its reworking of existing ideas and personal experience into a new synthesis in order to solve concrete problems in a specific cultural environment.[240]

Third, Al-Muqrin's work provides a blueprint for other regional insurgencies, or at least makes available a package of ideas to consider and to stimulate the thinking of would-be insurgents elsewhere. While others may not adopt his ideas wholesale, there is considerable material from which to select and adapt. In particular, the doctrine can be a vehicle for professional military education of *jihadi* insurgents and would-be insurgents, either as a substitute for combat experience or in combination with the latter. Those who ponder and internalize the principles and questions embedded in this document are likely to become more formidable adversaries in virtually every warfighting function.

Finally, Al-Muqrin's work should serve to remind everyone that we face a thinking adversary with an independent will, one who can adapt and innovate and one who should never be underestimated. The text under study here is a seminal doctrinal publication and provides a valuable insight into the thinking of such an adversary—in this case a *jihadi* movement. Al-Muqrin is likely to retain his relevance in the future, particularly as his work (including his other written, audio, and video products) continues to be made available by the QAP and other like-minded organizations, and indeed the QAP even has continued to promote his book as obligatory reading.[241] This ongoing visibility will contribute to ensure that Al-Muqrin's military thought will remain a factor to consider and contend with despite his death.

NOTES TO PART 1

1. Jarret M. Brachman and William F. McCants survey two such *jihadi* military writers in *Stealing Al-Qa'ida's Playbook*.
2. The literature on Al-Qa'ida is by now voluminous. Some of the studies dealing with Al-Qa'ida that can provide a useful context for this study include Ahmed S. Hashim, Rohan Gunaratna, Christopher Henzel, and Jane Corbin.
3. Others have also grappled with the same problem, resulting in such products of military thought as the Chinese work *Unrestricted Warfare* by Senior Colonel Qiao Liang and Senior Colonel Wang Xiangsui. This work was intended to provide a strategy for a developing country to defeat a technologically superior adversary, but in this case, of course, the authors envisioned conflict between two states, despite the unconventional asymmetric means contained in *Unrestricted Warfare*.
4. Milan Vego, "On Doctrine," 1–2.
5. A useful background resource on the situation in Saudi Arabia is Anthony H. Cordesman's magisterial research project, *Saudi Arabia Enters the 21st Century: Main Report*. Other analyses, encompassing various evaluations of the extent and seriousness of internal problems, include Sherifa Zuhur, As'ad Abukhalil, Mamoun Fandy, and Madawi Al-Rasheed.
6. *Al Qaeda Training Manual*. For a short overview of this document, see Jerrold M. Post, "Killing in the Name of God: Osama Bin Laden and Al Qaeda," 24–30.
7. Others, such as guerrilla war analyst Robert Taber, have also allowed for the overlapping of the two terms: "Guerrilla war, in the larger sense in which we have been discussing it, is *revolutionary war*, engaging a civilian population, or a significant part of such a population, against the military forces of established or usurpative governmental authority." Taber, *War of the Flea: The Classic Study of Guerrilla Warfare*, 4. Apolitical versions of guerrilla warfare, with all the military techniques but not the political objectives commonly associated with insurgencies, of course, also exist; see, for example, the account by a participant in the U.S.-led guerrilla operations in Burma during World War II, Roger Hilsman, "Guerrilla Warfare."

8. According to custom, his *kunya*—Abu Hajir—was taken from the name of his first-born child, in his case a girl, but it would have changed if and when a son was born.

9. Mushari Al-Dhaydi, "'Abd Al-'Aziz Al-Muqrin: kayf tahawwal min haris marma ila haris mawt?" ['Abd Al-'Aziz Al-Muqrin: How Did He Change from a Goal-keeper to a Defender of Death?] *Al-Sharq Al-Awsat* (June 18, 2005).

10. Interview with 'Abd Al-'Aziz Al-Muqrin, "Liqa' ma'a ahad al-matlubin al-19" [Interview with One of the Wanted 19], part 1, *Sawt al-jihad*, no. 1 (Sha'ban 1424/September–October 2003), 22–23. As was typical of many of his fellow-*mujahidin*, Al-Muqrin resented the fact that the Saudi government had supported the *mujahidin* earlier in Afghanistan but when they returned, as they saw it, had abandoned them and punished them for having gone abroad to fight in the *jihad*. For information on all Islamic terminology and concepts, the standard reference work is *The Encyclopaedia of Islam*, 2nd edition.

11. "Liqa' ma'a ahad al-matlubin al-19," part 1, 22–23

12. Interview with 'Abd Al-'Aziz Al-Muqrin, "Liqa' ma'a ahad al-matlubin al-19" [Interview with One of the Wanted 19], *Sawt al-jihad*, no. 2 (Sha'ban 1424 October–November 2003), 22.

13. According to an anonymous source who reportedly knew Al-Muqrin well, reported in Khalid 'Uways and Sa'd Al-Matrafi, "Al-Muqrin wa-rifaquhu: ma'lumat tunshar li-awwal marra" [Al-Muqrin and His Comrades: Information Published for the First Time], *Al-'Arabiya* (June 19, 2004). Also used for this biographical sketch was 'Ali al-Qahtani and 'Abd Allah Falah, "Latma jadida 'ala wajh al-irhab ba'd suway'at min maqtal al-amriki Junsun" [Another Slap to the Face of Terrorism Just a Few Short Hours after the Murder of the American Johnson], *Al-Watan* (June 19, 2004).

14. Sa'ud 'Abd Allah Al-Qahtani, "Hifz al-khawarij al-qur'an lam yamna'hum min takfir al-muslimin wa qatlihim" [Memorizing the Qur'an by the Kharijites Did Not Prevent Them from Declaring Other Muslims Infidels and Killing Them], *Al-Riyadh* (June 27, 2004).

15. "Turki Bin Fuhayd Al-Mutayri," *Sawt al-jihad*, no. 20 (Jumada I 1425/July 2003), 33.

16. "Liqa' ma'a ahad al-matlubin al-19," part 2, 23.

17. "Liqa' ma'a ahad al-matlubin al-19," part 2, 22. In particular, he was reportedly responsible for training new QAP recruits in the eastern and central parts of the country, in secret camps in the mountain and *wadi* wilderness areas. 'Ubayd Al-Suhaymi, "Shakhsiyat al-irhabiyin al-arba'a al-qatla" [The Personalities of the Four Terrorists Who Were Killed], *Al-Sharq Al-Awsat* (June 20, 2004). Al-Muqrin placed a high value on the role of trainers, and fully recognized how difficult that function was. Recalling his days in Afghanistan, he notes that many recruits had a hostile attitude toward their trainers, viewing them as arrogant, and that

patience is needed in order to deal with so many individual personalities, "Liqa' ma'a ahad al-matlubin al-19," part 1, 24.

18. As reported in Faris Bin Hazzam, "'Abd Al-'Aziz Al-Muqrin qa'id 'Al-Qa'ida' fi Al-Sa'udiya harrab asliha min Asbaniya li-l-Jaza'ir wa-u'tuqil fi Al-Sumal wa-qatal fi Afghanistan wa-l-Busna" ['Abd Al-'Aziz Al-Muqrin, the Leader of "Al-Qa'ida" in Saudi Arabia Smuggled Weapons from Spain to Algeria, Was Arrested in Somalia, and Fought in Afghanistan and Bosnia], *Al-Sharq Al-Awsat* (December 10, 2003).

19. Anthony H. Cordesman and Nawaf Obaid, *Al-Qaeda in Saudi Arabia; Asymmetric Threats and Islamist Extremists*, working draft, 4.

20. Al-Dhaydi, *Al-Sharq Al-Awsat*.

21. "Turki Bin Fuhayd Al-Mutayri," *Sawt al-jihad*, 34.

22. 'Abd Al-'Aziz Al-Muqrin, "'Ashar dhi al-hijja . . . wa-l-jihad fi sabil Allah" [The Tenth of Dhu Al-Hijja . . . and the *Jihad* in God's Cause], *Sawt al-jihad*, no. 9 (Dhu Al-Hijja 1424/January 2004), 3. Among the best overviews of the history and traditional concepts of *jihad* are Rudolph Peters and James Turner Johnson. A quick overview of some relevant concepts is also found in E[mile] Tyan, Douglas Streusand, and Youssef H. Aboul-Enein and Sherifa Zuhur.

23. Interview with Abu Jandal by Khalid 'Antar, "'Ulama'na wa-mashayikhna khadhaluna wa-takhallaw 'anna" [Our 'Ulama' and Shaykhs Betrayed and Abandoned Us], part 1, *26 Sibtimbir* (Sanaa, Yemen) (December 16, 2004). Abu Jandal at one time had been Usama Bin Ladin's bodyguard. The *huris* refer to the virgins awaiting martyrs in Paradise, according to Islamic doctrine.

24. Interview with Abu Jandal by Turki Al-Dakhil, "Dhayf al-halaqa" [Guest of the Series], *Al-'Arabiya*, *Al-Ida'at* TV program (April 30, 2007).

25. Al-Suhaymi, "Shakhsiyat al-irhabiyin al-arba'a al-qatla," 22.

26. Al-Dhaydi, *Al-Sharq Al-Awsat*. On a different level, some in Saudi Arabia have dismissed Al-Muqrin's military work because they view him as not professionally qualified, at least in conventional military terms. For example one mid-level Saudi National Guard officer told the author that Al-Muqrin was not to be taken seriously because "he has no military training; he was not a soldier," and posited that someone else must have penned his work for him, 2004.

27. See Usama bin 'Abd Al-'Aziz Al-Khalidi, "Madha yurid Al Sallul?" [What Do the Al Sallul Want?], *Sawt al-jihad*, no. 6 (Shawwal 1424/November–December 2003), 6.

28. 'Uways and Al-Matrafi, "Al-Muqrin wa-rifaquhu," *Al-'Arabiya*.

29. 'Abd Al-'Aziz Al-Muqrin, "Bayan li-l-umma" [Communique to the Ummah], n.d., printed text from the video entitled *Ayyuha Al-Amrikan* [Oh, You Americans!]

30. Ibid.

31. 'Abd Al-'Aziz Al-Muqrin, "Sariyat Al-Quds" [The Jerusalem Company], transcript

of an audio tape, (Rabi' II 1425/May–June 2004). Retrieved from www.qa3edoon. com/KotobWaBayanatWEB/SariyatAlquds.htm.

32. 'Abd Al-'Aziz Al-Muqrin, "Risala ila man tarak al-silah" [Letter to Those who Have Abandoned the Fight], undated audio tape transcribed by the *Sawt al-jihad* staff.

33. For example, although there are no solid unemployment figures for Saudi Arabia, estimates range from official ones of 12 percent to some as high as 30 percent, Tariq Al-Nawfal, "470 alf sa'udi 'atil 'an al-'amal yumaththilun 12% min ijmali quwwat al-'amal" [470 Thousand Unemployed Saudis Represent 12% of the Entire Labor Force], *Al-Watan* (April 14, 2007), and Milton Copulos, President of the National Defense Council Foundation, Testimony Before the House Re-sources Subcommittee on Energy and Mineral Resources, Washington, D.C., March 4, 2004, available online at www.nma.org/pdf/cong_test/ copulos_030404.pdf. Two-thirds of those unemployed were between twenty-one and thirty years old, and the prevailing belief among them was that what counted in finding work was "connections." 'Ali Al-'Umayri, "Dirasa 'ilmiya: 67% min al-'atilin a'marhum ma bayn 21–30 'am" [An Academic Study: 67% of the Unemployed Are Between 21–30 Years Old], *Al-Madina* (April 22, 2007). The age cohort under twenty-one, which seemed to provide a disproportionate number of QAP recruits, was particularly vulnerable to unemployment, with more than 60% of that age bracket unemployed, according to the Saudi Minister of Labor, Ghazi Al-Qusaybi, quoted in "Al-Qusaybi: Al-bitala bayn al-dhukur fi Al-Sa'udiya 9.1%" [Al-Qusaybi: Unemployment among Males in Saudi Arabia is 9.1%], *Al-Jazira TV* (November 21, 2006).

34. Al-Muqrin, "Bayan li-l-umma."

35. Al-Muqrin, *Ayyuha Al-Amrikan*.

36. In fact, some of his most pointed barbs were directed at former *mujahidin* who, after returning to Saudi Arabia, did not want to fight in their own country. Using appeals to honor, shame, love of God and the rewards of Paradise, as well as past comradeship, he sought to reactivate them, Al-Muqrin, "Risala ila man tarak al-silah."

37. "Al-Qissa al-kamila li-'wazir a'lam' Al-Qa'ida bi-l-Sa'udiya" [The Complete Story of the "Minister of Information" of Al-Qa'ida in Saudi Arabia], *Al-'Arabiya* (October 17, 2005).

38. 'Ali Al-Qahtani, "*Al-Watan* yanqul tafasil al-hadith min mawqi' al-hadath wa-amakin qatl al-irhabiyin" [*Al-Watan* Reports the Details of the Incident from the Scene and the Place Where the Terrorists Were Killed], *Al-Watan* (June 20, 2004). Also, see 'Abd Al-'Aziz Al-Shammari, "Kashaf Al-Watan tafasil al-lahadhat al-'asiba qabl al-injaz al-amni al-bahir" [*Al-Watan* Discovers the Details of the Critical Moments before the Brilliant Security Success], *Al-Watan* (June 21, 2004) and 'Abd Allah Bin Falah, "Rijal al-mabahith istadu al-irhabiyin fi-l-mahatta"

[The Secret Service Agents Caught the Terrorist at the Gas Station], *Al-Watan* (June 20, 2005).

39. These versions are discussed in the reporting by Maysar Al-Shammari and 'Abd Allah 'Assuj, "Sayyara mufakhkhakha am shabakat al-intarnat awqa'at Al-Muqrin wa-rifaqahu fi al-fakhkh?" [Was It A Booby-trapped Car or the Internet Which Led Al-Muqrin and His Comrades into a Trap?], *Al-Hayat* (June 20, 2004).

40. Khalid bin 'Abd Al-Latif Al-Mu'jal, "'Abd Al-'Aziz Al-Muqrin radhiya Allah 'anhu" ['Abd Al-'Aziz Al-Muqrin, May God Be Pleased with Him], *Sawt al-jihad*, no. 20 (Jumada I 1425/June–July 2004), 25.

41. Ibid.

42. *Mu'askar Al-Battar*, no. 13 (Jumada I 1425/July 2004), 2.

43. As posted on *Al-Sahat* forum, January 10, 2007. Retrieved from www.aafaq.org/blog/aa/654.htm.

44. Omar Nasiri, a Moroccan who trained in the *mujahidin* camps in Afghanistan, reports this, *Inside the Jihad: My Life With Al Qaeda: A Spy's Story*, 127.

45. A good dosage of Clausewitz would also seep through by means of any familiarization with Soviet doctrine, given the influence of Clausewitz on Lenin's strategic thinking. For an incisive analysis of Mao and other modern theorists and practitioners of revolutionary war, see John Shy and Thomas W. Collier, "Revolutionary War." The reference editions used here of these two military thinkers are Carl von Clausewitz, *On War*, and Mao Tse-tung, *Mao Tse-tung on Guerrilla Warfare*. For comparative purposes, reference will also be made to Sun Tzu, *The Art of War*.

46. According to his training tape, "Dars li-l-shaykh.al-shahid Yusuf Al-'Ayyiri rahimahu Allah 'an harb al-'asabat" [Lesson by Shaykh Yusuf Al-'Ayyiri, May God Have Mercy on Him, on Guerrilla War]. Retrieved from www.qa3edoon.com/vivi.htm.

47. (n.p.: Markaz al-dirasat wa-l-buhuth al-islamiya, n.d).

48. (n.p.: Markaz al-dirasat wa-l-buhuth al-islamiya, March 2004).

49. 'Abd Al-'Aziz bin Rashid Al-'Anazi, *Hukm istihdaf al-masalih al-naftiya* [Judgment on the Targeting of Oil Assets], n.p.: Markaz al-dirasat wa-l-buhuth al-islamiya, [2005].

50. "Al-Khatima" [Concluding Article], *Mu'askar Al-Battar*, no. 20 (Sha'ban 1425/September–October 2004).

51. In this sense, recognizing an expanded set of non-state belligerents, Al-Muqrin is closer to some current thinking in the West, such as found in the U.S. Marine Corps' *A Tentative Manual for Countering Irregular Threats; An Updated Approach to Counterinsurgency* in which war is defined as: "a violent clash of interests between or among *organized groups* characterized by the use of military force," 1.

52. See William F. Scott and Harriet Fast Scott, *Soviet Military Doctrine; Continuity, Formulation, and Dissemination*.

53. 'Abd Al-'Aziz Al-Muqrin, "Nida' al-nafir min al-shaykh Usama Bin Ladin" [The Call to Arms by Shaykh Usama Bin Ladin], *Sawt al-jihad*, (Dhu al-qa'da 1424/ December 2003–January 2004), 2.

54. Al-Muqrin, "Risala ila man tarak al-silah."

55. Al-Muqrin, "Bayan li-l-umma."

56. As Al-Muqrin put it, Al-Qa'ida is "the historical starting point for reestablishing the Islamic state," "Liqa'," part 2, 22. Elsewhere, Al-Muqrin explained that when God establishes the Rightly-guided Caliphate, the latter "will fill the world with fairness and justice, as it is now filled with injustice and tyranny." Al-Muqrin, "Risala ila man tarak al-silah."

57. Al-Muqrin, "Risala ila man tarak al-silah."

58. Al-Muqrin, "Bayan li-l-umma."

59. Al-Muqrin, "Sariyat Al-Quds."

60. 'Abd Al-'Aziz Al-Muqrin, "Asrana amana fi a'naqna" [Our Prisoners Will Be Free Or We Will Die], *Sawt al-jihad*, no. 12 (15 Muharram 1425/March 7, 2004), 3.

61. Al-Muqrin, "Bayan li-l-umma."

62. Al-Muqrin, "Liqa'," part 2, 22. The formulation of this goal relied on an extreme interpretation of a *hadith* attributed to Muhammad: "Expel the idolaters from the Arabian Peninsula," which is recorded in *Al-Jami' Al-Sahih*, Muhammad Al-Bukhari's (810–870) collection of *hadith*.

63. Al-Muqrin, "Liqa'," part 2, 25.

64. Al-Muqrin, "Nida' al-nafir," 2–3.

65. Ibid., 3. *Jahili* refers to the pre-Islamic period, which is seen by Muslims as an age of ignorance and paganism.

66. See Joseph A. Kechichian "The Role of the Ulama in the Politics of an Islamic State: The Case of Saudi Arabia," and Nawaf E. Obaid, "The Power of Saudi Arabia's Islamic Leaders."

67. Al-Muqrin, "Nida' al-nafir," 3.

68. The greatest disruption in this respect seems to have been inter-generational, between children and their parents, as often blood-ties among relatives of the same generation appear to have been a vehicle for QAP recruitment, as in the case of several of Al-Muqrin's relatives who joined the QAP. In one family, in fact, four members joined the QAP, despite the family patriarch's opposition. Muhammad Darraj and 'Asim Al-Ghamidi, "Usrat munaffidhi al-'amaliyat al-irhabiya fi Yanbu' takshif asraran jadida li-l-*Watan*" [The Family of Those Who Carried Out the Terrorist Operations in Yanbu' Reveal New Secrets to *Al-Watan*], *Al-Watan* (May 7, 2004).

69. A former female leader in the QAP noted that the latter engaged in an intensive campaign to recruit women, most of whom ended up working on the QAP's internet front. Interview with Umm Usama by Manal Al-Sharif, "*Al-Watan* tuhawir ra'isa sabiqa li-ahad tandhimat Al-Qa'ida al-nisa'iya" [*Al-Watan* Interviews a

Former Head of a Women's Organization in Al-Qa'ida], *Al-Watan* (February 19, 2005). Al-Muqrin himself was effusive in his praise of the role women were playing in the *jihad*, particularly in Saudi Arabia, calling them an example for the menfolk, 'Abd Al-'Aziz Al-Muqrin, "Nihayat al-fa'izin" [The End-State of the Victors] *Sawt al-jihad*, no. 18 (1 Rabi' I 1425/April 21, 2004), 3.

70. The QAP media, for example, highlighted the competition between loyalties to one's tribe and to the *jihadi* movement, arguing that one should shun individuals who placed "the evil of loyalty to their tribe and clan" above—and in opposition to—loyalty to "a unitarian Muslim *salafi mujahid* group." "Al-Fatiha" [Opening Article], *Mu'askar Al-Battar*, no. 15 (Jumada II 1425/July–August 2004), 26.

71. "Nihayat al-fa'izin," 3.

72. For example, in an interview, he said, "My wish, really, is for God to grant me this martyrdom." "Liqa'," part 2, 22.

73. 'Abd Al-'Aziz Al-Muqrin, "Rahimak Allah ya Aba Hazim" [God Have Mercy on You, Abu Hazim], *Sawt al-jihad*, no. 13 (1 Safar 1425/March 23, 2004), 3.

74. For Mao, guerrilla warfare is similarly "a weapon that a nation inferior in arms and military equipment may employ against a more powerful aggressor nation," 42.

75. As Clausewitz puts it, "Kind-hearted people might of course think there was some ingenious way to disarm or defeat an enemy without too much bloodshed. . . . Pleasant as it sounds, it is a fallacy that must be exposed," 75. Conversely, Sun Tzu, while recognizing the need to fight if necessary, nevertheless stressed that "To subdue the enemy without fighting is the acme of skill," 77.

76. Luways 'Atiyat Allah, "Al-Fitna" [Discord]. This consists of an interview with the QAP ideologue Luways 'Atiyat Allah, published in book form.

77. 'Abd Al-'Aziz Al-Muqrin speaking on video number 28, dealing with the QAP attack at Al-Khobar. Retrieved from www.al-qa3eedon.com.
    A protracted war is also key for Mao, 67, 69, 94, given his focus on guerrilla war, but anathema to Sun Tzu, who warns that "For there has never been a protracted was from which a country has benefited," 73.

78. Of course, the emphasis on the enemy echoes Sun Tzu's dictum "Know the enemy and know yourself; in a hundred battles you will never be in peril," 84.

79. Al-Muqrin, "Nida' al-nafir," 2.

80. Douglas Pike, *PAVN: People's Army of Vietnam*, 227.

81. See Pike, 222–230.

82. Al-'Ayyiri emphasizes even more forcefully the point about targeting and defeating the enemy's will, defining defeat as "the destruction of the will to fight." In his instructional tape on guerrilla war, he stresses that the U.S., for example, has a critical vulnerability in terms of casualties. He compares the Afghans—who he says lost one million in their war against the Soviets—and were victorious to the Americans—who he says lost only 72,000 to 73,000 (sic) dead in Vietnam—but were still defeated because of a loss of will. Video tape *Harb al-*

      'asabat [Guerrilla War], n.d., available online at www.qa3edoon.com.

83. For example, see Clausewitz, 259, 386, 421. Clausewitz, of course, speaking of decisive battles in the real world, noted that "such cases are rare," 625, and that victory may not occur with a single blow, but may require instead "managing a campaign," stressing that what counts is not each single engagement but "the ultimate success of the whole," 177.

84. Mao, 52.

85. For example, Al-Muqrin notes in *Guerrilla War* that the area of operations for what he terms "mountain forces" encompasses various aspects of difficult terrain, such as is found in the countryside, mountains, swamps, forests, and even the terrain in small towns.

86. In that respect, Al-Muqrin is closer to the Vietnamese Communist experience in using terrorism rather than to that of the Chinese Communists, who had largely avoided it; see Chalmers Johnson, "The Third Generation of Guerrilla Warfare," 442, 444–445.

87. The legal basis of this definition is Title 22 of the U.S. Code, 2656f(d), Department of State, Office of the Coordinator for Counterterrorism, *Country Reports on Terrorism 2005*, 9.

88. Ibid. The issue is complicated further by a more nuanced understanding of terrorism in the Middle East itself. For example, according to press reports, a recent highly-praised doctoral dissertation by the Saudi military attache in Egypt, Staff Brigadier 'Abd Al-Rahman 'Atiyat Allah Al-Dhahiri, focused on differentiating between terrorism and legitimate military actions based on whether those actions were conducted on behalf of "national resistance" and "national liberation," which would make such actions acceptable. Fathi 'Atwa, "Dirasa sa'udiya tad'u li-l-tafriq bayn al-irhab wa-haqq al-muqawama al-wataniya" [A Saudi Study Calls for Differentiating between Terrorism and the Right of National Resistance], *'Ukaz* (July 28, 2007). For further discussion of the issue of defining terrorism, see Bruce Hoffman, *Inside Terrorism*, and Martha Crenshaw Hutchinson, "The Concept of Revolutionary Terrorism."

89. 'Abd Al-'Aziz Al-Muqrin, "Fa-sharrid bihim man khalfahum" [Disperse with Them Those Who Follow Them], *Sawt al-jihad*, no. 20 (Jumada I 1425/June 2004), 3–4. The title is taken from Qur'an, VIII/57. Al-Muqrin was also anxious to dispel government reports that the QAP had used civilians as human shields when they attacked foreign oil personnel in Al-Khobar, 'Abd Al-'Aziz Al-Muqrin, "Dhalik min fadhl Allah 'alayna wa-'ala al-nas" [That Is by God's Grace to Us and to the Rest], *Sawt al-jihad*, no. 18 (Rabi' II 1425/May–June 2004), 3.

90. "Tasa'ulat hawl jihad al-salibiyin fi Jazirat Al-'Arab" [Second-guessing about the *Jihad* against the Crusaders on the Arabian Peninsula], part 3, *Sawt al-jihad*, no. 11 (Muharram 1425/March–April 2004), 29.

91. As Taber also stressed, in order for people to join a movement, with all the risks

involved, they must have a "reasonable expectation of success," 23.

92. Indeed, Al-Muqrin was disappointed that so few people met his demanding standards for practicing Islam, as he complained of "the small number of those who practice this religion the way God expects." 'Abd Al-'Aziz Al-Muqrin, "Rabah al-bay'ya shabab Yanbu'" [It Was a Success, Youth of Yanbu'], *Sawt al-jihad*, no. 16 (15 Rabi' I 1425/May 5, 2004), 3.

93. Al-Faruq Al-'Amiri, "Ma huwa wajibna tujah ummatna?" [What Is Our Obligation to Our Ummah?], *Mu'askar Al-Battar*, no. 16 (Jumada II 1425/August–September 2004), 3–4, and "Hamlat naz' al-silah" [The Campaign to Disarm], *Mu'askar Al-Battar*, no. 17 (Rajab 1425/August–September 2004), 3–4.

94. George Tenet, *At the Center of the Storm: My Years at the CIA*, 248.

95. Al-Muqrin, "Liqa'," part 2, 23.

96. Ibid.

97. Al-Muqrin, "Nida' al-nafir," 2.

98. "Risala min al-mujahid Al-Turki Al-Mutayri rahimahu Allah ila al-shaykh Usama Bin Ladin hafidhahu Allah" [A Letter from the Mujahid Al-Turki Al-Mutayri, May God Have Mercy on Him, To the Shaykh Usama Bin Ladin, May God Preserve Him], *Sawt al-jihad*, no. 20 (Jumada I 1425/June 2004), 35.

99. Muhammad Bin 'Abd Allah Al-Nasir, "Bal al-'aqiba li-l-muttaqin ya Al Sallul!" [Oh Al Sallul, It Is the Pious Ones Who Will Be Victorious], *Sawt al-jihad*, no. 30 (Muharram 1428/January–February 2007), 4.

100. One of the leaders of the QAP's women's section, who was involved in the organization's communications, notes that during the later period only inexperienced cadres remained, and claimed that Bin Ladin's messages containing coded guidance became longer and more detailed in order to compensate for that loss in local leadership. Interview with Umm Usama.

101. QAP Communique of 28 Muharram 1427/February 27, 2006.

102. Interview with Umm Usama.

103. Reported in Hasan Al-Amir, "Najah fasl al-qa'id 'an al-qa'ida" [Success in Separating the Leader from the Base], *Al-Watan* (May 16, 2007).

104. In fact, he reportedly selected subordinate leaders from those militants he knew from his time in Afghanistan. Faris Bin Hazzam, "Qissat ta'sis Al-Qa'ida fi Al-Sa'udiya" [The Story of the Establishment of Al-Qa'ida in Saudi Arabia], part 2, *Al-Riyadh* (October 6, 2005).

105. Al-Muqrin, "Liqa'," part 2, 26.

106. Marc Sageman, *Understanding Terrorist Networks*, 139–140.

107. On patrimonialism in the region, see James A. Bill and Robert Springborg, *Politics and the Middle East*, 5th ed., especially 112–129.

108. As a case in point, such personal ties seem to have been able to trump at times even that of national origin for the QAP, with at least three of its top leaders having come originally from foreign countries (Yemen and Morocco), as was

also true of a number of its rank-and-file. For example, on the list of thirty-six wanted QAP operatives released in 2005, six were foreigners (three from Chad, one from Kuwait, one from Yemen, and one from Mauritania). Maysar Al-Shammari, "21 minhum kharij al-mamlaka," [21 of Them Are Outside the Kingdom], *Al-Hayat* (June 29, 2005).

109. Faris Bin Hazzam, "Kayf ikhtaru qadathum wa-man qa'idhum al-jadid?" [How Did They Select Their Leadership and Who Is Their New Leader?], *Al-Riyadh* (July 25, 2006).

110. Faris Bin Hazzam, "Qissat ta'sis Al-Qa'ida fi Al-Sa'udiya" [The Story of the Establishment of Al-Qa'ida in Saudi Arabia], part 1, *Al-Riyadh* (September 27, 2005).

111. For example, in 1998, the Saudi government reportedly disrupted a plan organized by Bin Ladin to target U.S. forces in the Kingdom using man-portable missiles, leading to the arrest of scores of people. *The 9/11 Investigations; Staff Reports of the 9/11 Commission*, ed. Steven Strasser, 69. Tenet appears mistaken when he claims that Bin Ladin had banned such attacks in Saudi Arabia before 9/11, 248. Likewise, the 1995 attack against the Saudi Arabian National Guard training facility, in which several Americans were killed, may have been the work of Bin Ladin although, as was typical of Saudi policy in the early years, the event was hushed up and not investigated to the U.S.'s satisfaction. See Thomas W. Lippman, *Inside the Mirage; America's Fragile Partnership with Saudi Arabia*, 322.

112. Bin Hazzam, "Qissat ta'sis Al-Qa'ida," part 1.

113. Bin Hazzam, "Qissat ta'sis Al-Qa'ida," part 2.

114. Bandar bin 'Abd Al-Rahman Al-Dakhil, "Faysal bin 'Abd Al-Rahman Al-Dakhil . . . musa"ir harb" [Faysal bin 'Abd Al-Rahman Al-Dakhil . . . War Starter], *Sawt al-jihad*, no. 28 (Ramadan 1425/October 2004), 14.

115. "Turki Bin Fuhayd Al-Mutayri," 33.

116. Khalid Al-Zaydan, "*Al-Riyadh* tunaqish asrar al-khaliya wa-l-tandhim" [*Al-Riyadh* Examines the Secrets of the Cell and the Organization], *Al-Riyadh*, part 6 (October 3, 2005).

117. Interview with Umm Usama.

118. 'Abd Al-'Aziz Al-Muqrin, "Li-kull al-raghibin fi al-jihad 'ala ardh Al-Jazira Al-'Arabiya" [To All Those Wishing to Fight in the Jihad in the Arabian Peninsula], *Mu'askar Al-Battar*, no. 10 (Rabi' I 1425/April–May 2004), 19.

119. Ibid., 18.

120. Ibid.

121. Al-Muqrin, "Risala ila man tarak al-silah." The influence of such pre-existing personal ties is normal, since knowing someone's abilities and personality first-hand is important for any military or political organization.

122. A holistic functional approach of blurring between the military and civilian sectors was also characteristic of the Soviet system, although not as extreme as in

the QAP's case. See William E. Odom, "Soviet Military Doctrine."

123. This reliance on deception parallels Sun Tzu's dictum that "All war is based on deception,"66.

124. "Rasa'il wa-rudud" [Letters and Responses], *Mu'askar Al-Battar*, no. 21 (Ramadan 1425/October–November 2004), 40.

125. Al-Zaydan, "*Al-Riyadh* tunaqish," part 6.

126. Typically, Bin Ladin argued that foreigners were stealing Saudi Arabia's oil and were preventing the price of oil to rise to its rightful price of at least $100/barrel. In fact, he exhorted the *mujahidin* in Saudi Arabia to "do everything you possibly can in order to stop the greatest theft in history." "Al-Risala ila al-muslimin fi Bilad Al-Haramayn khassatan wa-ila al-muslimin fi ghayrha 'ammatan" [Letter to the Muslims in the Land of the Two Shrines in Particular and to Muslims Elsewhere in General], December 15, 2004.

127. For example, even as a youth Al-Muqrin would not watch television, as a sign of devotion, 'Uways and Al-Matrafi.

128. For example, Saudi security officials estimate that the QAP achieves 80 percent of its recruitment by means of the Internet. Huda Al-Salih, "80% min 'amaliyat tajnid al-tandhimat al-mutashaddida tatimm 'abr al-intarnat" [80% of the Extremist Organizations' Recruitment Is Done on the Internet], *Al-Sharq Al-Awsat* (April 29, 2007).

129. According to the interview with Umm Usama.

130. Steven Simon makes a case that the religious mainspring of terrorist groups, such as Al-Qa'ida, imprints them with qualitative characteristics different from those of more conventional terrorist groups. This is apparent insofar as objectives and tactics are concerned but, one could add, the religious imprint also provides a basis for cohesion and for command and control, given the extreme sense of commitment, as one can sense in Al-Muqrin's doctrine. Steven Simon, "The New Terrorism: Securing the Nation against a Messianic Foe."

131. On the ideological continuum within the Saudi clerical establishment, see International Crisis Group, *Saudi Arabia Backgrounder: Who Are the Islamists?*

132. Al-Muqrin, "Rahimak Allah ya Aba Hazim," 3.

133. Shy and Collier, 823. Of course, one needs to add a similar East Asian source of influence too.

134. Such a situation should not be seen in any sense as unique to an Islamic context. To cite but one example of the possible amalgam of extreme religiosity and pragmatism, Lt. Gen. William G. Boykin, eventually the U.S. Deputy Undersecretary of Defense for Intelligence, cast the war on terrorism in apocalyptic dimensions and explained other political events in similar religious terms, but otherwise could still function in a professional manner. See Richard Leiby, "Christian Soldier," *Washington Post* (November 6, 2003), C1.

135. Al-Muqrin, "Liqa'," part 2, 22.

136. According to the interview with Umm Usama.

137. As *Sawt al-jihad* noted later, "After September 11, guidance came for the *mujahidin* to initiate operations in the Peninsula and to prepare for that." "Tasa'ulat hawl jihad al-salibiyin," *Sawt al-jihad*, part 3, 29.

138. Tenet, 248.

139. Ibid.

140. This was Al-'Ayyiri's position in representing QAP interests to Bin Ladin, as reported in Bin Hazzam, "Qissat ta'sis Al-Qa'ida," part 1, *Al-Riyadh*.

141. *Ibid.* This version is confirmed based on information reportedly obtained by U.S. sigint intercepts, Ron Suskind, *The One Percent Doctrine; Deep Inside America's Pursuit of Its Enemies Since 9/11*, 235–36. An Egyptian lawyer who knew Al-Zawahiri provides insights into the difficult task those who disagreed with the latter must have had in arguing with Al-Zawahiri: "Zawahiri has always insistently preferred his own opinion despite his humbleness. He has always tended to get into clashes with those who do not agree with him, despite his tolerance." Montasser Al-Zayyat, *The Road to Al-Qaeda; The Story of Bin Laden's Right-Hand Man*, 104. It appears that Al-Zawahiri likewise continued being adventuristic in his aggressive approach toward confronting the Musharraf regime in Pakistan in 2007, to the chagrin of more cautious elements within Al-Qa'ida. See Sami Yousafzai and Ron Moreau, "Al Qaeda: Internal Power Struggle Looms," *Newsweek* (July 30, 2007), retrieved from www. msnbc.msn.com.

142. For example, in *Fursan taht rayat al-nabiy* [Knights under the Banner of the Prophet], Al-Zawahiri had stressed that initiating a *jihad* could not be rushed, and that this required a preliminary building of a territorial base, mobilizing resources and supporters, drafting plans, and selecting when to fight. In fact, as he tells it, when someone in Egypt had proposed launching a guerrilla war during Sadat's time, Al-Zawahiri had dissuaded him from doing so and had offered him a book on guerrilla war, presumably to instill in the proponent of the guerrilla war a greater sense of reality.

143. Though there were many instances of this phenomenon, the subordination of the interests of the local Communist parties in the Middle East to Moscow's policy of developing strong relationships with radical, but nationalist, local regimes— as in Egypt, Syria, and Iraq—was a particularly glaring long-term example.

144. This account is taken form Al-Muqrin, "Liqa'," part 2, 24. The Yemeni *jihadi* activist Abu Jandal, who knew Al-Muqrin, confirms that the latter had been "completely opposed" to operations in Saudi Arabia. Interview with Abu Jandal Nasir Al-Bahri, "Tawassatt li-tazwij Bin Ladin min fatat yamaniya" [I Was the Go-Between for Bin Ladin's Marriage to a Yemeni Woman], *Al-Quds* (London) (August 3, 2004), 4. Of course, deciding if and when to initiate a war has been acknowledged as a difficult decision by such varied military thinkers as Thucydides and Clausewitz and, as Shy and Collier point out, this decision has

been as much a dilemma for revolutionary movements as for states, 820, 828.

145. Al-Muqrin, "Bayan li-l-umma."

146. Ibid.

147. Luways 'Atiyat Allah, "Al-Tajriba al-jihadiya" [*Jihadi* Experience]. Retrieved from www.qa3edoon.com/KotobWaBayanatWEB/Shobohat-08.htm.

148. Neil A. Lewis, "U.S. Court Asserts Authority over American in Saudi Jail," *New York Times* (December 17, 2004), A17, and "The Case of Ahmed Omar Abu Ali," *New York Times* (February 24, 2005), A22.

149. The QAP's focus on Saudi Arabia is not to preclude coordination and coopera- tion with sister cells in neighboring countries. For example, Yemeni security believed that Al-Muqrin was possibly connected to the attack on the *U.S.S. Cole* in Aden harbor, based on the fact that when Saudi security captured one of those wanted by Yemen as a suspect in the attack, the latter turned out to be one of Al- Muqrin's aides. "Al-Kashf 'an 'alaqa lil-l-Muqrin bi-tafjir 'Cole'" [Discovering a Link between Al-Muqrin and the Blowing Up of the *Cole*], *Al-'Arabiya* (June 20, 2004).

150. Al-Muqrin, "Nida' al-nafir," 2. It was a common view within the QAP that the latter was involved in a global war between Islam and Infidelity. Akhu Man Ta' Allah ['Abd Al-'Aziz Al-'Anazi], "Hal baqiya ma yuqal 'an 11 sibtimbir?" [Is There Anything Left to Say about September 11?], part 2, no. 26, *Sawt al-jihad* (Sha'ban 1425/September–October 2004), 25–30.

151. Al-Muqrin, "Li-kull al-raghibin," 19.

152. "Tasa'ulat hawl jihad al-salibiyin," part 3, 28.

153. Ibid., 29.

154. Al-Muqrin, "Liqa'," part 1, 25.

155. Ibid.

156. See Nawaf Obaid and Anthony Cordesman, *Saudi Militants in Iraq: Assessment and Kingdom's Response*.

157. Sulayman Al-Dawsari, "Al-Iftitahiyya" [Opening Article], *Sawt al-jihad*, no. 1 (Sha'ban 1424/October 2003), 3.

158. Even one of the QAP's inner circle, 'Abd Allah Al-Rashudi, reportedly went to Iraq. Hasan Al-Sharif, "Najah 'amaliyat Al-Rass ahbat mukhattatat Majid wa- Sultan Al-Harisi" [The Success of the Al-Rass Operation Frustrated the Plans of Majid and Sultan Al-Harisi], *Al-Madina* (July 2, 2005). Eventually, Al-Rashudi lost his life in Iraq; his obituary appeared on Al-Firdaws Forum. Retrieved from http://203.223.152.151/~alfiradws/vb/showthread.php?t=6795.

159. This occurred in an audio tape by Salih Al-'Awfi, "Risala ila al-mujahidin fi Al- 'Iraq" [Letter to the *Mujahidin* in Iraq] (6 Safar 1426/March 17, 2005). Re- trieved from www.qa3edoon.com/KotobWaBayanatWEB/ResalatA13ofee-3.htm.

160. Abu Thabit Al-Najdi, "Labbayka ya Falluja" [At Your Service, Oh Falluja], *Mu'askar Al-Battar*, no. 8 (Safar 1425/April 2004), 3.

161. For a good discussion of this concept, see Jennie L. Johnson, "Exploiting Weakness in the Far Enemy Ideology."

162. Akhu Man Ta' Allah, "Hal baqya ma yuqal," 29. That reflects Mao's dictum to "avoid the solid, hit the hollow," 46, or Sun Tzu, to the effect that "an army avoids strength and strikes weakness," 101.

163. Sulayman Al-Dawsari, "Al-Iftitahiya" [Opening Article], *Sawt al-jihad*, no. 2 (Sha'ban 1424/October 2003), 2.

164. Al-Muqrin, "Liqa'," part 2, 25.

165. Ibid. Indeed, he had concluded that "this [Saudi] state" had declared war on all the *mujahidin*. Al-Muqrin, "Liqa'," part 2, 24.

166. 'Abd Al-'Aziz Al-Muqrin, "Bayan hawl 'adam mas'uliyat tandhim Al-Qa'ida 'an tafjir mabna qiyadat al-tawari'" [Communique Stating Al-Qa'ida Is Not Responsible for the Bombing of the Emergency Force Headquarters Building], (Rabi' I 1425/April–May 2004). Retrieved from www.qa3edoon.com/KotobWaBayanatWEB/Tawaree.htm.

167. Al-Muqrin, "Bayan li-l-umma."

168. Ibid.

169. 'Abd Al-'Aziz Al-Muqrin, "Tahni'atan bi-l-'id" [Holiday Wishes], *Sawt al-jihad*, no. 10 (1 Dhu Al-Hijja 1424/February 2004), 4.

170. Abu Jandal Al-Azadi [Faris Bin Ahmad Al Shuwayl Al-Zahrani], *Al-Bahith 'an hukm qatl afrad wa-dhubbat al-mabahith* [The Researcher and the Judgment on the Killing of Mabahith Personnel and Officers]. The Saudi Mabahith is equivalent to the U.S. FBI.

171. Al-Muqrin, "Li-kull al-raghibin," 19.

172. "Tasa'ulat hawl jihad," part 3, 29.

173. "Rasa'il wa-rudud" [Letters and Responses], *Mu'askar Al-Battar*, no. 21 (Ramadan 1425/October–November 2004), 40.

174. Shy and Collier, 844.

175. As even a liberal Saudi editor, Jamal Khashoggi, noted: "Saudi Arabia is proud of its independence and sovereignty. . . . It was very awkward for us throughout to have American troops in the kingdom." Quoted in Dave Montgomery, "U.S. to Remove Almost All Troops from Saudi Arabia," *Stars and Stripes* (Washington, DC), April, 30 2003. Retrieved from http://stripes.com. Of course, as other observers have posited, there were additional factors, beside the growing QAP threat, involved in this development, which resulted from long-term trends in U.S.-Saudi relations. See W. Andrew Terrill, *Regional Fears of Western Primacy and the Future of U.S. Middle Eastern Basing Policy*, 36–38. Since 2004, Saudi Arabia has been an unaccompanied post for American personnel because of security concerns. Moreover, as an official "Travel Warning" by the U.S. Department of State's Bureau of Consular Affairs pointed out (June 14, 2007), "Due to concerns about the possibility of additional terrorist activity directed

against American citizens and interests, the Department of State continues to warn U.S. citizens to defer non-essential travel to Saudi Arabia."

176. As was recognized even by analysts on the Left, the application of Marxist-based theory for revolutionary war ran the gamut of environments and varied widely in how it was applied and in its results and, indeed, required extensive revisions and modifications depending on local conditions. William J. Pomeroy, "Introduction," in William J. Pomeroy, ed., *Guerrilla Warfare and Marxism*.

177. Al-Muqrin, "Bayan li-l-umma."

178. Al-Muqrin, "Li-kull al-raghibin," 19.

179. Yusuf Al-'Ayyiri, video tape *Harb al-'asabat* [Guerrilla War]. Retrieved from www.qa3edoon.com

180. Hazzam, Faris Bin, "Qissat ta'sis Al-Qa'ida," part 2.

181. For example, roughly one in twenty-nine Saudi males serves in the conventional armed forces, as compared to one in 128 in the U.S.; these numbers are intended to provide only an order of rough magnitude and are based on the male population as a whole, irrespective of age.

182. See Anthony H. Cordesman, *Saudi Arabia Enters the 21st Century: Military and Internal Security Issues, IX, Saudi Paramilitary and Internal Security Forces*.

183. According to a senior ARAMCO official, briefing received by the author during a visit to Saudi Arabia under the auspices of The National Council on U.S.-Arab Relations, 2000.

184. According to their Director, the *mutawwi'a* (or more formally the Committee to Promote Virtue and Prevent Vice) conduct studies, engage in propaganda, and cooperate with the security apparatus as part of their mission to counteract terrorism; see interview by 'Abd Allah bin 'Abd Al-Rahman Al-Khariji with Shaykh Ibrahim bin 'Abd Allah Al-Ghayth, "Al-Ra'is al-'amm li-hay'at al-amr bi-l-ma'ruf wa-l-nahy 'an al-munkar" [The Director General of the Committee to Promote Virtue and Prevent Vice]. The Saudi Minister of the Interior, Prince Nayif, who has always been a strong supporter of the *mutawwi'a*, in fact, envisions the latter playing an even greater role in security affairs, as he announced in a recent speech, "Tahmilun mas'uliyat al-difa' 'an al-din wa-'an al-'aqida al-salafiya," [You Bear the Responsibility of Defending Religion and the *Salafi* Doctrine], *Al-Yawm* (June 21, 2007).

185. Al-Muqrin, "Li-kull al-raghibin," 19.

186. Based on statistics provided by Saudi Arabia's Ministries of Labor and the Civil Service, 652,935 Saudis work in the country's public sector and 609,767 in the private sector, Salim Al Sahman, "Shabab kharij al-sirb al-wadhifi" [Youth Outside the Employment Picture], *'Ukaz* (April 3, 2007).

187. On censorship in the Saudi media, see John R. Bradley, *Saudi Arabia Exposed; Inside a Kingdom in Crisis*, 181–204. Government control of communications has made possible the untrammeled tapping of phones and the internet, leading

to further QAP arrests, 'Ali Al-Qahtani, "Al-Dharabat al-istibaqiya dalil tawaffur al-ma'lumat al-daqiqa" [The Preemptive Strikes Are an Indication of Having Precise Intelligence], *Al-Watan* (June 25, 2005). For overviews of the Saudi government's counterterrorism effort, see Cordesman and Obaid, Joshua Teitelbaum, and John R. Bradley.

188. For example, this was the case with the tribe of QAP leader Salih Al-'Awfi, whose tribal leaders assured the government that the tribe would provide him no help, "Tadhyiq al-khanaq 'ala Al-'Awfi ba'd muhasarat awkarahih wa-tabarru' qabilatih min af'alih" [The Noose Tightens around Al-'Awfi after His Den Is Surrounded and His Tribe Distances Itself from His Misdeeds], *Al-Watan* (April 7, 2005).

189. For an official Saudi government summary of its efforts to counter the QAP, see the Royal Embassy of Saudi Arabia, Information Office, *Initiatives and Actions Taken by the Government of Saudi Arabia to Combat Terrorism*. Also see Anthony H. Cordesman and Nawaf Obaid, *Saudi Counter Terrorism Efforts: The Changing Paramilitary and Domestic Security Apparatus*.

190. Ahmad Al-Jami'a, "Ba'd lahdhat min maqtil al-irhabi al-matlub" [A Few Moments Drawn from the Killing of the Wanted Terrorist], *Al-Riyadh* (June 19, 2004).

191. 'Abd Al-Wahhab Salih Al-'Arbad, "Ma'an dhidd al-irhab" [Together against Terrorism], *Al-Yawm* (February 5, 2005). Another account, however, claims that it was U.S. sigint intercepts which uncovered the emerging QAP threat and which were communicated to the Saudi government, Suskind, 234–235.

192. As of late 2007, 2200 QAP sympathizers had been released from prison, according to a Ministry of the Interior official, Major General Mansur Al-Turki, after "cleansing their minds;" there had also been an earlier release of 1,500 people, and those set free may not include the hard-core militants. See Sa'ud Al-Shibani, "Al-Liwa' Al-Turki li *'Al-Jazira'*: Al-Injaz al-amni tahaqqaq 'ala yad rijal al-amn ba'd mutaba'a istamarrat 4 ashhur" [Major General Al-Turki to *Al-Jazira*: The Security Success Was Achieved Thanks to the Security Personnel Following a Pursuit Which Lasted for Four Months], *Al-Jazira* (November 30, 2007).

193. Al-Muqrin, "Li-kull al-raghibin," 19.

194. A good overview for a common base of understanding of such analytical concepts is found in Joe Strange, *Centers of Gravity & Critical Vulnerabilities*.

195. Bard E. O'Neill, *Insurgency & Terrorism*, 2nd ed., 56. This concept is a refinement of the more traditional concept of "focosim," popularized by Che Guevara, who believed that—like a fire—the use of violence itself could mobilize popular support instead of having to develop a preliminary political base; see Shy and Collier, 849–852.

196. 'Abd Al-'Aziz Al-Muqrin, "'Am jadid wa-sahwat umma" [A New Year and the Awakening of an *Ummah*], *Sawt al-jihad*, no. 11 (Muharram 1425/February 2004), 4.

197. 'Abd Al-'Aziz Al-Muqrin, "Dhalik min fadhl Allah 'alayna wa-'ala al-nas" [That Is by God's Grace to Us and to the Rest], *Sawt al-jihad*, no. 18 (Rabi' II 1425/ May–June 2004), 4.

198. A typical comment after Saudi security personnel were attacked was: "Today, they [i.e., the QAP] targeted their brothers, cousins and relatives. I'm trying to understand the miserable thinking of these militants," quoted in Megan K. Stack, "Bomb Targets Saudi Police Headquarters," *Los Angeles Times* (April 22, 2004), A1. Another average Saudi stressed that "There's not one American in this entire area. . . . Not one! What kind of jihad is this?" Megan K. Stack, "Saudis Bewildered by Attack in Riyadh; Many Don't See Insurgency as a Holy War," *The Seattle Times* (April 26, 2004), A14. Also see Margaret Coker, "Saudi Relations: For Islamist Terrorists, Haven Becomes a Hot Seat," *Atlanta Journal-Constitution* (February 27, 2005), E4. A Saudi schoolteacher, for his part, accused the QAP of "not having a heart, since they target those who are protected and the innocent, as well as the police," quoted in Fahd Yusuf and Salman Al-Sabi'i, "Al-Jami' yarfudhun al-irhab wa-yasifun al-fi'a al-dhalla b-inghilaq" [Everyone Rejects Terrorism and Accuses the Misguided Band of Being Incomprehensible], *Al-Yawm* (May 30, 2004).

199. "Al-'Amaliya al-'askariya 'ala mujamma' al-salibiyin bi-iskan Al-Muhayya" [The Military Operation against the Crusader Compound of Al-Muhayya], *Sawt al-jihad*, no. 5 (Shawwal 1424/December 2003), 7–10. This subject continued to come up repeatedly in the QAP media.

200. "Liqa' ma'a al-ustadh Luways 'Atiyat Allah, hafidhahu Allah" [Interview with Professor Luways 'Atiyat Allah, May God Preserve Him], *Sawt al-jihad*, no. 6 (Shawwal 1424/November–December 2003), 15.

201. Al-Muqrin, "Fa-sharrid bihim," 3–4.

202. For example, the government alleged that the QAP members did not pray at the designated times, used false documents, were ignorant of Islamic doctrine, were spendthrifts, and were indifferent to their own wounded personnel, "Al-Juz' al-thani min film *Haqa'iq khassa min dakhil al-khaliya* yakshif mazid min al-tafsil" [Part Two of the Film *Secrets from Inside the Cell* Reveals More Details], *Al-Watan* (October 2, 2004).

203. Pro-government Saudi *shaykhs* went so far as to blame foreign forces for Islamic extremism. Shaykh Safar Al-Hawali, himself a "repented" radical, for example, accused "international Zionism" of "deceiving the minds of some youths and citizens," Majid Al-Bassam, "Al-Hawali yakshif li-l-*Watan* tafasil 120 daqiqa qadhaha Al-'Umari fi manzil al-amir Muhammad bin Nayif" [Al-Hawali Reveals the Details of the 120 Minutes Which Al-'Umari Spent in Prince Muhammad bin Nayif's House], *Al-Watan* (June 30, 2004). Another cleric, Ibn Dulaym, compared Al-Qa'ida to "a poisoned dagger that the Jews and the Christians have stuck into the side of the *Ummah*." "Fi bayan yastanid ila ahdath wa-waqai' al-

tarikh al-islami al-qadim wa-l-mu'asir Ibn Dulaym yastahithth al-shabab al-ladhin yaz'amun al-intima' li-l-jihad wa-Bin Ladin 'ala al-ruju' 'an al-tatarruf wa-l-inhiraf" [In a Communique Based on Ancient and Contemporary Islamic History, Ibn Dulaym Exhorts Those Youth Who Claim to Follow the *Jihad* and Bin Ladin to Repent of Extremism and Deviance], *Al-Watan* (July 12, 2005).

204. "Mushahadat" [Observations], *Sawt al-jihad*, no. 29 (Rabi' I 1426/April–May 2005), 5–7.

205. For example, the Saudi Arabian National Guard's official journal carried an editorial entitled "Ba'd al-malhama al-butuliya li-rijal al-amn fi Al-Rass al-irhab fi-l-mamlaka ya'ish lahadhatih al-akhira" [After the Heroically Fierce Battle by the Security Personnel at Al-Rass, Terrorism in the Kingdom Is in Its Last Throes], *Al-Haras al-watani* (March 1, 2005). The Minister of the Interior, Prince Nayif bin 'Abd Al-'Aziz, likewise claimed that the QAP was now "paralyzed," as reported in Sadiq Salman, "Al-Qa'ida mas'ula 'an a'mal al-takhrib fi al-duwal al-'arabiya wa-Isra'il wa-l-sahyuniya taqifan wara'aha" [Al-Qa'ida Is Responsible for the Acts of Sabotage in the Arab Countries, while Israel and Zionism Are Behind It].

206. Shaddad Bin 'Antara Al-Ayyubi, "Qa'idat al-jihad fi Bilad al-Haramayn wa-l-hudu' alladhi yasbuq al-'asifa" [The Jihadi Al-Qa'ida in the Land of the Two Shrines and the Quiet before the Storm], *Al-Nusra* (March 2006), Retrieved from http://www.alnusra.net/vb/showthread.php?t=5151.

207. See "Al-Dakhiliya: al-qabdh 'ala 172 muwatinan wa-muqiman mimman ittakhadhu takfir al-muslimin wasila li-istibahat al-dima' wa-al-amwal" The [Ministry of the] Interior: 172 Citizens and Residents Arrested, Who Used the Condemnation of Muslims as Infidels as a Pretext to Making The Latter's Blood and Property Fair Game], *Al-Watan* (April 28, 2007), and "Baynahum khabir fi itlaq al-sawarikh wa-mumawwilun wa-khaliya i'lamiya" [Among Them Are an Expert in Firing Rockets, Financiers, and a Media Cell], *Al-'Arabiya* (November 28, 2007).

208. For one of the best accounts of the Chinese events, see Roy Hofheinz, Jr., "The Autumn Harvest Insurrection," *The China Quarterly*, no. 32 (October–December 1967), 37–87.

209. "Mustaqbal al-'amal al-'askari fi Jazirat Al-'Arab" [The Future of Military Activity in the Arabian Peninsula]. Indicative of the porous nature of Saudi Arabia's borders, and especially with Yemen, according to the Commander of the Saudi Border Guards, Staff Lieutenant General Talal 'Anqawi, about half a million individuals crossing the border illegally are intercepted successfully every year, though it is impossible to ascertain how many individuals get through. Salim Murishid, "Akthar min 500 alf mutasallil yatimm al-qabdh 'alayhim sanawiyan 'abr hududna" [More than 500 Thousand Illegal Crossers Are Stopped at Our Borders Every Year], *Al-Riyadh* (April 5, 2007).

210. For example, four men wanted for terrorism were arrested in a tent in the desert in Hafr Al-Batin province, Salman Al-Sabi'i, "Al-Qabdh 'ala 4 matlubin amniyan bi-sahra' Hafr Al-Batin" [Four Wanted Men Arrested in the Hafr Al-Batin Desert], *Al-Yawm* (June 25, 2006).

211. Sa'id Al-Thubayti, 'Ata' Allah Al-Ju'ayd, and Muhammad Darraj, "Al-Matluban atlaqa al-nar 'ala rijal al-amn wa-ladha bi-l-farar dakhil al-ahrash" [The Wanted Men Fired at the Police and Then Fled into the Woods], *Al-Watan* (June 3, 2004).

212. 'Ali Al-Qahtani, "Mu'akkidan ann al-qa'ima al-haliya tatadhamman 'adad mimman lahum khibra sabiqa fi al-'amal al-midani mas'ul amni yatawaqqa' farar 'adad min al-matlubin ila al-kharij harban min al-mulahaqa al-amniya" [Confirming That the Current List Contains a Number of Those with Previous Operational Experience, a Security Official Expects a Number of Those Who Are Wanted to Flee Abroad to Avoid the Security Catching Up with Them], *Al-Watan* (June 30, 2005).

213. Mushari Al-Dhaydi, "Dharb al-khalaya al-sab'iya ahbat muhawala jadida li-ihya' khalaya Al-Qa'ida" [The Blow to the Predatory Cells Prevented a New Attempt to Revive Al-Qa'ida's Cells], *Al-Sharq Al-Awsat* (April 29, 2007).

214. See "Quwwat al-amn tuhbit 'amaliyat irhabiya istahdafat mansha'a naftiya" [The Security Forces Prevent Terrorist Operations Which Targeted an Oil Facility], *Al-Riyadh* (November 29, 2007).

215. However, the Saudi government subsequently did discourage foreigners from traveling outside of cities, "Dhamm Al-Muhammadi wa-l-Balawi ila qa'imat al-matlubin" [Al-Muhammadi and Al-Balawi Added to the Wanted List], *Al-'Arabiya* (March 7, 2007).

216. "Turki Bin Fuhayd Al-Mutayri," 33.

217. "Al-Khatima" [Concluding Article], *Mu'askar Al-Battar*, no. 2 (15 Dhu Al-Qa'da 1424/January 8, 2004), 2. The title itself of the magazine—*Mu'askar*—suggests a "training camp" and was indicative of its intended function as a virtual training site. *Al-Battar* referred to the first QAP leader, Yusuf Al-'Ayyiri, whose *nom de guerre* was Shaykh Al-Battar, or "the sharp sword."

218. "Al-Salamu 'alaykum" [Greetings], *Mu'askar Al-Battar*, no. 1 (Dhu al-qa'da 1424/December 2003–January 2004), 2, and "Al-Iftitahiya" [Opening Remarks], *ibid.*, 3. The editors of *Mu'askar Al-Battar* continued to stress that their magazine was not just to be read passively or just to gain general knowledge, but that the information was there in order to be put into practice, "Al-Salamu 'alaykum" [Greetings], no. 19 (Sha'ban 1425/September–October 2004), 2. In a sense, the Saudi youth's lack of military knowledge suggests the need for greater nuance in one of the key conclusions in a recent study, to the effect that in traditional societies "all men of age in a tribe, clan, or communal group learn through societal norms and legacies to fight in specific ways and to fight well, if required."

Richard H. Shultz, Jr. and Andrea J. Dew, *Insurgents, Terrorists, and Militias: The Warriors of Contemporary Combat*, 262.

219. From the author's experience of having taken such courses and seeing those around him do so, it is clear that such courses lack the necessary human interaction and practical exercises, and encourage instead a mechanical approach designed to facilitate a *pro-forma* completion of a course.

220. "Rasa'il wa-rudud," *Mu'askar Al-Battar*, 41.

221. There had been 330,843 hits as of November 15, 2006 on the QAP's website, and 412,274 by July 15, 2007, or an average of over 10,000 per month. In July 2007, the official website was closed down, replaced with a cryptic message advising, "Please contact the billing/support department as soon as possible."

222. For example, one anti-extremist forum which called his document "the communique of the deviant Al-Muqrin" nevertheless publicized his ideas, despite the negative accompanying commentary. Retrieved from http://66.113.178.143/vb3/ showthread. php?t=1559.

223. The work in question is entitled *Nasa'ih wa-tawjihat 'askariya li-l-mujahidin fi Ardh Al-Rafidayn* [*Advice and Instructions to the Mujahidin in Mesopotamia*]. Internal evidence, however, reveals the book was written after the U.S. entry in Baghdad, but before the final collapse of the Iraqi regime in April 2003. The work carried the signature of the "Ansar al-jihad" (Partisans of the Jihad), subsequently a shadowy front probably for Al-Qa'ida. The origin of the work was made even clearer by the fact that it was published by the Center for Islamic Studies and Research [Markaz al-dirasat wa-l-buhuth al-islamiya], another shadowy in-house enterprise which routinely has published works by the mother Al-Qa'ida and the QAP, and which may in fact have been managed by the latter, given the latter's more active intellectual and publishing activity.

224. For an overview of tactics and techniques used by insurgents in Iraq, often paralleling those proposed by Al-Muqrin, see Ahmed S. Hashim, *Insurgency and Counter-insurgency in Iraq*, especially 188–200.

225. The piece was entitled "Guerrilla War," although Al-Muqrin as the source was not identified. *Al-Fursan*, no. 6 (Ramadan 1426/October 2005), 12.

226. For example, the Director of the Scientific Branch of Saudi Arabia's Counter-radical Sakina (Calm) internet team, who is also a member of the Ministry of Interior's Counter-radical Re-Education Committee, rued the fact that the internet phenomenon now provided would-be terrorists with rapid training in such skill areas as fund-raising, intelligence collection, observation, weapons handling, and explosives, as well as instruction in guerrilla warfare and military operations in urban terrain, areas, one might add, where Al-Muqrin made particular contributions. Interview with Shaykh Majid Al-Mursal, "Idhtirab al-mintaqa wa-l-taqniya wa-l-ittisalat sahhalat al-mahamma" [The Region's Instability, Technology, and Communications Have Made the Task Easier], *Al-Watan* (April 28,

2007). As a mid-level Saudi Army officer told the author in 2005, Al-Muqrin's work is "dangerous . . . because others can read it and learn from it."

227. Often, access to these websites is replaced by vacuous ads for dating services or requests to contact the server in order to renew access.

228. On the issue of having to deal with Al-Qa'ida in general as an insurgency, see Lt. Col. Michael F. Morris' perceptive essay, "Al Qaeda as Insurgency."

229. See Michael Scott Doran, "The Saudi Paradox;" and Madawi Al-Rasheed, *Contesting the Saudi State: Islamic Voices from a New Generation*. For example, in the war of ideas, despite the stated intention to remove teachers deemed to be extremist, this might prove difficult, as the Saudi press pointed out that such teachers are so numerous that if they were removed half of the country's schools would then become inoperable, Abeer Mishkhas, "Patching the Wounds Is Not Enough," *Arab News* (March 8, 2007). Likewise, despite a government initiative to remove some 2000 radical clerics from their posts, the press reported that most eventually returned to their mosques. Craig Whitlock, "Saudis Confront Extremist Ideologies," *Washington Post* (February 6, 2005), A18.

230. See Toby Jones, "Seeking a Social Contract for Saudi Arabia," *Middle East Report*. Thus, as a disturbing indicator for the Saudi regime, it was the Islamist Dhahabiya ("Golden") coalition which swept the limited experimental local municipal elections held in 2005, defeating their liberal and tribal rivals, Steve Coll, "Islamic Activists Sweep Saudi Council Elections," *Washington Post* (April 24, 2005), A17.

231. See "All Puffed Up and Stalling on Reform; Saudi Arabia. Why Saudi Arabia Is Newly Confident," *The Economist* (March 3, 2007). Retrieved from www.economist.com.

232. On the role of socio-economic factors in affecting the wider pool of potential supporters of radical movements, see Alan Richards, *Socio-economic Roots of Radicalism? Towards Explaining the Appeal of Islamic Radicals*.

233. This Clausewitzian precept is illustrated well by Wray R. Johnson in relation to the U.S.'s misreading of the Vietnam War, "War, Culture, and the Interpretation of History: The Vietnam War Reconsidered," *Small Wars and Insurgencies*.

234. For expositions of 4th generation warfare by its proponents, see William S. Lind, Keith M. Nightengale, John F. Schmitt, Colonel Joseph W. Sutton, and Lieutenant Colonel G. I. Wilson, "The Changing Face of War into the Fourth Generation;" and William S. Lind, Major John F. Schmitt, and Colonel Gary I. Wilson, "Fourth Generation Warfare: Another Look," *Marine Corps Gazette*.

235. For a convincing deconstruction of such ideas, see Antulio J. Echeverria II's *Fourth-generation War and Other Myths*. The insightful work by Adam Lowther also revolves around his thesis that "many of the strategic and tactical concepts of modern asymmetry are restatements of concepts developed decades, centuries, and millennia ago." *Asymmetric Warfare and Military Thought*, 4.

236. For a sound interpretation of the enduring nature of Clausewitz's concept of the Trinity, emphasizing the latter's understanding of forces—not time-specific institutions—as the essence of the shifting balance of the "Trinity," see Edward J. Villacres and Christopher Bassford, "Reclaiming the Clausewitzian Trinity," *Parameters*.

237. Such a statement, however, does not denote a rejection of the concept of the state, but is a reflection of operational reality. That is, even in conventional wars such as World War I and II, operations, of necessity, extended across—and often ignored—state borders.

238. Muhammad bin Ahmad Al-Salim, "La tadhabu li-l-'Iraq" [Do Not Go to Iraq], *Sawt al-jihad*, no. 17 (Dhu al-hijja 1424/January–February 2004), 23. Indicative of this recognition of reality, one QAP writer although putting "Saudi people" (*al-sha'b al-sa'udi*) in quotation marks nevertheless used that entity as his unit of analysis in addressing his audience when writing, 'Abd Al-Ilah bin Sulayman Al-Badri, "Sha'b Al-Jazira wa-marahil al-tadjin" [The People of the Peninsula and the Phases of Domestication], *Sawt al-jihad*, no. 25 (Sha'ban 1425/September–October 2004), 45.

239. According to the transcript of a Saudi TV documentary showcasing *mujahidin* who had repented, reported in Mishari Al-Mash'al, "I'tirafat muthira li-l-musharikin fi film *Tajarib bi-ism al-jihad*" [Unsettling Confessions by Those Taking Part in the Film *Experiences in the Name of the Jihad*], *Al-Wifaq* (December 8, 2005). One can detect a sense of "Saudi" pride even in Bin Ladin, who was said to have "envisioned a Saudi leadership in the struggle against the West." Uriya Shavit, "Islamist Ideology; Al-Qaeda's Saudi Origins," *Middle East Quarterly*, 12. Characteristically, Bin Ladin was incensed that "the Crusaders" dominated Saudi Arabia, which he called "our country [*biladna*]." See his "Al-Risala ila al-muslimin fi Bilad Al-Haramayn khassatan wa-ila al-muslimin fi ghayrha 'ammatan" [Message to the Muslims in the Land of the Two Shrines in Particular, and to Muslims Elsewhere in General]. On the distinct characteristics of national pride in Saudi Arabia, see Joseph Nevo, "Religion and National Identity in Saudi Arabia."

240. E. L. Katzenbach, Jr. gives a similar evaluation of Mao's thinking in, "Time, Space, and Will: The Political-military Views of Mao Tse-tung," originally published in *Marine Corps Gazette*, reprinted in U.S. Marine Corps, *The Guerrilla and How to Fight Him*.

241. For example, *Mu'askar Al-Battar* stressed to its readers that "It is vital to absorb *A Practical Course for Guerrilla War* which was written by the martyred leader Abu Hajir (may God have mercy upon him), as it contains the essential basics for urban warfare and important detailed information on assassinations, ambushes, and the means to resist. This is an obligatory work for anyone who wants to engage in any activity," and touted the book as "the indispensable reference."

"Rasa'il wa-rudud" (Letters and Replies), *Mu'askar Al-Battar*, no. 21 (Ramadan 1425/October–November 2004), special issue, 40.

.

Part 2:

Mu'askar Al-Battar

Mu'askar Al-Battar Book
Military Courses Publications

Number 1
Sha'ban 1425 a. h. [September 2004]

A PRACTICAL COURSE
FOR GUERRILLA WAR

Written by the Martyred Leader
Abu Hajir 'Abd Al-'Aziz Al-Muqrin

Translated by Norman Cigar

CONTENTS

In the name of God, the Merciful, the Compassionate

To the Reader:

Praise be to God, Lord of all creation, and prayers and salvation on the noblest of the prophets and messengers, our prophet Muhammad, and on all his family and Companions. Brother *mujahidin*, we are beginning this blessed *Kitab Al-Battar* (the Al-Battar book) series, every one of which consists of a specialized course.[1] Thus, one is a course on pistols, another on small arms, still another on physical conditioning, etc.

After these topics had come to you in the form of articles in the issues of the magazine *Mu'askar Al-Battar* (Al-Battar Training Camp) God made it possible for your brothers on the Military Committee of the Al-Qa'ida Organization on the Arabian Peninsula to collect these issues by topic, to revise and add to some of them, and to publish them in more splendid garb so that they would be available to the lovers of martyrdom and suitors for the maidens of paradise (*hur*).[2]

In issue number 19 of *Mu'askar Al-Battar*, we carried out a survey to ascertain the best way to publish such topics, that is, whether to do so in bound volumes of *Mu'askar Al-Battar*, which would include the entire issues [of the magazine]. The answer from many of the brothers was that it would be better to publish the [articles on] military science in separate volumes, since this would be more self-contained and easier to use. That was how this series came to be, and it would not have been possible but for God's help, His granting of success, and His kindness and mercy.

We should not forget to stress to our brothers in God that this series and others are part of that knowledge about which believers will be questioned on Resurrection Day. As God's Prophet (God's prayers and salvation be upon him) said, "The two feet of (God's) servant shall not move at all on the Day of Judgment until that servant is asked about how he spent his life and to what end he used his knowledge." Al-Tirmidhi reported this, with a line of transmission from Abu Barza Al-Aslami (may God be pleased with him). Al-Tirmidhi said, "This is a sound and true *hadith*."[3]

God forbid, Islamic youth, that God should have something of which to reprove you. Rise up as if a single man in order to remove this humiliation and shame from your *Ummah*.[4]

My *Ummah*, struggle has become a duty . . . abandon feebleness and clamor.

And abandon hesitation. He who wavers and sits back will not be helped (by God).

We yearn for numerous tongues and people who are eloquent.

Unbelief has become acute . . . why then are you fighting and struggling against each other?

To continue . . . This is the first volume of this blessed series of Al-Battar books, and contains the practical course on urban warfare and an introduction to the various types of wars. It was written by the heroic martyred leader (although, of course, only God knows who the true martyrs are) Abu Hajir 'Abd Al-'Aziz bin 'Isa bin 'Abd Al-Muhsin Al-Muqrin, who was killed on the [Arabian] Peninsula's soil after he had engraved letters of glory and pride with his deep-red blood.

Abu Hajir (may God have mercy on him) said, Praise be to the Lord of all creation, and prayers and salvation be upon the noblest of the prophets and messengers, our prophet Muhammad, and upon all his family and companions.

WAR

THE DEFINITION OF WAR

War is a state of conflict that erupts between two communities, factions, or states, or between two individuals and, in general terms, between two armed camps, with the purpose of achieving political, economic, or ideological gains or for expansionist goals. Usually, this is the last card in statesmen's hands.

THE OBJECTIVES OF WARS

1. For the belligerent to destroy the force that is confronting him and to compel that force to submit to him.
2. To eliminate the enemy opposing him and to uproot him.
3. For self-preservation.

THE CAUSES OF WAR

In general, the causes of wars can be divided into two:

1. Just wars are those wars that a party or peoples deprived of power, who are oppressed and wronged, wage against an oppressive aggressor or a tyrannical ruler. The objective is to end injustice and aggression, and to fight for the sake of God to make the *shari'a* the law of the land and for the word of God to become supreme. Examples of this kind of war are the wars in the Land of the Two Holy Shrines [i.e., Saudi Arabia], Palestine, Afghanistan, Iraq, Chechnya, Kashmir, the Philippines, and others.
2. Unjust wars are those wars that unjust powers wage against the dispossessed. The objective is to dominate other belief systems, to replace the prescriptions of religious laws, to seize territory, and to plunder (others') riches.

A TAXONOMY OF WARS BASED ON MILITARY AND HUMAN FACTORS

1. Conventional Wars
2. Total Wars
3. Cold Wars
4. Unconventional Wars

We will discuss each type of war (God willing), and we will discuss, in particular, unconventional wars at length (God willing).

Conventional Wars

These are wars in which all weapons are used, with the exception of weapons of mass destruction, and this is a war waged between two conventional armies. Examples of this type of war include the 10th of Ramadan War [i.e., the 1973 October War or Yom Kippur War] between Egypt and Israel, the Korean War, and the Iran-Iraq War.

Total Wars

These are wars in which unconventional weapons are used (weapons of mass destruction such as biological and nuclear weapons) but this type of war is considered unlikely because it leads to mass destruction, which could spell the end of all of mankind.

Cold Wars

These are wars in which there is no direct combat between the two parties. An example of this was what happened between the Soviet Union and America after the end of World War Two.

The Means Used in Cold Wars

1. Supporting unrest occurring within the adversary's country and encouraging the breakout of unrest and demonstrations, and provoking strife, as is occurring on Eritrea's part against the Sudan. There, we have the Eritrean government supporting the Sudanese People's Liberation Movement, which is led by a Christian, John Garang, while on the other side the Sudanese government supports the *jihadi* movements in Eritrea.[5] There is also another similar cold war in which such means are being used, the one between the Sudan and Ethiopia. Wars such as these two are called "proxy wars."

2. Obstructing construction and production plans, whether in the field of economic development or in the military field, as occurred when the Iraqi government sought to develop its nuclear program and was targeted by an air strike. Like-

wise, Yahya Al-Mashadd[i] was assassinated in order to derail the Iraqi nuclear program.[6] Examples of such means include America's use of economic embargoes against Libya and Syria.

3. Spreading defeatist ideas, theories, and susceptibilities throughout the society of the targeted nations, as the Zionist-Crusader alliance is doing at present against the Muslims. The international media is being used by the Jews and the Christians in order to achieve this objective, and it is mostly the Muslims who have been influenced by this partisan media (we seek God's help). This is why one sees the current American administration spending billions of dollars on the media and on networks that claim to be credible and unbiased!

4. Provoking the helpless to rise up and revolt against their rulers, and supporting and sheltering the external opposition.

5. Generating dissension within the ranks, creating disorder in others' efforts, setting up fifth columns, and sowing the seeds of division and disunity, as the West is doing now in the Muslim world by using the leading Muslim champions of secularism, modernity, and Westernization, who want to spread such abominations among the faithful. The intent of setting up this fifth column is to groom the latter to become the rulers in the Islamic countries at a more advanced stage of the struggle, as is the case with [Afghan President Hamid] Karzay and the Transitional Governing Council in Iraq.

---

[i] Egyptian nuclear scientist in charge of Iraq's nuclear program.

1
UNCONVENTIONAL WAR (GUERRILLA WAR)

DEFINITIONS

Definition One

A [guerrilla war] is a revolutionary war mobilizing the civilian population, or part of it, against the military power of the current authority in power, whether a local or an invading foreign one. Those rising up are a section of the local people who oppose the government's program, ideology, and legitimacy. The motivation for the population may be national or tribal, as was the case in Ethiopia between the Oromo tribe (who are in the majority) and the Tigre tribe who held power.

Definition Two

A [guerrilla war] is a war waged by a poor and weak party using the simplest methods and the cheapest means against a strong opponent who has a superiority in arms and equipment. It is called guerrilla war, or the war of the flea and the dog. Fleas keep on biting the dog and inflict wounds on it, and then flee. The dog then bites itself and scratches its own skin, but the fleas return and resume biting the dog and continue until the dog loses its balance and the fleas exhaust it and kill it.

[STRATEGIC] GOALS OF GUERRILLA WARS

As far as the *mujahidin* are concerned, the goal for which they are striving is a high and noble one, namely the call for a pure Islamic system free from defects and infidel elements, one based on the Book [i.e., the *Qur'an*] and the *Sunnah*. Among the *mujahidin*'s goals is also that of liberating the oppressed Muslim peoples from the yoke and the tyranny of oppressive and despotic infidel regimes, whether local or foreign ones. The *mujahidin* also call for a new social system that will draw its legitimacy from the light of the Book and the *Sunnah*. As a result, one finds that most Islamic movements agree on the definition and the goals.

[OPERATIONAL] OBJECTIVES OF GUERRILLA WARS

The guerrillas have important goals, namely:

1. To prolong the length of the war in order to create a successful resistance, which any fighting guerrilla movement in the world will seek to do.

   Factors that help promote a protracted war include avoiding some targets that the *mujahidin* could strike, because were they to attack them, they would lose the majority of their cadres and organizational structure. Therefore, such actions are to be postponed. This happened in Tajikistan, when the *mujahidin* led by Khattab did not attack a Russian military base that had three thousand personnel, as he had only forty *mujahidin* with him.[7] Had the latter attacked directly, everything would have been over for them, unless God willed otherwise. Instead, Khattab chose to shell the enemy from distant rear areas and from well-camouflaged positions. It was this which (with God's favor) enabled him to develop his staying power and to survive longer. An example of successful resistance is that by Abu 'Abd Allah Shaykh Usama Bin Ladin and Dr. Ayman Al-Zawahiri and the *mujahidin* with them. Of course, such resistance comes at a price and there are setbacks. The second objective follows from this one.

2. Acquiring combat proficiency, which comes gradually through practice, drilling, and hard work. This objective is based on the first and contributes to raising morale. As a result of this successful resistance[ii] and of these acquired combat skills,[iii] we will automatically move to the third objective, which is:

3. Achieving successful phasing[iv] and the building of impressive forces despite the enemy's superiority and the latter's efforts to prevent that. When the *Ummah* sees that the war is protracted and that the *mujahidin* are equal to their opponents—the international Crusaders—people will realize how strong the *mujahidin* are. As a consequence, they will begin to join the winning side.[v]

4. Based on the three preceding objectives, achieving them will lead to the fourth objective, which is that of building military power throughout the country, which will constitute the nucleus of an army. We can therefore say that the fourth objective is that of building an army. This army will be built on modern and

---

[ii]   The first objective.

[iii] The second objective.

[iv] "Phasing" (*tamarhul*) is the successful transition from one phase of guerrilla war to the next. We will address the phases of guerrilla wars after we deal with the topic of objectives (God willing).

[v]   **Important Note**: The correct transitioning between phases and avoiding rushing the transition from one phase to the next are vitally important in order to survive.

innovative foundations. This is the final phase, and the army at this phase will be capable (God willing) of confronting conventional forces using the same tactics as the latter.

Note: During this last phase, it is vital to retain guerrilla units because the *mujahidin* may need them in some instances.[vi] If God decrees that the *mujahidin* revert from one phase to a preceding one, it is the guerrillas who will be key for that earlier phase.

THE PHASES OF GUERRILLA WAR

Phase One: Attrition (Strategic Defense)

The reason for the appearance of this phase, as far as the *mujahidin* are concerned, almost always is the defense of Islam, Muslims, sacred places, and honor.

Phase Two: Relative Strategic Balance (Policy of a Thousand Cuts)

Phase Three: Military Decision (Final Attack)

It is the leadership (that is the *mujahidin* leadership) who will determine how the *mujahidin* fit into each phase. Although war may begin with the attrition phase, the enemy may not be able to resist, and one finds him collapsing already during this first phase (this is thanks to God's goodness) or the enemy may collapse during phase two. However, one must caution here not to rush with the transition from one phase to the next. Rather, it is necessary to be patient and to assess all the factors. As an example we can offer here what happened to the brothers in Algeria when they rushed in transitioning from phase one, which is that of attrition, to phase two, which is the phase of achieving a relative balance. This led to a setback for the movement and a return to the attrition phase again. This occurred in the 1995–97 period.

Each one of these phases is distinct in its political and military characteristics, which are subject to maneuver and variation by both the enemy and the *mujahidin*. One also finds that both the enemy and the *mujahidin* have bases during this phase. There is also the question of negotiations during every phase. We will deal with all these issues in detail (by God's grace).

PHASE ONE: ATTRITION (STRATEGIC DEFENSE)

Political Characteristics

A. *Political Characteristics with Respect to the Enemy.* Continuous fierce and frantic campaigns to distort the image of the guerrillas or the *mujahidin* and to mislead the public, and the launching of deceptive propaganda about the guerrillas or *mujahidin*.

---

vi   They also have other names, such as "commandos" or "insurgents."

An example of this is the [enemy's] claim that the *mujahidin* are criminal killers who were failures in life and who have despaired of life. For this, the enemy uses the media, which it controls. Any reader or observer of the situation in the region today can see for himself these mad campaigns against the *mujahidin* in the Islamic countries and in the Land of the Two Holy Shrines [i.e., Saudi Arabia]. And, they can see the sordid use of religion to oppose the *mujahidin*, and to distort the image of the *mujahidin*. The Saudi regime recently even used the leading figures of Islamic movements who until recently had been calling for opposition to the oppressors. The objective of this disinformation and diversion is to expel the *mujahidin* from the ranks of society and to cut off the logistic and material support that the people provide to the *mujahidin*. However, how preposterous that is! "Fain would they extinguish Allah's Light with their mouths, but Allah will not allow but that His Light should be perfected, even though the Unbelievers may detest it."[8]

Among the political characteristics of this phase are secret offers to negotiate and throw down one's weapons in exchange for a blanket amnesty or exile from the country, or something similar. Such offers are usually made to the leadership of the guerrillas or to those in charge of the military or the political campaign. Examples of this are the offers which Safar Al-Hawali or [Muhsin] Al-'Awaji are making today to the *mujahidin* on the Arabian Peninsula.[9]

Political Characteristics with Respect to the Mujahidin

The *mujahidin* exploit military strikes during this phase in order to smash the prestige of the regime and to clarify the picture for the members of the *Ummah* to the effect that the enemy is incapable of stopping the military strikes by the *mujahidin*, in other words, to encourage people to oppose the enemy.

The *mujahidin* also take advantage of this phase to make clear the truth about the current struggle in the region (the struggle against the Jews and Christians) or about the brutal enemy occupying their lands. It is for that reason that when the *mujahidin* delay in striking, they justify such delays because they have to select significant, critical, and "clean" targets (that is, Jewish and Christian targets) in order to embarrass the state in the people's eyes and in order that the public see clearly the regime's collaboration. This is the reason why during this phase the *mujahidin*'s media apparatus promotes the *mujahidin* and urges the people to resist the Crusaders and Jews and to help the *mujahidin*. It also spreads news of the *mujahidin*'s heroic deeds and of their operations or clashes that have occurred and highlights them to the people so that the latter can follow news of their brothers, the *mujahidin*, and can have a clear picture.

Among the political characteristics during this phase, as far as the *mujahidin* are concerned, is that of making allies (that is, the *mujahidin* outside the area of conflict) and strengthening the bonds of cooperation with those *mujahidin*, while neutralizing as far as possible those enemies not involved directly. This is done in order to prevent the opening of multiple fronts simultaneously against the *mujahidin*.

Military Characteristics

Military Characteristics with Respect to the Enemy

Fierce, violent, intense, unrelenting campaigns intended to put an end to the power of the *mujahidin* once and for all. One will find the enemy using everything he can and all his military power to achieve this objective. At the same time, one will find that the enemy will try to lure the *mujahidin* into open battles and engagements in order to do away with them, even if that leads to heavy losses for his own forces.

Military Characteristics with Respect to the Mujahidin

During this phase, the *mujahidin* attempt to expand, diversify, and concentrate their attacks against the enemy, and to distribute these attacks throughout the country. Even if these attacks are small-scale ones, they will be widespread and dispersed and will, as a result, spread out, overextend, and disperse the enemy's effort.

These attacks generally depend on the tactic of attack and withdraw (hit and run) and, during this phase, a *jihadi* group may need to conduct spectacular operations, which will create a positive media impact. The objectives of such operations will be to demonstrate the existence or power of these groups, as well as to rub the enemy's nose in the dirt, and to embolden the people to fight and to energize the youth to take up arms against the enemy—the Jews and the Christians, and their lackeys. Examples of the propaganda use of such spectacular operations include:

1. What the enemy of God, the American Attorney General [John] Ashcroft, said about the ongoing information war between America and the *mujahidin*. "We were helping the Al-Qaeda organization without realizing it," since the Americans were providing excellent media coverage of the operations that Al-Qa'ida carried out.

2. What the enemy of God Turki Al-Faysal said: "Usama Bin Ladin was able to create a historic cleavage between the United States and the Kingdom of Saudi Arabia."[10] This cleavage would not have been possible (by God's grace and power) if the attacks of September 11 had not been so spectacular.

3. Members of Al-Qa'ida benefit from the public when the latter see the heroic actions of their brother *mujahidin* and their spectacular operations, as this strengthens determination and motivates the public, as happened after the attacks on the USS *Cole*, the attack in Nairobi, and September 11, which mobilized the *Ummah* and raised the morale of the Muslim youth.

Bases during This Phase

A. *With Respect to the Enemy*: The enemy's bases during this phase are fixed and well-known.

B. *With Respect to the Mujahidin*: Their bases are mobile, not fixed, and lightly equipped, that is, they can be moved easily and are light to transport.

Negotiations during This Phase

Negotiations during this phase are prohibited and are absolutely forbidden (no negotiations, no military truce, no abandoning your military bases, no dialogue) because the principle of fighting and the appearance of the *jihadi* movement are based on irreconcilable differences, since the conflict is between the Muslims and the Crusaders, and between the *mujahidin* and the apostates, so that there is no room for compromise solutions.

PHASE TWO: RELATIVE STRATEGIC BALANCE

After the movement's success in proving its staying power, in diffusing the enemy's effort, and in attriting and paralyzing the latter's power, and after the people develop trust in the soundness of the *mujahidin*'s program and develop a clear picture, and after the combatants and auxiliaries rally in mass around the organization and the *mujahidin*, we will transition spontaneously to the second phase of guerrilla war, which is the phase of relative strategic balance or what is known as the strategy of a thousand cuts.

Political Characteristics of This Phase

A. *With Respect to the Enemy*: After a protracted war of attrition, the enemy of God will feel that it is impossible to eliminate the *mujahidin*'s military power. As a result, one finds the enemy during this phase turning to political solutions as a potential means to find a way out of this conflict, which he feels will otherwise inevitably overwhelm him. However, owing to the deep-rooted circumstances during this phase, one will find that the military establishment within the regime frequently derails the political establishment's plans. The military may be the cause for the politicians' losing everything, the reason being that the military will not acknowledge the existence of a language with which to talk to the *mujahidin* except the language of blood. There is the possibility of internal coups because of the military's stubbornness and arrogance. The military may convince the politicians to ask for help from foreign forces during this phase, as occurred when the late Najib in Afghanistan asked for the Communist Russians' help.[vii, 11]

B. *With Respect to the Mujahidin*: In light of this frantic and fumbling policy on the enemy's part, the *mujahidin* realize that they are on their way to setting up the

---

[vii]   Perhaps someone who follows the situation in the Arab world and the activity of the apostate governments, and especially those [countries] in which there are movements for reform and armed opposition to those infidel governments, sees the fumbling that besets [these governments]. At times, you will see [these governments] acting according to the characteristics of phase one of a guerrilla war, and at other times moving to the characteristics of phase two, and then transitioning to phase three, and so on. One of the clearest indications of this is, for example, the fact that you see some traitors today

state of the Islamic Caliphate, and one finds them escalating their political campaign in parallel with the military campaign. The intent is to clarify the nature of the struggle being waged between the *mujahidin* and the main enemy—the Jews, the Christians, and their agents. It will be difficult during this period for the collaborators to hide the reality of the Christian and Jewish presence in the Muslim countries, since the *mujahidin* will intensify their attacks against the bases and other places where the enemy is found to such an extent that there can be no doubt left as to the enemy's presence across the length and breadth of the country.

From their liberated areas, their administrative installations, and their media centers, the *mujahidin* must also continue their agitation to reveal the weakness and inability of the collaborationist regime to crush the *mujahidin*. During this phase, the *mujahidin* must also send diplomatic messages by means of political statements or with the language of blood and fire to all the foreign governments that support the collaborationist regime and make the situation clear to them that if they continue to support the regime they will also become legitimate targets for the *mujahidin*'s attacks. The *mujahidin* must address public opinion in those countries to the effect that their governments have embroiled them in wars and struggles in which they have no business being involved. Examples of this are the statements of Abu 'Abd Allah Shaykh Usama Bin Ladin (may God preserve him) some of which are directed to specific nations, such as to the Japanese people and to some other nations.

Military Characteristics of This Phase
   A. *With Respect to the Enemy*: After the *mujahidin*'s tireless activity, their attacks, their successful protracted resistance, and their paralyzing the regime's power and their mobilization of new cadres, the enemy almost ends his military actions, or their number is reduced, in those areas where the *mujahidin*'s influence is strong and where the power of God's believing servants has gained the upper hand. The enemy is content with launching air strikes in those areas and against the *mujahidin*'s supply routes, and is forced to withdraw to more secure areas. This happened in many areas of the world, with operations by the regime's forces reduced to long-range shelling in the case of mountains. As for

---

having recourse to mercenaries and hired guns, even when they know that the movement is only in its infancy. There are also those who say, "If America pulls back and abandons us to confront terrorism, we cannot be responsible for what will happen then." Therefore, one must be careful that these characteristics not become a rigid template (*qawalib jamida*) or a "school solution" (*umur munzala*) but, rather, that they remain adaptable to developments in the region.

cities, the enemy's presence will decrease in those cities where the *mujahidin* are strong and where they have established their control over most of a city. The enemy's obvious inability to repel the *mujahidin*'s repeated attacks will become apparent.

B. *With Respect to the Mujahidin*: Along with the escalation of the *mujahidin*'s military operations and the direct utilization of the experience gained from the engagements, or what is called firsthand experience, and taking advantage of those regions where the regime's presence is limited or weak, the *mujahidin* will set up conventional forces able to extend security and replace the regime in the liberated areas. And, at the same time, they will be able to stand up to the enemy's conventional forces. At that point, the *mujahidin*'s power will grow by leaps and bounds day by day.

Bases during This Phase

A. *With Respect to the Enemy*: As we noted, the enemy's presence will decrease in rugged areas and in those areas where the *mujahidin* are present.

B. *With Respect to the Mujahidin*: During this phase, the *mujahidin* will establish administrative installations and bases in the liberated areas that have fallen under the *mujahidin*'s complete control. There, the *mujahidin* will set up base camps, hospitals, *shari'a* courts, and broadcasting stations, as well as a jumping-off point for military and political actions.

Negotiations during This Phase

After this sequence of events, the enemy will be very anxious to negotiate, in order to stop the *mujahidin*'s military operations and to attempt to regain his breath and rebuild his strength. During this phase, the *mujahidin* can accept to negotiate on condition that military operations continue. One finds that when negotiations begin each side will try to mount violent military attacks before, after, or during the negotiations. That is done in order to demonstrate a continuing presence and one's strength at the negotiating table, and to begin negotiating from a position of strength. In other words, each side will try to score military victories in order to translate them into political gains. We advise the *mujahidin* during this phase, if they have control over the area of operations, to continue military operations because that is what will break the enemy's back and force him to accede to the *mujahidin*'s demands.

During these negotiations—should they happen—conditions for the enemy's surrender should be discussed (since that will break the enemy's morale) so they relinquish power one way or another! That is to be done in return for a trial in accordance with God's *shari'a*. One will observe that the enemy may propose to the *mujahidin* during this phase power-sharing in the government (as happened in Yemen, and as happened recently in the Sudan between Al-Bashir and Garang).[12] This is to be rejected totally and out of hand, as there is no compromising.

PHASE THREE: THE DECISIVE PHASE

This phase is that of the final attack and of finishing off the enemy (by God's will and help).

Political Characteristics of This Phase

A. *With Respect to the Enemy*: This phase, insofar as the enemy is concerned, is considered an extremely critical one and is the final phase with respect to the latter. The regime now is in its throes of agony and is going through a process of political and economic collapse, as well as of internal divisions. There will be internal struggles between the military and the politicians, with each blaming the other, or there may be struggles between different political factions (moderates against hard-liners). During this phase, there may also be military coups for the reasons given above. This collapse will happen notwithstanding major foreign help, which will increase steadily, as happened with the support of the French and Saudi governments for the Algerian government when the latter was about to fall owing to the blows from the *mujahidin*. A similar thing happened to the former regimes in Vietnam and elsewhere. Or, one may find that a regime cannot survive without foreign support and the continuous supply of aid, as is the case with our Arab governments today, even given the fact that in most cases there has not yet appeared a movement for change or armed resistance.

B. *With Respect to the Mujahidin*: During this phase, there is an increase in defections and mutinies in the enemy's military units and administrative apparatus. The *mujahidin* must take advantage as much as possible of those who flee, and reorganize and make use of them (but with due caution against spies and plants). During this phase, the *mujahidin* intensify their links to the *mujahidin* outside the theater of operations and use them to spread their ideas everywhere. If the *mujahidin*'s situation stabilizes, they will then pursue the *jihad* and the liberation all the Islamic countries from oppression and occupation by the Jews and Christians, and will then undertake to revive the neglected religious duty, that of preemptive *jihad* (*jihad al-talab*).

Military Characteristics of This Phase

A. *With Respect to the Enemy*: During this phase, the enemy's influence will be rolled back and will shrink to a very great extent from most of the countryside, the mountains, and other rugged and remote areas because as the *mujahidin* intensify their operations in many of those areas, one finds that the enemy will withdraw and retreat to the principal cities and will transform them into huge armed camps. This process was seen on many fronts throughout history. For example, this is what happened in Afghanistan during Najib's rule when the *mujahidin*'s attacks escalated and their control over many areas spread, and the enemy was compelled to withdraw to the big cities.

The enemy will attempt strenuously to retain control over the lines of communication linking all the cities, and for the main roads to neighboring countries to remain open, which is also what the Afghan government did, even though the majority of support and supplies were transported by air because of the *mujahidin*'s control over the land lines of communication and the constant threat to them. Therefore, the *mujahidin* must not permit the enemy to accomplish this objective. During this phase, land-based attacks against the *mujahidin*'s bases will cease, but air operations or long-range shelling will continue.

B. *With Respect to the Mujahidin*: With respect to the *mujahidin*, this phase is considered one of successes and victory. During the preceding phase (the balance phase), the *mujahidin* were able to create conventional-like forces that will be transformed gradually into conventional forces with modern units. By "modern" I mean that they will be completely familiar with conventional war and with an army's order of battle and how it operates in the field. [These units] will not be used as is the case with those military regimes and military tribunals, and ape the infidel West in ways that everyone knows. However, the *mujahidin* must also retain guerrilla fighters (commandos, insurgents).

By means of these *mujahidin* conventional forces, the *mujahidin* will begin to attack smaller cities and exploit in the media their successes and victories in order to raise the morale of the *mujahidin* and the people in general and to demoralize the enemy. The reason for the *mujahidin*'s targeting of smaller cities is that when the enemy's forces see the fall of cities into the *mujahidin*'s hands with such ease their morale will collapse and they will become convinced that they are incapable of dealing with the *mujahidin*. This happened in Afghanistan, after Khost fell, and then Gardez, into the *mujahidin*'s hands, and then one city after the other followed, culminating in the fall of Kabul.

Note: The army will not fight during this phase, and its leadership will negotiate with the *mujahidin* to save their own necks. We want to caution you here that the main [*mujahidin*] bases in the mountains have to retain strong garrisons; otherwise, the *mujahidin* will be blinded by their successes and abandon their secure bases. One must retain strong garrisons in order to prevent the enemy from exploiting the evacuation of these bases by the *mujahidin* and mounting an air descent in the rear. For that reason, we noted earlier that the *mujahidin* must always retain a guerrilla capability that will always be in a state of readiness.

Bases during This Phase

A. *With Respect to the Enemy*: The enemy will begin to withdraw from his bases in the countryside, in the mountains, and areas in which the *mujahidin* are strong and in which there are frequent operations by the latter. The enemy will be compelled to hunker down in the main cities and to turn them into fortified bases and huge defensive garrisons.

B. *With Respect to the Mujahidin*: The *mujahidin*'s bases will be in the liberated areas, both in the smaller cities and in the countryside, while the *mujahidin* will retain their rear bases and defend them, and will locate their base camps, hospitals, and various combat service support assets there.

Negotiations during This Phase

All negotiations with the enemy cease, and enemy personnel are to be intimidated [by stressing] the inevitability of surrender. *Shari'a* courts are to be established to try all the apostates who have rebelled against religion in fair *shari'a* trials.

Now that we have explained what guerrilla war is and laid down the objectives, targets, and phases of a guerrilla war, we still have to address important issues and the basic preconditions for launching a successful guerrilla war.

2

THE BASIC PRECONDITIONS FOR CONDUCTING A SUCCESSFUL GUERRILLA WAR

LEADERSHIP CADRE

The first [precondition] is a leadership cadre that is homogeneous in terms of mind, spirit, thought, program, and, of course, belief. Leadership is what unifies, shapes, and executes. Leaders unify in the sense that they integrate under one umbrella all the cadres, efforts, capabilities, and experience that the movement possesses. By shaper is meant the one who formulates a strategy for work and action, and who organizes the cadres and material assets, and who assigns them to the right places. It is also the executor, in the sense that this leadership cadre has the capability of taking bold concrete steps to put into action its plans and ideas. The leaders will consist of individuals who have experience, expertise, situational awareness, knowledge, and the fear of God, the Great, the Almighty. "The strong believer is better and more loved by God than the weak believer."[13] Therefore, one finds that such an organization (God willing) will be successful if the right leaders are chosen. Common beliefs are also a key precondition for the leadership and for the entire movement as a whole. How many unified organizations quickly fall into disagreement and split up! Examples of successful leaders include Muhammad (God bless him and his noble Companions and grant them salvation) and, in our days, Shaykh Abu 'Abd Allah [Usama Bin Ladin] and Dr. Ayman [Al-Zawahiri] (may God protect them from the enemy's trickery).

I. SUITABLE CONDITIONS

Second, suitable conditions [are required], which are those circumstances, events, and current trends in the region of conflict or in the region where the *jihadi* movement springs up, that is, what has occurred there up to now. For example, there are within this region new circumstances and events every day, and you must keep your eye on these conditions and circumstances and exploit the best moment to launch your *jihadi* movement. Let us note as an example of this point what happened in Algeria after the Islamic Salvation Front won in the elections and its results were voided and the Army intervened and imposed its control over the country. In the wake of that, a sort of popular rage developed, and the people at all levels were in sympathy with the Islamic Salvation Front, since in people's minds the latter had been robbed of its rights and had a right to be the government. The *mujahidin* in the Jama'a Islamiya and in the Islamic Salvation Front took advantage of these conditions to recruit supporters and to launch armed actions (although what the Islamic Salvation Front did was not according to the *shari'a,* since parliaments and election committees are all rulers to whom God did not grant power and it is not permissible to join them). As God (may He be praised and glorified) said, "Already had He sent you in the Book, that when ye hear the Message of Allah held in defiance and ridicule, ye are not to sit with them unless they turn to a different theme: if ye did, ye would be like them. For Allah will collect the Hypocrites and those who defy Faith—all in Hell."[14] The situation in the Arabian Peninsula was similar. Ten years ago, the situation there was not ready for military activity. However, there have been new developments in the region, and unprecedented situations and events have occurred in succession beginning with the blessed explosion at Al-'Ulya in 1416 a.h. (November 1995 AD) and continuing with the destruction of the World Trade Center, and culminating with the invasion and plundering and exploitation of the [region's] riches by the Americans and the latter's launching [of attacks] from the Peninsula to strike at our brother Muslims in the East and West under the auspices of their servants, the Al Sallul.[15] Before that, there was the replacement of religious laws and the government with those that God had not instituted. Events and transformations continued to occur until the environment became thoroughly ready for the launching of the *jihadi* movement in the Land of Muhammad (God's prayers and salvation be on him).

Therefore, any budding movement or any group that wants to wage a successful guerrilla war must pay attention to the situation of the ordinary people, and address their rights and needs, and it is necessary to live with [the ordinary people] and to share in their sorrows and joys. If the movement reaches this stage, it has earned the right to be accepted by the people, which is what we call the popular response. The *mujahidin* must be mindful that the majority of people are preoccupied with their day-to-day lives and expend their energies chasing their daily bread. In light of this, the *mujahidin* can be sure that they will not get much support, unless God wills otherwise. The basic issue for us in this respect is: "Those who have abandoned them will not be able to harm them; neither will those who differ from them."[16] It is up to the *mujahidin* to create the appropriate conditions by undertaking spectacular operations (as, for example, that of September 11) and by their efforts in organized media activity.

Before doing all that, the leadership must undertake an exhaustive study of the situation, of conditions, variables, and trends in the region, and then determine whether the time for action and to begin a successful guerrilla war has arrived or not. It is vital to examine all the issues very carefully. The *mujahidin* are fighting for the *Ummah* as a whole, to preserve its religion, holy places, the blood of its sons, and the latter's possessions, honor, and lands, and defending the *Ummah* from injustice and aggression. It is necessary—this being the case—for the *mujahidin* to pay attention to all the details that could affect negatively the conduct of operations. It is all right to postpone action if there is real benefit in delaying it until the preconditions, preparations, and favorable circumstances are ripe, of course provided [the *mujahidin*] are making a great effort, with perseverance, in preparing and training, and creating the appropriate atmosphere, and fulfilling the remaining preconditions and requirements for undertaking a successful guerrilla war.

II. THE POPULAR RESPONSE

By popular response we mean engendering a state of mind and convincing the majority of citizens to accept the principle of *jihadi* action and of military operations and ousting the invaders. They will also agree to participate materially and morally and extend their support to fill any needs or gaps. Usually, such a response only appears in a subjugated and helpless people. Therefore, the *mujahidin* must undertake to relieve the injustices from those who are oppressed and restore their rights.

Elements of the Popular Response

1. *Passive*: When individuals or groups (or some of them) refrain from sharing in bearing the risks, burdens, and hardships to a sufficient degree, it is because they are afraid and hesitant to engage in action or initiative. However, they nevertheless provide material and logistic support, and individuals of this type will provide money, food, and information to the *mujahidin*. There are many such as these in our Islamic society, thank God. They are very close to joining the organization, and a successful organization has only to motivate them to move them to an active response, but the group will not be able to accomplish that unless it demonstrates to these people its ability to manage and control matters effectively.

2. *Active*: This is when supporters provide volunteers for combat and provide to the *mujahidin* moral and financial aid, as well as sensitive intelligence, shelter, and food and drink. To describe their position, they would say, "We are with you body and soul." Such a response usually happens after every successful operation by the *mujahidin*. One finds those responding submitting themselves to the *jihadi* leadership; they are obedient, and they bear a significant portion of the risks, burdens, and hardships.

III. THE MEANS OF USING FORCE (WEAPONS AND MUNITIONS)

There is no *jihad* without force, and there is no war without resources to guarantee the outburst and continuation of this force. There is no *jihad* without creating a great force and increasing it, and it is vital to have both a human force and military equipment.

If we have youths without weapons, that is of no use, unless God wills otherwise. Likewise, it is necessary, if there are weapons, to have someone wield them. Weapons are of no use without someone to use them to their full potential, with expertise and skill. In addition, there must be high moral standards, noble-mindedness, and knowledge of the *shari'a*. These are the most effective weapons, first and foremost. *Mujahidin* who do not possess knowledge of the *shari'a* will end up being nothing but bandits.

The matter of preparation and getting weapons and munitions should be done to the greatest degree possible. "Against them make ready your strength to the utmost of your power."[17] This is a good reply to the slackers and slanderers, that is, we are preparing to our utmost and we begin in God's name and with His blessings.

The leadership must acquire military equipment and distribute it to the personnel, and also allocate the personnel correctly, and may the start [of the *jihad*] be with God's blessings.

The leadership must seek to distribute small groups and cells with few people. The number of individuals in a cell normally should not exceed four to six. This is to be done as feasible, and the intent is to reduce potential losses and to increase the organization's flexibility. For that reason, the leadership should disperse depots and caches for supplies and weapons in scattered locations in relation to the distribution of the cells and groups, so that each cell can be responsible for its own cache and supplies. The intent is that if there is a misfortune or an attack (God forbid), it will be limited to a specific cell or group. Or, the leaders should set up more support and supply units, so that that there will be multiple logistics cells in the region. It is a prerequisite under these circumstances that the cells do not know or are linked with each other, in order to ensure continuity of action for the collective and the organization. Successful leaders must instill the *jihadi* idea within the *jihadi* groups and must make clear the program and the beliefs to all the members of the cells for the following reasons:

1. Soundness of thought and belief.
2. Cohesion.
3. If the leaders are killed or captured, the torch will continue to be carried by those who succeed them without any problem (God willing).

Leaders must transform these forces and armed groups into forces kneaded in blood, bones, and sweat. These fighters must fear no one but God and must be willing to sacrifice everything they have for the sake of promoting God's word. They must be committed to discomfiting the enemies of God, believing in God's victory, confident in His promises, and be known for their noble-mindedness, high morals, and loyalty to other believers. "Lowly with the Believers, mighty against the Rejecters."[18]

All these matters and these positive characteristics develop over time and through battles and adversity, which reveal men's true mettle. These forces must be endowed with high morals and good behavior. A *mujahid* must be a beacon showing the path to the people and a leader to those brothers who follow him. He must be careful that God the Exalted's words not apply to him to the effect that "Do ye enjoin right conduct on the people, and forget (to practice it) yourselves?"[19] Without these qualities, the Islamic group's affairs will not progress and it is the preceding qualities that are the real weapons and ammunition.

After we addressed in the preceding lesson Phase Two and its military and political characteristics with respect to the enemy and the *mujahidin*, and the foundations of that phase, we addressed the military and political characteristics of Phase Three with respect to the enemy and the *mujahidin*, and the foundations of that phase. We then addressed the basic preconditions to launching a successful guerrilla war and identified three main preconditions: a leadership cadre that is homogeneous in terms of intellect, spirit, thought, and program, suitable conditions, and the means of exerting force. In this installment, we will wrap up with the fourth and final precondition, which is:

IV. KNOWLEDGE OF THE ART OF CONVENTIONAL AND UNCONVENTIONAL WEAPONS

A. With Respect to the Leadership and the Fundamental Rules Relative to Action

1. The First Issue: Leadership and Fundamental Principles

Among the basic requirements of leaders is the capability to be creative and innovative and to have the moral preparation for the worst. Leaders must always prepare themselves to face danger and stand up to it, and they must have mastery over the spectrum of combat skills, procedures, and methods, in accordance with the conditions and terrain in the region, that is, the theater of conflict. An example of that is conducting a *jihadi* movement on territory that is mostly desert, in which the *jihadi* movement must exploit the cities expertly and carry out operations inside the latter. Military operations within cities will be conducted without deploying forest forces, since forests do not exist in the area of operations.

A movement must adapt itself to the existing geographic conditions and be able to attack in the mountains, just as it attacks on the plains, in the cities, and along the coasts. For each [of these environments], there are specific techniques, operating procedures, and tactics. One finds that history is replete with examples of popular revolts against unjust dictatorial rulers. However, most unfortunately, there is a repetition of failed attempts. The situation reaches a crisis, and one finds that there is a sort of fumbling about and despair on the part of individuals in the *Ummah*. The cause for that situation is a lack of leaders who know the art of conventional and unconventional warfare, and leaders who are incapable of organizing and building cohesion.

Leadership, however, has improved throughout history, and we will summarize the specific areas where there has been improvement:

1. The correct assessment of a situation.
2. A sound estimate of the general and the specific situation (a correct reading of the internal and foreign situation).
3. Establishing dynamic and effective systems and operations, with the leadership itself an operational cell.
4. Establishing a common political doctrine applicable to the whole organization (setting the broad guidelines that the organization will follow).
5. Study of and planning operations and assigning missions and tasks.

Overall, leaders must fulfill the following conditions for a successful guerrilla war:

1. Propaganda and Propagandists: Propaganda for this program is to be clear and will address all levels of society. Propagandists for this program must be energized and their influence over society's different classes utilized. The program for this [propaganda] is the Book and the *Sunnah*. Propaganda by sound *'ulama'* and clerics is vital.
2. Messengers and Correspondence: This depends on conditions and on the security situation. The movement must dispatch messengers before it launches the war so that the movement can determine who is for it or against it. These messengers and these messages may take various forms. This may be done covertly rather than openly in recognition of your security situation and having to avoid burning your papers. The enemy's correspondence may be a way to keep an eye on the latter. There is a technique and method for everything.
3. Collecting, Securing, Managing, and Accounting for Funds: Any *jihadi* movement in the world has nerves, muscles, and bone. The muscle are the leaders, the cadres, and experience. The bone is the *mujahidin* who bear arms. Money is the nervous system of the *jihad*. Therefore, one finds that the *jihad* eats money in a prodigious manner. It is imperative that before any *jihadi* action or before setting up a movement for change that money be collected, that it be secured, and that good provision be made for its sources. It should be made to flow in an orderly manner so that the organization's needs are met in the future, because the enemy during the first phase of a guerrilla war (the attrition phase) will try his utmost and use all means to cut off the flow of this money and will mount a vigorous campaign to dry up the sources of funding and to freeze accounts.
4. Bases, Depots, and Caches: There should be bases, depots, and caches in all areas (bases are not limited only to the mountains, as **a base is any secure spot in which the *mujahidin* can hide and from which they can operate**). It is vital to have depots and caches that the movement can use.
5. Seeking Out Members and Auxiliaries: Successful and outstanding leaders must always be on the lookout for [new] members and auxiliaries.
6. Organizing Units for Defense and Deterrence: Their mission is to protect reli-

gion and honor and to uproot the sources of evil and corruption that are causing corruption in the country, such as apostates who insult God and His prophet, or those who mock God's religion, or the apostate officers who openly fight against God and His prophet. It is necessary to uproot them in order to deter others and in order that the *Ummah* see that the tyrant's day of reckoning is near.

Important Note: Owing to the degenerate times and sad state of affairs, as well as to the public's unclear picture of the struggle and of the truth about the struggle, nascent movements must avoid [targeting] agents who are the servants of the Crusaders and begin first with the Jews and Crusaders and confront the *Ummah* with its foreign enemy who invaded the land and replaced the *shari'a*. The *Ummah* always unites against a foreign enemy, and the *mujahidin* at the same time should try to expose those agents and use the *mujahidin* media to achieve this objective. Let the *Ummah* know who its real enemy is.

7. Organizing propaganda and the media at home and abroad and setting up an integrated media apparatus capable of transmitting the voice of the *mujahidin* at home and abroad.

8. Something that is very important: Creating an Islamic intelligence apparatus. This will have the task of oversight over recruitment of individuals and of protecting the organization from being penetrated. It will also set the security plans for individuals, the leadership, and installations.

9. Setting up base camps and training centers with the mission of providing practical training to cells so that they can become operational.

The second issue related to this topic is knowledge of the art of conventional and unconventional war.

This consists of the political program for conducting a *jihad*: There are two basic aspects in any political war.

1. One aspect is not open to debate or compromise, which is that of beliefs; there is no debate or discussion about beliefs.

2. The second aspect is modified according to the situation and conditions. This aspect is usually that of military operations conducted against the opponent. For example, there are operations such as hostage-taking, and the negotiations conducted in relation to them. Such matters are open to compromise. These operations are military, because they are conducted in order to attain specific objectives, whether political or economic. Such operations are also mounted as a way of sending diplomatic messages to various intended recipients.

The third issue: Leaders Must Make Use of the Capabilities, Energy, and Cadres, and Activate and Train Them on the Basics and Order of Battle of Conventional Wars.

Leaders must know the enemy whom they are fighting, because the enemy can maneuver and has sensitive nodes that enable him to function, and because when conventional forces in our region maneuver they do so with specific formations. Therefore, it is imperative that leaders know how the enemy fights in order to be able to strike at the latter. As experts know, armies are organized either in a Western or Eastern mode. Armies have a number of units, beginning with the smallest, being the squad (nine to twelve individuals), above which comes the platoon, which consists of three or more squads. Above that is the company, which consists of three platoons, and has between 100 and 150 men. Above that is the battalion, which consists of three or four companies. Above the battalion is the brigade, which is made up of three or four battalions, and above that is the division, which is made up of three or four brigades. Above the division is the corps, which is made up of three or four divisions. Above that is the army, which is most often composed of three or four corps. These echelons are known by different terms depending on the specific army.

Armed forces are made up of three services: land, sea, and air. Usually, one finds that there is mutual support among these three services. For example, one finds a land battalion being supported by naval forces or by air defense, etc. For that reason, leaders must learn how to do this well and study it and take an interest in any new area of knowledge or innovation in this field, and must also train personnel in this area of knowledge.

With this, we end the section on the basic conditions for conducting a successful guerrilla war, and we will continue with a study of the guerrilla force structure.

3

GUERRILLA FORCE STRUCTURE

1. Mountain forces
2. Urban forces (clandestine action groups)
3. Auxiliaries

MOUNTAIN FORCES

Defining Mountain Forces: By mountain forces we mean those small units without permanent bases inside the country where the conflict is taking place. However, they may have permanent bases in neighboring countries, as did the *mujahidin* formerly in Afghanistan, who had bases in Pakistan, or as is the case with the Chechens, who have bases and support installations on Georgian territory. As we noted above, these forces are always on the move and do not spend more than forty-eight hours in a single place. As a result, the personnel belonging to these forces carry everything they need on their backs (weapons, water, food, bedding, and other necessities).

The area of operations for these forces is in those lands where government forces are not in complete control, which are usually those [areas] with difficult terrain such as mountains, forests, swamps, or similar terrain. It is this [terrain] that constitutes the maneuver and movement space for these units. Their method of operations is that of continuous movement, hitting the enemy, and then movement again. That is the way of the flea and the dog, inducing the enemy to make moves that are not well thought out, whereupon he falls into ambushes that the mountain fighters have set. We also see that mountain forces do not operate in cities, but that they operate, instead, in less populated areas, such as in the countryside, in mountainous areas, forests, and small towns. Personnel in these units are physically fit and are sufficiently healthy to enable them to live in the open for long periods of time. These units have a high level of endurance and patience in putting up with hardships and with difficult climatic conditions. They are able to march eighteen to twenty hours a day while not eating very much.

The Organization of Mountain Force: The squad (*jama'a*) is the nucleus and nerves of mountain forces and is the unit that enables the guerrillas to engage the enemy. Every six mountain squads form a guerrilla company (*sariya*), which is the largest guerrilla formation in a sector. Four guerrilla companies form a guerrilla battalion (*katiba*), and a guerrilla battalion is the largest guerrilla formation, with one guerrilla battalion in each operational zone.

Squad Organization

1. The squad commander, armed with a Kalashnikov.
2. Deputy squad commander, armed with a Kalashnikov.
3. Light machine gunner (PK), armed with a pistol for personal protection.[20]
4. Individual armed with a Kalashnikov, assistant to the light machine gunner.
5. Individual armed with an RPG, and with a pistol for personal protection.
6. Individual armed with a Kalashnikov, assistant to the RPG operator.
7. One communications man, armed with a Kalashnikov.
8. One medic, armed with a Kalashnikov.
9. One medic, armed with a Kalashnikov.
10. One sharpshooter.
11. One terrain analysis specialist, armed with a Kalashnikov.
12. Individual armed with a Kalashnikov.

The amount of ammunition carried by each individual in the squad:

1. Each rifleman: 300 rounds.
2. Light machine gunner (PK): 1,000 rounds, which his assistant will help carry.
3. RPG operator: ten rockets, which his assistant will help carry.

Hand grenades and anti-armor munitions:

1. Hand grenades for defense and offense: every individual in the squad will carry at least one defensive grenade and one offensive one.
2. Anti-armor munitions: every rifleman, with the exception of the light machine gunner (PK) and the RPG operator, will carry one anti-tank round.

Logistics for the Squad:

1. Food: every individual in the squad while on the move will carry enough food for forty-eight hours at a minimum, and preferably carry on his back enough food for a whole week.
2. Water: each individual will carry two liters of water (in two canteens), which is enough for forty-eight hours.

Medical First Aid:
The squad will bring a first-aid kit, which an individual trained in first aid will carry.
Contents of the backpack for each member of the squad:

1. An extra track suit (extra clothes).[21]
2. Personal toiletries: soap, thread, etc.
3. Food.
4. Other supplies not stocked in the depots.
5. Harness, rope, and descending rings.
6. A small shovel.

Contents of the waist pack for every rifleman:

1. Supplies.
2. Hand grenades and anti-armor grenades.
3. Any specialized technical equipment, such as a compass, binoculars, a cell phone, Magellan GPS.

Technical Equipment at the Squad Level:

1. Two compasses.
2. Two pairs of binoculars.
3. Two cell phones.
4. Wireless communications gear to be used for communicating between the company commander and the component squads.
5. A Magellan GPS to determine locations.

Notes:

1. The squad may carry more hand grenades, depending on the type of mission.
2. When attacking a target, heavy packs (backpacks) will be left at the nearest secure area. Anything not used in the fighting will be left behind.
3. RPG rounds will be secured on the outside of the backpack. There must be twenty rounds in a squad. The RPG operator will carry three rounds in his own bag, so that seventeen rounds remain for others in the squad. The RPG operator's assistant will carry three in the operator's spare bag, so that fourteen remain, which will be distributed among the rest of the squad's personnel.

Training for the squad will culminate in how to execute various missions, and include how to handle supporting weapons. As a result, training will be sequential, as follows:

1. Guerrilla formations and units and each individual's tasks in the formation.
2. Various mobile formations for all types of terrain.
3. How to react when encountering the enemy while on the march.
4. Mission support sites.
5. What to do in various areas (assembly, nearest cover, rallying points).
6. Reconnaissance patrols.
7. Combat patrols (raids, ambushes).
8. Guerrilla tactics in fighting against conventional forces.
9. Guerrilla tactics in fighting against guerrilla forces.
10. Various combat missions required of guerrillas.

All team personnel participate in this training.

After having discussed in the preceding lesson the fourth, and last, precondition for undertaking a successful and organized guerrilla war, and after having discussed the force structure of guerrilla forces, and a short diversion in the section on mountain forces, we will finish (God willing) the discussion on mountain forces later.

Selecting a Guerrilla Base (A Place to Assemble and from Which to Launch)

In special situations and circumstances, guerrillas may establish a permanent base within the enemy's zone or in their own forward zones, which will facilitate launching more patrols and their return to base. This occurs in combat in the mountains and forests, since having such a base makes it easier to protect patrols both when they leave and when they return, and provides the advantage of evacuating the wounded and prisoners to the rear, and facilitates having secure communications. A condition for choosing a base is that it be impregnable and easily defensible. Activity and movement in it should be limited so that it does not become vulnerable to discovery. Otherwise, the enemy will intervene and attack it. The mission support site is a position that the guerrillas occupy for a short period in order to conduct operations in an area. A combat base resembles the mission support site, but is designed for use by all the guerrillas and is intended for multiple patrols, not just one.

The Location of the Base

The following conditions are required for the location of a base:

1. That it be in the best location for the execution of the mission.
2. That it be in a location that is easily defensible for a period sufficient to carry out an exfiltration of forces.
3. That it be sufficiently distant from roads and paths in the zone.
4. That it be in a location with easy communications.
5. That it be near sources of water.

6. That it be in a zone where there is ample cover and concealment.

Security (Base Security); Required Security Measures for a Base
A guerrilla base is vitally dependent on secrecy for its defense and a security plan must include the following items:

1. Distance from roads, patrols, and inhabited areas.
2. Choice of only a single way to enter and exit the base; this track must be very well camouflaged.
3. The location must provide good protection for the *mujahidin* from airpower.
4. The location must facilitate the preparation of plans for flexible defense (all-point defense), by which is meant the ability to defend in all directions and the ability to control egress and fields of fire so that the entire base is covered by defensive fires.

Reconnaissance and Defense of the Zone Surrounding a Base

1. A reconnaissance team will go out to a predetermined distance in a specific direction and conduct reconnaissance of the zone around the base.
2. A reconnaissance team will undertake to make sure there are no civilians or enemy in the zone and will determine the following points through reconnaissance:
   a. The appropriate locations for observation and defense points.
   b. Listening posts.
   c. Exfiltration routes.
4. Appropriate rally points, observation and defensive points, and exfiltration routes are to be determined based on the reconnaissance patrol's information.[22]

Factors in Selecting a Base

1. *The presence of potable water* year-round (wells, springs, stream, river, rainwater accumulation, etc.)
2. *Knowledge of the local people* (country folk, village and city dwellers, nomads) and the degree of the people's loyalty, whether to the enemy or to the *mujahidin*.
3. *The enemy*: Identifying the enemy.
   a. *Who is he?* What kind of units does he have, and what size are they?
   b. *Location*: Where is he? What is he doing?
   c. *His organization*: How is he organized? What is his force structure?
   d. *Strength*: What is his strength in comparison to our strength?
   e. *Morale*: How is his morale, level of experience, and level of training?
   f. *Type of forces*: Are they reserves or active-duty forces?

g. *Airpower*: Does he use tactical airpower? Does he use paratroops or attack helicopters?

h. *Order of battle*: Do his forces include tanks, infantry (light, mechanized) artillery, or supporting arms?

i. *Artillery*: What type is used? How is it used—the type of fires, caliber, and when?

4. Rugged terrain, specifically:

a. *Key [Terrain] Features*: [Terrain] features are key in relation to the mission. Key features are those locations that when controlled or occupied give one side an advantage over the other. This is key terrain in relation to carrying out a mission; by controlling it, one prevents the enemy from doing so. Examples include high mountain peaks and valley passes.

b. *Observation and Fires*: Observation means seeing, and fires means striking. When you evaluate a specific piece of terrain, ask yourself the following question: "What can I see and what can I hit from here?" The answer to that question will determine for you the locations that will be used as observation points and the appropriate points for defensive positions and also determine dead zones and positions. The relationship of these locations to the avenues of approach is a very important one. If the avenue of approach is in a dead zone, it will favor the attacker, while if it can be observed and can be hit from multiple positions, it favors the defender. If the defensive positions are not mutually supportive and cannot be reinforced due to poor observation and poor fields of fire, that favors the attacker.

c. *Obstacles*: All sorts of man-made and natural obstacles are to be considered, such as minefields, road obstacles, anti-tank ditches, and other anti-tank obstacles that are emplaced in order to destroy, delay, and hinder the enemy.[viii] All obstacles that are used in the defense must be covered by fires. Natural obstacles have a lesser impact on infantry than they do on other types of forces.

d. *Cover and Concealment*: Cover is the protection of a unit from enemy fires. Concealment is protection of a unit from enemy observation. All advantages that the terrain provides for cover and concealment must be exploited, such as caves, caverns, and thickly wooded areas.

e. *Avenues of Approach and Supply Routes*: Avenues of approach must be considered as well as supply routes and defensive and offensive opera-

---

viii "M/d" [*mudhadd li-l-dabbabat*] here means "anti-tank," since impassable ditches especially made to block the advance of mechanized and armor vehicles are put in place. When one sees the abbreviation "m/t" [*mudhadd li-l-ta'irat*], that designates "air defense."

tions with respect to our forces and the enemy's forces. An analysis of the enemy's avenues of approach has to focus on the areas on which he can maneuver, the number of enemy units that can use these positions, the obstacles that are emplaced, and the positions from which our forces can hinder, delay, destroy, and defeat the enemy.

5. *The Beasts of Burden Appropriate for the Zone*: horses, mules, camels, donkeys, vehicles, etc.

THE TACTICS OF MOUNTAIN COMBAT

Tactics in guerrilla war take two main forms: ambushes and raids. Each of these is subject to general rules that must be followed in guerrilla tactics, whatever form they may take. We will return below to some general considerations that govern guerrilla tactics. Subsequently, we will direct our attention to both ambushes and raids.

General Considerations That Govern Guerrilla Tactics

1. The tactical objective of operations is resistance and surviving successfully in order to bring about victory. Therefore, one must always be alert that the enemy not encircle us and to break contact immediately when it is the enemy who has the initiative.
2. On the offensive, one must always be fully alert while taking care to deceive the enemy into thinking, for example, that the attack is in the West, while the main attack is really in the East, **so that the enemy is kept busy with a supporting attack from one direction and is surprised from another direction**.
3. There must be complete reliance on blending in and on the effective penetration and intermingling with the local population.
4. Bases for launching operations must be well-fortified with natural defenses and be prepared with engineering works for defense if needed. In addition, these bases must be provided with easy secret escape routes, and defense and escape plans will be drafted.
5. When moving or stopping for rest or to spend the night, care must be taken not to leave behind any trace or indications that will point to the guerrillas' having been there.
6. Well-concealed small mission support sites must be established around the target area before an attack in order to use such sites to shelter the wounded in preparation for transferring them to more secure areas.
7. The issue of food and supplies is to be solved by using small camouflaged caches whose location only a small number of fighters know. Items are to be stored in moisture-resistant containers made of plastic, metal, or glass so that they are not ruined by water and humidity.
8. Complete secrecy must be maintained. Only a small number of personnel need

to know the plans for movement and the location of forward assembly areas and alternative bases, besides the main ones, of course.

9. It is necessary to avoid routine and repetition in executing various operations. Instead, originality and creativity are vital. Rashness and carelessness are totally unacceptable in guerrilla tactics. Rather, patience and taking into consideration all the factors are vital.

10. Surprise, speed, and determination are important factors in guerrilla tactics.

11. Attacking the enemy while he is on the march is best, because he is most vulnerable then.

12. Attacking isolated installations is best because of its impact on morale, in addition to forcing the enemy to disperse and to overextend his forces and to allocate relatively large quantities of supplies and weapons [to such installations].

13. Weapons and documents must be removed from guerrillas who are killed so that the enemy cannot exploit them.

Next, we will deal with ambushes and raids.

A. The Ambush

The ambush, as a combat tactic, is used by both guerrilla and conventional forces. Indeed, special forces in conventional armies use ambushes frequently for the purpose of capturing prisoners, seizing documents, assassinations, or hindering the advance of an army. Ambushes are the same in basic tactical terms, whether set by guerrillas or by conventional forces. However, ambushes that guerrillas set do differ in specific ways, the most important of which is reliance on local support from the local population for concealment, exfiltration, and storing the necessary weapons and supplies, as well as compensating for the required material capabilities with high morale and local knowledge.

"Ambush" means concealment in a good location in which one waits for the arrival of the enemy in a situation where the latter will be vulnerable. The forces lying in ambush will burst out with the intent of wiping out the enemy or seizing prisoners, documents, weapons, or supplies, quite apart from harassing, provoking, and intimidating the enemy, of course. In order for an ambush to succeed, guerrilla forces proceed to split the ambush force into three squads: reconnaissance, assault, and one for security and for blocking the road. Examples of some types of ambushes include

1. The ambush force splits into four units, each one of which takes a position along four specified geographic directions, where they hunker down to await the enemy. When the enemy comes upon one of these units, the latter proceeds to open fire and, if attacked, withdraws while another unit hits the enemy with fire. The four units alternate with attacks and withdrawals until the enemy's morale collapses and the latter becomes fixed in one spot, making him easy prey in the end

for the ambush. The time of day is not important in carrying out this mission, as it could be either at night or during the daytime, but the distances should be reduced if this maneuver is carried out at night.

2. The ambush force is split into two, in the shape of an L, and both detachments should be prepared to attack if the enemy falls into the ambush. In this type of ambush, it is especially important to deconflict fires. Of course, there are also many other types of ambushes.

B. The Raid

The technical difference between an ambush and a raid is that an ambush consists of lying in wait in a good position, whereas a raid is a planned and organized attack on a target selected with precision and care. In a raid, the attacking detachment advances using total concealment along the avenue of approach toward the preselected objective. [The detachment] must be proficient at infiltrating, approaching, and concealment, and in taking advantage of natural conditions. This force then attacks the objective in a manner appropriate to the intelligence and according to the plan that was drafted beforehand. Of course, the general objective of every raid is to harass, put pressure on, and intimidate the enemy. Every raid also has its own specific objectives, which may be to acquire prisoners, documents, weapons, supplies, equipment, or even simply the destruction of, blowing up, or sabotaging the targeted objective. It is worth mentioning that exfiltrating after a raid is considered one of the most important phases of a raid, as the enemy will spare no effort to pursue if at all possible, while the raiding force enjoys no cover or heavy covering fires, since guerrillas usually do not have that luxury. Therefore, guerrillas must compensate for that by using difficult, rugged routes, predesignated in the plan, with the escape routes sown with small booby traps that will hinder the enemy's progress in pursuit of the exfiltrating force.

In concluding this section on ambushes and raids, we will note that both may be conducted from mission support sites placed among the enemy's units. Likewise, they may be conducted by using infiltration and fanning out within the enemy's lines. In general, all this applies to the tactics and organization of mountain forces. If we wanted to deal with this in detail, that would require a longer discussion. However, these are the most important points and issues relevant to this type of guerrilla forces, may God grace us with that knowledge and make it an argument in our favor rather than against us on Judgment Day, and [grant] that to be a means of fighting, defeating, and humiliating the infidels. He is able to do all things and can grant one's prayers.

4

COVERT OPERATIONS UNITS IN CITIES

Urban operations require small independent units whose number of personnel usually does not exceed four. They will come from the people of the city where they are operating because urbanites know a city's ways and geography. However, this stipulation is not absolute, since country folk moving to big cities may be a common occurrence. Urban dwellers must be able to move easily about the city because a city is full of eyes and spies, given that most of the targets are in the cities and given that government officials, businessmen, and the wealthy are there. It is the cities that usually represent a state's prestige. Covert operations units should not be launched in cities without the necessary training, the necessary identity documents, and excellent hideouts. Individuals must be well-trained. Offices for the forging of documents must be established. Therefore, the organization's best personnel in terms of education, sophistication, and training should operate in cities, because that will make it easier for them to move around and operate. Urban operations also require a great deal of financial support because of the higher cost of living in cities in comparison to that in the mountains—cities burn up money. Even safe houses can be very expensive. If the house is located in a fashionable neighborhood, an appropriate car must also be bought to blend in with the neighborhood's atmosphere.

Note: There is an error that most *jihadi* groups have fallen into, namely that an individual in the organization knows everything about the organization, including its secret affairs. Or, one finds that one of the operational groups knows everything from A to Z about a specific activity or a specific operation, since it collects intelligence, plans, executes, and commands. Instead, the *mujahidin* must profit from their previous brothers' experience and pick up where they left off. The one who collects the intelligence should not know what the target is by collecting the intelligence about an individual or installation. Nor should he know how the operation is to be carried out, nor the means to be used in the operation or how they are to be brought to the operation's location. Likewise, the logistician should not know why certain weapons were collected or why certain explosives are being prepared.

FORCE STRUCTURE WITHIN A CITY

More than one form of force structure can be used in a city, including pyramid force structure and that like the centerpiece of a set of worry beads.[23] Any group must engage in action and set up the organization structure chart depending on the circumstances in which the group has to operate, and these are matters that the leadership usually determines. Among these formations are:

1. The command element (*majmu'a*)
2. The intelligence collection element
3. The logistics element
4. The assault element

These [elements] may also be called the command team (*taqim*), assault team, etc.

A. Field Command Element

This element consists of two or three individuals.

Its functions: Controls the tasks of the operations team and provides guidance and administration for the other three elements. The field command element usually gets its instructions from higher headquarters by means of dead drops or by other means of indirect contact.[ix] The dead drop is any means by which indirect communications are carried out between two parties. The commander in the field also sends instructions to the other teams by means of dead drops.

Individuals in this element [field command] must know thoroughly how to plan operations in cities. Therefore, they must be selected from among the best elements within the organization. Those who are the most knowledgeable and have the greatest familiarity with military science will be promoted over those who are better in the field of religious learning. Individuals in this element will be selected based on their planning capabilities, their intelligence, and their managerial skills.

The training for this element consists of the following:

1. Assessment and analysis of the intelligence obtained from the intelligence collection element. Personnel must be able to analyze and anticipate all contingencies that might happen before they happen.
2. Study, analysis, and planning of military operations, and the drafting of the plans needed for the offense, withdrawal, emergencies, and defense, and the assessment of the utility, and the positives and negatives resulting from an action.
3. The members of this element must train using secret communications in all its

---

[ix]   By "higher headquarters" what is meant here is the organization's senior leadership, which gives the orders to the field commanders who are distributed in various regions.

forms (all types of devices for receiving and sending), and they must be thoroughly proficient in how to meet securely and secretly, as well as in other skills such as detecting and eluding surveillance.

4. A thorough mastery of the work of the other teams: intelligence collection, logistics, and assault.

The *mujahidin* need a strong Islamic counterintelligence apparatus in order to counter the threat that surrounds secret activity in cities. Usually, an urban operational group's intelligence apparatus consists of four individuals who are trained in the counterintelligence and security matters they require. This cell must also undertake the functions of other cells too, such as planning and execution. One of the members of the intelligence cell may also belong to the leadership cell, and therefore, the selection of the intelligence cell's members must be very rigorous.

B. The Intelligence Collection Element

One of the appropriate ways for this [intelligence collection] element to carry out its mission is for it to collect using two individuals. If the target is a major one, the entire element will collect the intelligence. If the target is bigger still, half of another team will support them, as is to be decided by the leadership. Roles must be assigned to this element, as well as to the sectors and installations, for example. Their training consists of the following:

5. Individual specialization, so that the team's activity as a whole does not stop. This specialization will consist of:

   a. A computer specialist, with the ability to enter and download information as required, whether this be images, videos, secret documents, statements, or textual reports. In general, he must be an expert in operating a computer.

   b. An individual to organize information (what is meant here is raw intelligence), whose task it is to organize and catalog raw intelligence after which he will pass it on to the computer expert to enter and archive it, if the leadership directs that the information be archived on a computer. This issue leads us to the importance of archives and preserving information collected by the intelligence collection element in order to make use of it at a subsequent time.

   c. A photographic lab specialist. We have to keep in mind here that photography advanced greatly during the late 1990s and that it is continuing to do so, and that photographic technology has reached a very advanced stage. It is no longer necessary at all to use the old methods of photography (developing), and one can use instead digital cameras linked to computers. This method is more secure and easier to use, and it is easier to enlarge or reduce photos, as well as having other advantages that it wouldn't be appropriate to discuss here.

    d. A communications specialist. He will be responsible for preparing the dead drops, as well as for secret meetings and communications.

Of course, it is vital that every individual specialize in a field, but all individuals must also be familiar with all these technical areas.

  6. It is vital that this element be trained in collecting raw operational intelligence using all methods, as well as in writing intelligence reports and photography (still photographs and film). They must not underestimate any information they find in the field (their observation posts) because the leadership may be able to make use of it, since it could be used as a diversion or it could benefit the assault team in conducting a mission. Therefore, it is vital to collect all available information in the collection area and to pass it on to the analyst, who in turn will pass it on to the leadership to use.

Important Note: The biggest thing that destroys organizations is the issue of communications (wire, wireless, direct, indirect). Therefore, one must pay attention to this problem and plan for this, keeping up with technological developments related to the means of communication. If communications between the leadership and the rank-and-file are solid and stable, then operations can proceed in the right way.

A Practical Lesson: When the Al Sallul released the names of twenty-six *mujahidin*, one of the Al Sallul's main objectives . . . in addition to [revealing] their impotence, the exhaustion of their means, and the failure of their security apparatus to apprehend the *mujahidin*, was to paralyze the people and to buy off their consciences.[24] The [Saudi government] also publicized the photographs of those who were wanted. One of the objectives of this step was to disrupt communications between these individuals and those who were working under their leadership. That is, if they made their photographs available in public, communications would decrease, as well as their movement and their contacts with the outside world. Therefore, communications are always considered one of the most important elements, and each side will work hard to strike at the other's communications.

C. The Logistics Element or Team

This element is composed of two to four individuals. As a rule, this element requires those who have experience with the methods of logistics and those who have ties with the Mafia or other smugglers because the latter have previous experience and can be very useful to you. The role of this element is to supply everything that the other units need in terms of weapons, tools, equipment, documents, safe houses, vehicles, etc.

Training for this element is wide-ranging and advanced. They will be given a specialized course called the logistics course, in which they will receive training in:

1. Procuring vehicles, that is, the enemy's vehicles, which are considered [legitimate] booty, not stolen, as well as leasing and buying vehicles, and procuring speedboats, sailboats, and other common types of transportation.[x]
2. Smuggling, which is something that requires bravery and boldness, as well as caution and sharp wits, and someone who will not lose his composure at inspection points or elsewhere.
3. Ways of buying and delivering weapons and munitions.
4. Forgery and how to acquire what is necessary for a bureau of identity documents with all its equipment and supplies.
5. They will also be trained in selecting appropriate cover and safe houses for operations. Every zone will have its own cover; for example, they will cooperate with the smugglers so that they will not give away that they are Islamists.

In reality, the role of this element is immense; we will not forget here what God's prophet (God bless him and grant him salvation) said to 'Uthman (May God be pleased with him) on the day when the latter equipped the 'Usra army: "Nothing shall harm Ibn 'Affan after what he did today," repeating that more than once. This was reported by Ahmad Al-Tirmidhi.[25]

D. The Assault Element or Team

This is the strike force and the cell's devastating punch. Many would like to join it. If this element is weak, then the whole organization is weak, because it is the military instrument and it is the organization's defense and deterrence unit. This element, as a cell, is composed of two to four individuals.

The mission of this element is the actual execution of operations. Training for its personnel encompasses everything that involves conducting operations in cities (assassinations, kidnapping, explosions, sabotage, infiltration, and freeing hostages).

Before we deal with the tasks of these teams, we will address the means of transmitting and receiving information between the teams operating in the field.

The Direction Flow for Transmitting Orders and Information

1. Orders are issued by the higher command to the field command based on the reports which the latter elevate to the higher command.
2. The team tasked with collecting intelligence receives its orders from the field

---

[x] Ahmad, Abu Ya'la, Al-Tabarani, Al-Bayhaqi, and the scholar Al-Tirmidhi all transmit from [Muhammad's Companion] Ibn 'Umar: "I have been sent with the sword between my hands to ensure that no one but Allah is worshipped, Allah who put my livelihood under the shadow of my spear and who inflicts humiliation and scorn on those who disobey my orders."

command to observe a specific target and collects the intelligence, which it then forwards to the field command.

3. The field command transmits the order to the logistics element to provide the materials to be used in an operation. When the materials have been provided, the element forwards a report on the readiness of the materials.

4. The field command transmits a warning order for readiness and for rehearsals to the assault element. Once the training is completed, the assault team sends a report on its readiness level to execute the mission, whereupon the field command will then send the order to the assault team to execute.

Important Notes:
1. It is very important that the higher command be in a completely secure location because, if it were to be struck, that would mean a serious blow to the organization.

2. It is also important to attract the *'ulama'* and to protect them because they have an important role in recruiting the youth and in raising money, as well as having significant social influence. They also play an important role in agitating the populace.

5

HOW MAJOR CITIES ARE DIVIDED

Major cities are divided into several sectors according to their area and importance. A single cell operates in each sector (command, intelligence collection, logistics, assault). Two factors determine the distribution of sectors:

1. The targets.
2. Security considerations.

THE IMPACT OF TERRAIN ON THE TYPE OF GUERRILLA WAR

The types of guerrilla war are to be based on the type of terrain on which the operations are conducted. For example, I cannot conduct mountain warfare in the Najd. However, there are some countries that have a variety of terrain features (mountains, woods and forests, swamps, cities) and it is then possible in such countries to conduct operations in the first-mentioned sector (mountains), which is what happened, in fact, in several countries, including Chechnya, Afghanistan, and the Philippines. If, on the other hand, in a specific country you do not have any appropriate areas for operations, such as mountains or forests, you must make do with urban forces and auxiliaries.

Note: Auxiliaries are to be found as a common denominator in all three [*sic*] types [of guerrilla wars], and, as we have noted, it is the winning card for an organization.

6

OBJECTIVES IN CITIES

Introduction: Attacks within cities are considered to be diplomatic-military. This type of diplomacy is normally written in blood, decorated with corpses, and perfumed with gunpowder. It has a political meaning connected to the nature of the ideological struggle. That is, it is considered the way to send messages to multiple audiences. Therefore, the choice of targets must be made extremely carefully (as Al-Qa'ida does with its explosions). One of the best examples of this is what four of our brothers did. When the heroes Khalid Al-Sa'id, Riyadh Al-Hajiri, 'Abd Al-'Aziz Al-Mi'thim, and Muslih Al-Shamrani (may God have mercy on their souls) set off the explosion, it was the opening shot.[26] Their choice of target was superbly felicitous, as the building belonged to the CIA. This was the initial spark and the beginning of the awakening of the *jihadi* youth, while the *Ummah* could also see there was a Zionist-Crusader presence in the Land of Muhammad (God bless him and grant him salvation).

There was also the East Riyadh operation in 1424/2003, which had great significance and sent a message to the enemy to the effect that "Well, we hit Vinnell in 1416/1995, and now we hit it again in 1424/2003. However you try to hide yourselves, we are at your backs." The clear message was that the enemy cannot dream of quiet in the Land of Muhammad (God bless him and grant him salvation). Then there was the attack which our brothers 'Ali Al-Mu'abbadi and Nasir Al-Sayyari (may God have mercy on their souls) carried out against the intelligence den of serpents.[27] This is proof that military operations are diplomatic messages mixed with blood and corpses and decorated and perfumed with gunpowder and lead.

TYPES OF TARGETS WITHIN CITIES

A. Targets of an Ideological Character

At the beginning of any *jihadi* military venture, it is not recommended that force be used against religious targets except in some exceptional circumstances, such as:

1. In cases of Christian missionary activity in purely Islamic societies, as happened in

Yemen with the killing of the Christian missionaries, and as is happening in Iraq—with the elimination of missionaries seeking to convert Muslims to Christianity—who are proselytizing on behalf of their religion throughout Mesopotamia.[28] This is also happening in the Land of the Two Holy Places, specifically in Riyadh, where copies of the Bible were distributed to homes recently. In such cases, if it is possible to hunt down those who are doing such things, that is good. Actually, the *mujahidin* know who is doing such things [i.e., missionary work], and we ask God to make it easy to hunt them down.

2. Undercover spying operations, even if under a religious cover. However, one should not have anything to do with those Muslims who are considered to be people of learning and religion lest [attacks] against them elicit a violent response from the Muslims whom those agents have bamboozled. If they are spies (may God help us), then any attack against those members of the learned and religious community will only bring them glory, increase their renown, and make heroes of them (may God's wrath be upon them).

3. Other exceptions [for attacking] religious targets is when priests, monks, rabbis, and other religious figures engage in propaganda attacks against Islam or Muslims, as happened when that damned American clergyman insulted the Prophet (God bless him and grant him salvation) recently; we ask God to grant that His swords reach his neck. And, likewise, [there is an exception], as Sayyid Nusayr (may God free him from prison) did by killing Rabbi Kahane, may God damn anyone who insults the Prophet (God bless him and grant him salvation).[29]

4. Other exceptional circumstances include when religious figures (Jews or Christians) undertake financial and military mobilization or incitement against Muslims, as happened during the Crusades in the past.

B. Economic Targets

The objective of [attacking economic] targets is to shake the security and sense of stability necessary for work to go forward and for the economic wheels to turn, as happened with the attack against the oil wells and pipelines in Iraq, which caused foreign companies to pull out. Or, at the very least, [the objective is] to create a sense of a lack of security and stability necessary for the plundering of the Muslims' riches. Other objectives include the withdrawal of foreign capital from local markets. Among the benefits is also that of the economic impact on the operations being conducted in the zone of conflict, as happened a short while ago with the economic impact of the blessed Madrid attacks on the European economy as a whole owing to the attack. In that respect, economic attacks against the regime of a Crusader, Jewish, or apostate country have a dual impact. Examples of economic attacks include:

1. Attacking Crusader and Jewish investments in Muslim lands.
2. Attacking international companies.

3. Attacking international economic experts.

4. Attacking imports coming from enemy Crusading countries, either by military means (as happened when some American restaurants were blown up and burned) or by political means, such as a boycott.

5. Attacking raw materials stolen from Muslim countries, as in the case of the French tanker carrying oil or as with the attacks against the oil pipelines in Iraq.[30] The senior leadership determines the timing for this type of economic attack, because it is the latter who determines timing and the appropriate moment.

6. Killing and eliminating Jews working in the economic sphere, and teaching a lesson to anyone cooperating with them in economic terms, but only after giving the latter a warning. Only those collaborators whose apostasy has been proved are to be killed.

C. Human Targets

We must target and kill Jews and Christians. To anyone who is an enemy of God and His Prophet we say, "We have come to slaughter you." In today's circumstances, borders must not separate us nor geography keep us apart, so that every Muslim country is our country and their lands are also our lands. We must turn the idolaters' countries into a living hell just as they have done to the Muslims' countries ("Be proportionate to the wrong that has been done to you").[31] Therefore, all the active cells in every corner of the world must pay no attention to geographic borders that the enemies have drawn. Instead, these cells must make every effort to transform the infidel countries into battlefronts and to force the infidel and collaborationist countries to deal with that. Just as the Muslim countries have been turned into test labs for their weapons and inventions, so also their countries must be turned into hell and destruction. The sons of the Islamic *Ummah* are capable of doing that (God willing).

The top priority in these operations is to be given to the Jews and the Christians who have an official position in the Muslim countries. The objective of that is to prevent them from enjoying any quiet in the Muslims' lands. It is advisable in the beginning to target soft, undefended, objectives, with the priority going to citizens of infidel countries directly involved in supporting the local apostates. For example, in the Land of the Two Holy Shrines [i.e., Saudi Arabia] Americans are to be targeted first, then the Britons; in Iraq, the Americans; in Afghanistan, the Americans; in Algeria, the French; in Indonesia, the Australians, and so on.

Prioritizing Human Targets by Order of Importance

1. *Jews*: They are to be divided into various categories, according to their importance. The Jews of America and Israel are to be targeted first, then the Jews from Britain, then those from France, and so forth.

2. *Christians*: They are ranked according to their importance in the following categories:
   - Americans
   - Britons
   - Spaniards
   - Australians
   - Canadians
   - Italians

   These groups are further subdivided thus, according to their importance:
   a. Those involved in finance, economics, and business, given the international importance of money in our age.
   b. Diplomats, statesmen, academics, analysts, and political delegations.
   c. Scientists, managers, and experts.
   d. Military commanders and military personnel.
   e. Tourists and recreational delegations, and everyone who receives a warning from the *mujahidin* not to enter or remain in Muslim territory.

3. *Apostates*: Their ranking is the following, in terms of importance:
   a. Those who are close to the Jewish and Christian governments are to be considered among the most important targets, such as Husni Mubarak and the rulers on the Arabian Peninsula and their advisers.
   b. Innovators and secularists, who spread corruption among the believers and who mock religion. Those Zindiq-s are to be considered the hypocrites of the fifteenth [hijra] century [i.e., twenty to twenty-first centuries AD].[32]
   c. Spies and intelligence agents, who are the armor and shield of the Jews and the Christians, and the striking fist of the apostate rulers.

The Objective in Attacking Human Targets

1. Making clear what the ideological struggle is about. Thus, when we target the Jews and Christians we make clear the religious nature of the struggle.
2. Making clear who the main enemy is, which may be seen as part of the first objective.
3. Doing away with the apostates' arrogance, purifying the land, and providing relief to the countries and the people from their presence, and deterring any of their likes.
4. Spreading terror within the enemy's ranks. This is established in God's *shari'a* and is a mandatory duty, as required by the holy verse [of the *Qur'an*] "Against them make ready your strength to the utmost of your power."[33]
5. To lift the morale of the Islamic *Ummah*.
6. To shatter the prestige of that regime which was targeted by the attacks. Thus,

following the New York and Washington attacks, America's nose was ground in the dirt.

7. To obstruct the infidels' and the apostates' political plans, as happened when Italy refrained from deploying [further] forces to Iraq after the Italians were blown up in Baghdad, and as happened recently when the Spanish prime minister's rivals promised to withdraw [Spanish] forces from Iraq as a result of the explosions in Madrid.

8. Retaliation for their killing of Muslims. God the Exalted said, "Be proportionate to the wrong that has been done to you."[34]

ADVANTAGES OF URBAN OPERATIONS

1. Raise the *Ummah*'s and the *mujahidin*'s morale, and lower or even shatter the enemy's morale (by God's grace).

2. Affirm the group's credibility within society. Since the operations are in cities, people will see them and will see the targets that are attacked, so that the media will not then be able to lie about them.

3. Deter and paralyze the regime.

4. Highlighting the meaning of the creed "there is only one God and Muhammad is the prophet of God," and bringing about the worship of one God.

5. Losses in terms of personnel and ancient symbols sensitive to those countries and organizations.

6. The impact on these countries' economy.

7. The *mujahidin* will acquire capabilities and skills that will enable them to lead the *Ummah* at a later date.

8. The study and analysis of mistakes, and their correction in future operations (God willing).

9. Preparing the *Ummah* and individuals within the group for the confrontations and fierce battles that the Prophet (God bless him and grant him salvation) spoke of.

10. Gaining supporters with each successful operation and an increase in the popularity of the *mujahidin*.

11. Forcing the regime to change its policy.

12. Undermining the confidence of those in the regime and, as we noted already, the [increased] possibility of a confrontation between the military and political wings [within the regime] or clashes between political parties. If such clashes increase (God willing), those in power will not have any confidence in each other.

DISADVANTAGES OF SPECIAL OPERATIONS WITHIN CITIES

We ask of God as few [negative results as possible] for the *jihadi* groups. However, we note them here in order to avoid them:

1. The killing of the *jihadi* groups' leaders and cadres if these operations are uncovered.
2. Heavy material and human losses.
3. A decline in morale among the *mujahidin* in case of failure. Therefore, a shrewd commander is one who raises the morale of his men no matter what happens since, as is well known, the fortunes of war fluctuate and one cannot win every time.
4. Giving the regime an opportunity to take advantage of the operations to target innocent people.
5. Raising morale within the regime and among its adherents when they achieve a victory in any engagement or battle. However, one cannot win every time and the fortunes of war fluctuate.
6. The capture of some cadres or personnel may lead to the disclosure of some operational secrets.
7. A weakening of confidence among some of the people and within the organization if there are repeated instances of failure.

After having presented the foregoing outline of urban targets and of their importance, and after having laid out the advantages of special operations within cities, as well as the negative aspects of such operations, and before we turn to the assault force or assault team, we must address here the means of secure communications among the various operational groups. We say (may God help us) that we noted previously that the means of communications to be used between cells within a city is that of a dead drop. The commanders of these cells receive their instructions from higher headquarters by means of a dead drop, an indirect means of contact. The field command also transmits instructions to the rest of the units using dead drops. A "dead drop" is any means by which two parties conduct their indirect communications, and we will address it in detail in the next chapter.

7

THE DEAD DROP

DEFINITION

[A "dead drop" is] a location where it is practicable to leave whatever type of item (intelligence reports, arms, logistics materials, and so forth) so that someone else can retrieve it without there having to be direct contact between the two operatives.

CRITERIA FOR SELECTING A DEAD DROP

1. The dead drop must provide sufficient cover, that is, the appropriate security to protect both the one who makes the drop and the one who makes the pickup. It is vital to have secure and plausible cover for visits by both operatives without arousing the least suspicion or any doubts.
2. The ability to get to it quickly, because leaving something cached for a long time facilitates its discovery or its ruin.
3. Ease in recognizing the dead drop, so that the one making the pickup can recognize it easily.
4. It must be protected from the elements.
5. It must allow sufficient time for individuals to be able to make the drop and pickup.
6. It must allow for the placing of "flags" nearby for both operatives, because that will be the secret code (such "flags" may consist of e-mails or other means of communications and signaling).
7. It must be difficult for the enemy and security forces to monitor, such as public places that are frequented by many people.

BEST LOCATIONS FOR DEAD DROPS

Gardens, museums, mosques, restaurants, hospitals, public places, restroom facilities.

ADVANTAGES OF DEAD DROPS

1. The one who makes the drop and the one who picks up do not know each other. This is an especially significant advantage in urban warfare, since this reduces casualties.
2. The security forces (the intelligence services, for example) do not see known individuals meeting with each other.
3. It reduces casualties. If one of the operatives is put out of action, the other operative (God willing) will notice that by means of the "flags," which we will explain subsequently (God willing).

DISADVANTAGES OF DEAD DROPS

1. The amount of time needed may not guarantee total secrecy.
2. The amount of time for dropping off and retrieving.
3. The difficulty of dealing with the dead drop in the shadows, that is, the difficulty of managing it behind the scenes.
4. The inability to control it sometimes, and the possibility of losing the contents to an outside party, for example, if a child takes them.

SECURITY PRECAUTIONS

1. Making sure that there is no surveillance of the dead drop location. It is vital to have a high sense of operational security without, however, going overboard to the extent of arousing suspicion.
2. It is necessary to have the appropriate cover when going to the drop and pick-up area (the dead drop).
3. Concealing the items during the drop operation so that they are not conspicuous and do not draw attention.
4. You must determine the amount of time sufficient to accomplish the drop and pickup, in order for the brothers to avoid meeting each other.
5. Do not take the same route or go at the same time over extended periods of time.
6. Do not leave items for extended periods of time between the drop and pickup.
7. The system of flags must be used in a location that is highly secure at all times, both in the general and immediate area.
8. This is important: the location must not be one where a police presence is suspected (where there is drug dealing or prostitution or, for example, places associated with what are called Islamic militants); and, do not go near places where there are preachers calling for the *jihad*.

CRITERIA THAT ARE NECESSARY FOR ITEMS DROPPED OFF AT DEAD DROPS

1. If it is a message, it must be in code, because it may seized, and it must be encoded securely.
2. Items must not draw attention. If they consist of military materials, they should be packaged, and preferably not be assembled. For example, if they are Kalashnikovs, they should be broken down into pieces.
3. The items should not present a danger if they are deposited there (such as explosives and lightning). Explosives must be insulated against lightning; otherwise they could make a noise when they are placed in a box, and they must be packaged so that they can be moved repeatedly.

THE DROPPING-OFF AND PICKING-UP OPERATION

Definition of Making a Drop: placing items at a dead drop location by the operative making a drop.

Definition of Making a Pickup: taking items from the dead drop by the operative picking up.

Steps in Making a Drop

1. The operative dropping off goes to the dead drop and places a "flag" signaling a contact (which is a signal that the operative making the drop leaves in an agreed-upon location so that the operative making the pickup can see it and know that the former has been there). This flag does not have to be a visual one; it could be an auditory one or an e-mail or any other prearranged signal. However, it must be distinct and clear. All these flags should be chosen with inventiveness and originality, and they must be agreed upon by both operatives for a specified place. The flag signaling a drop should be relatively far away from the dead drop so that one can be sure that the leadership or the one making the pickup received it and understood it.
2. Before the operative making the drop places a flag signaling a drop has been made, he must take measures to break off any surveillance before going to the area of the dead drop.[35]
3. Entering the area of the dead drop in order to make the drop.
4. Going straight to the dead drop.
5. Dropping the items at the dead drop.
6. Leaving the place after the drop and placing the drop flag (this is a signal that indicates that items have been placed at the dead drop and that the drop is complete) in the place designated by both operatives. Usually, this is near the dead drop.

7. Final departure from the area and making sure there is no surveillance.

8. Placing the all-clear flag in the appropriate place to confirm that the place is secure. This pretty much marks the end of the operation by the one making the drop.

9. Going to check on the flag signaling that a pick-up has been made after the operative making the pickup has done his work because, in case the operative making the pickup has not been able to do so—for example, if he is not able to enter the area—the operative who made the drop must return and retrieve the message or the items from the dead drop and not leave them behind. Now, we come to the one making the pickup.

Steps in Making a Pickup

1. The one making the pickup proceeds to the place where the flag indicating activity is and uses that to make sure that the brother making the drop has left the items.

2. He proceeds to the area with the security flag and takes it, being careful to look out for any surveillance. Of course, the leadership will determine the precise time for him to go, so that the one making the drop has enough time to make the drop at the dead drop, clear the area, and set up the all-clear flag without meeting the one making the pickup.

3. After seeing the all-clear flag, he proceeds to the place where the drop flag is located, which is usually near the dead drop, being careful to take steps to shake off any surveillance, and sees from that flag that the items are there and have been dropped off.

4. He proceeds to the dead drop, remembering to shake any surveillance.

5. He makes the pickup (taking the items from the dead drop).

6. He shakes off any surveillance, then places the flag indicating a pickup.

7. He departs the area for good.

Important Notes:

1. If either operative (the one making the drop or the one making the pickup) senses any danger, he should not go through with the operation, even if the threat has nothing to do with the operation—for example, if there is a quarrel near the place of the dead drop and the police intervenes to put an end to the scuffle. For that reason, we mentioned in the criteria for selecting a dead drop that it not be in questionable locations in which there are frequent problems.

2. No flags are to be put in place until the operation is complete. For example, the flag for a drop should not be put in place the day before for a pickup the following day unless there was an agreement about that.

3. No curiosity or excessive reconnaissance, and no remaining in the area of the dead drop after the drop or after any operation. Perhaps a brother may be over-

come by curiosity after making a drop, wanting to know who the brother making the pickup is; here, the leadership plays a role in making the right selection [of operatives] and in stressing this point.

4. Confirmation of detection or breaking surveillance after every step of the operation. We will deal with detecting surveillance operations in detail (God willing) in subsequent issues [of the magazine].

FLAGS

Conditions that must be met for flags.

1. They must not be anything frivolous and not be perishable. For example, a flag cannot be a quick scrawl on a wall since, given the great number of fools and those who love to write graffiti on walls, one of them might come along and erase it or write comments or additions to it!
2. They must be common and not attract attention.
3. They must not draw the attention of others, but only of the one meant to notice it.
4. The two operatives must agree on them beforehand.

TYPES OF FLAGS

1. Flag indicating a need to go to a drop. The one making a drop places it, and that means that the latter went to the dead drop in order to make a drop of an item. The flag should be relatively distant from the place.
2. Flag indicating a drop has been made. The one making the drop places it, and that means that the drop has been made. This flag is the closest one to the dead drop.
3. Flag indicating the all-clear. The one making the drop places this, and it means that the latter sees the situation as suitable and secure so that the one making the pickup can carry out the pickup operation.
4. Flag indicating the completion of a pickup. The one making the pickup places this in a secure location far from the security forces after completing the pickup. Its utility is in informing the intended recipient—whether the one making the drop or another designated by the leadership—that the operation has been completed.

THE DEAD DROP PLAN

One of the greatest factors for successful intelligence activity is a sound plan. Any plan for this type of operation must contain two plans, the first for the one making the drop, and the second for the one making the pickup. The two plans must include the following information on coordination:

1. Appropriate cover while on the way to the dead drop.
2. A survey of the routes leading to the dead drop point and a diagram of the area. There must be multiple routes, so that if either of the operatives is arrested or killed (God forbid), everyone who enters the place will not be tracked.
3. The brother should have explained to him in detail the location of the flags and the dead drop spot. The explanation must contain the following information:
   a. A general description of the area
   b. A clearly delimited description of the of the map grid that has the location of the flags or of the dead drop.
   c. An exact designation of the place for the flag or for the dead drop.
   d. Specifying in a straightforward manner the flags themselves or the dead drop and the signal for it.
4. Specifying the times. As far as the one making the drop, it is necessary to specify the following times:
   a. Setting the time for the ready flag to be placed.
   b. Setting the time for the drop to be made at the dead drop.
   c. Setting the time for the flag to be placed signaling the drop has been made.
   d. Setting the time for the all-clear flag to be placed.
   e. Setting the time for confirming the pickup has been made, if the one who made the drop is also tasked with confirming this flag.

   As far as the one picking up, the following times have to be set:
   a. Setting the time for confirming the ready flag.
   b. Setting the time for confirming the all-clear flag.
   c. Setting the time for the pickup.
   d. Setting the time for the completed pickup flag to be placed.

   It is preferable to have a diagram of the dead drop, of the flags, and of the general area. A plan should be drawn up to keep the place under observation before any operation is undertaken. And, may God bless and grant salvation to our Prophet Muhammad, to his family, and to all his Companions.

THE ASSAULT ELEMENT OR TEAM

Its Size

The size [of the assault element or team] depends on the size of the operation, but the size of a single operational team is four individuals. You may find an assault element with thirty individuals, but it will be subdivided into several teams.

Its Task

Its task is to carry out any orders or military tasks assigned to it (that is, to execute operations).

This Element's Characteristics

1. Patience, and the ability to bear hardships and inconveniences. Physical endurance is a requirement for its members, because more than anyone else they will be exposed to operations in which they are hunted down and pursued. If the tyrants' forces know that any one of the brothers took part in killing or assassination operations, they may put pressure on his relatives or may arrest them and torture them. Although we are in agreement that such conduct is vile and despicable, a brother must nevertheless withstand this pressure, and he must be patient and endure this." O ye who believe! Persevere in patience and constancy; vie in such perseverance; strengthen each other; and fear Allah; that ye may prosper."[36]

2. Courage, a lack of fear of death, and trust in God.

3. Boldness and a spirit of self-sacrifice, so that he has that spirit which will motivate him to give up his life for the cause of God.

4. A spirit of self-sacrifice for the cause of God and to prevent harm from coming to his brothers, and a willingness to give his life for the sake of his brothers.

5. Good conduct and quick-thinking.

6. Important: discipline, earnestness, and a willingness to hear and obey both when it suits him and when it does not. Resolve and determination. He should be resolute in carrying out an order and be convinced of its legitimacy, and determined to see it carried out (God, his master, willing).

8. Professionalism in using small arms. He must be proficient with all small arms (pistols, submachine guns, machine guns, some types of light antitank weapons).

9. The ability to fight at close range, to kill quietly, and to strike with a knife.

10. Proficiency in attacking, hand-to-hand fighting, and disengaging.

11. Proficiency in driving a motorcycle. It is vital that he be able to drive a motorcycle, because that will be very useful, as motorcycles are used in many of the operations.

12. Proficiency in driving all different sizes of motor vehicles. He must be very good at driving at high speeds and to know evasive driving, what is known in the colloquial as "drifting" (*tafhit*),[37] and be able to fight while driving.

13. Proficiency in sailing boats, for those brothers who live on the coast.

14. Proficiency in piloting hang-gliders and civilian aircraft, insofar as is possible. Computer programs teaching piloting have become common, and they are very useful in this respect. The nineteen brothers (we pray that God welcome them) who brought down America's [World Trade Center] Towers made use of them. There are also devices in some countries called simulators, which are like an airplane cockpit and training in them is like training in a real airplane. Such courses are available to anyone, even though they are now subject to some restrictions and some have been cancelled in the wake of the blessed attacks [i.e., of September 11].

Advice and Admonitions

1. It is the leadership that selects this [assault] element, and only the leadership knows who its members are.

2. The groups are separate from one another, so that any team does not know anything about any other.

3. It is advised—indeed we stress it—that communications be between the leadership and the units, not between the units themselves.

4. It is important that the members of this element carry on with their normal lives (at least part of the time) and go to work and go on about all their business in a normal fashion.

5. The smaller the number of individuals in a cell, the more successful it will be, because a small number facilitates control over the units.

6. The more timely the provision of information within a cell, the greater the likelihood of that cell's carrying out its action successfully (God willing). There must be some balance in this matter. The cell members will not be provided information on the timing of an operation much before it occurs, but they will be provided information useful for the operation and that will enable them to prepare for the operation, but that will not be of use to the tyrants if one of the brothers should fall captive.

7. Boldness by the members of this element is considered commonplace, and execution is easy, because they have been promised victory or martyrdom (God willing). However, attention must be paid to withdrawal operations, which is one of the most difficult and most dangerous procedures. The leadership must prepare a plan for withdrawal in every operation, and must devote special care to this. Only those who absolutely must go on an operation should be involved. The leadership must secure for those individuals a safe disengagement, so that *jihadi* activity can continue and so that individuals can be take part again in other operations (God willing).

8. If any member of a team is compromised or becomes known, the leadership must take the appropriate security measures. For example, the leadership will send him to join the brothers in the mountains or send him to another region or another city.

WEAPONS USED IN CITIES

For the most part, [the weapons used in cities] consist of small arms, such as knives, pistols, rifles, machine guns, submachine guns, antitank and anti-air weapons, and rockets. Poisons and explosives are also used. Actually, the assault team is able to convert any civilian item into a deadly weapon, such as booby traps, the idea of using civilian aircraft on September 11, or the making of Molotov cocktails from everyday civilian materials.

8

ASSASSINATIONS

Assassinations are part of our Prophet Muhammad's *Sunnah* (may God bless him and grant him salvation). Al-Bukhari (may God have mercy on him) reports a *hadith* from Al-Barra' bin 'Azib (may God be pleased with him), who said, "The prophet of God (may God grant him blessings and salvation) sent one of his Ansar [Companions] to Abu Rafi' the Jew," and reports the *hadith*, to the effect that they killed him and then informed the prophet of God (may God grant him blessings and salvation) of that.[38] In Al-Bukhari's *Sahih*, there is also the report from Jabir bin 'Abd Allah (may God be pleased with both of them), who said, "The prophet of God, may God grant him blessings and salvation, said, 'Who will kill Ka'b bin Al-Ashraf, as he has insulted God and His Apostle?' inciting his Companions to kill him. It was Muhammad bin Maslama (may God be pleased with him) who did the deed.'"[39] Likewise, Muhammad sent 'Abd Allah bin Unays (may God be pleased with him) to kill Khalid Al-Hudhali, as is found in the *Sunan* of Abu Da'ud.[40]

Definition of Assassination: An operation involving a surprise killing of a designated target, done in order to eliminate the harm someone is doing and to deter others like him.

MOTIVES FOR ASSASSINATION

1. *Ideological Motive*: For example, in case of an apostate or an infidel who attacks what is sacred in religion or infringes on God's domain, or plots to fight against the Muslims and aids those fighting against the Muslims, it is necessary to assassinate him. This was the case when Sayyid Nusayr (may God set him free) assassinated the Jewish rabbi [Meir] Kahane, and as the four lions of Islam—Khalid Al-Islambuli, 'Ata Tayil, Husayn 'Abbas, and 'Abd Al-Hamid 'Abd Al-'Ali—assassinated the tyrant who was doomed to perdition, Anwar [Sadat] of the Jews. Likewise, the vicious journalist Farag Foda (may God damn him) was assassinated.[41] Some of the operations, which the brothers in the Battalions of the Two Holy Places carry out targeting the chiefs of the putrid intelligence service within the Lands of the Two Holy Places, belong here too.

2. *Political Motive*: For example, to suppress a specific idea or sect, or the spread of an idea counter to that of a state, or as a last resort in a political game, as happened with the assassination of the nuclear scientist Yahya Al-Mushadd, who was in charge of the Iraqi nuclear program.
3. *Economic Motive*: An assassination may occur in order to get money, or for reasons of economic competition between large companies.
4. *Psychological Motives*: [This involves] an individual who is mentally ill, for example an individual who has a psychological complex about women or about specific groups of people. This is a phenomenon that is common in the infidel countries of the West, where one finds frequent killings resulting from these motives.

CHARACTERISTICS THAT THOSE UNDERTAKING ASSASSINATIONS MUST POSSESS (HIT SQUADS)

1. Complete conviction that this activity is legitimate.
2. High levels of physical conditioning and of combat skills.
3. Mastery of weapons used in assassinations and hostage-taking.
4. It is essential that they have quickness of mind and the ability to deal with contingencies and with anything unexpected.
5. High security awareness. Caution and alertness are essential, as well as not talking about matters related to military activity with relatives, friends, or other *mujahidin*.
6. A warrior mentality (war-fighting spirit). One finds that some brothers are happy and thank God that such missions are assigned to them.
7. Bravery, steady nerves, and an ability not to rush.

CHARACTERISTICS OF ASSASSINATION OPERATIONS

1. Complete secrecy, which is the basis for the second characteristic.
2. Surprise and shock.
3. Speed and coolness in execution, rapid but cool in executing and in focusing.
4. Deterring anyone who fights against God and His prophet.

THE PHASES IN ASSASSINATION OPERATIONS

Phase One

Designating the target precisely. It is imperative when designating a target to highlight the latter's crimes and enmity toward Islam and the Muslims in order to convince the squad to kill him.

Phase Two

Collecting sufficient intelligence about the target, and collating the following information:

A. Personal information: his name, age, his photograph, his home address, his car (the make, color, license plate number, model), his daily routine (such as he usually leaves his house at 8:00 in the morning and returns at 2:00 in the afternoon, and then goes back out at 4:00, and so on), his weekly routine (he may have a day every week when his security is reduced and he changes his routine, or he may be an individual who likes debauchery and fun and eludes his guards and escorts in order to make it easier to pursue his depravity, which is a good opportunity to get at him), where he spends his vacations, whether he has training or not, whether he is armed or not, whether he has bodyguards or not (if the answer is in the affirmative, what is the number of guards, what are their duty shifts, are they trained or just anybody, and how are they armed).

B. These are some of the questions that must be asked about the security detail surrounding the target:

    1. What does the security detail do when the target leaves the house?
    2. What does the security detail do when the target gets in his car?
    3. On his way from the house to the car on foot what does the security detail do?
    4. What route does the motorcade take during the drive?
    5. Does the security detail try to evade surveillance or not?
    6. Does the security detail vary the route every day?
    7. How many cars do the security guards have?
    8. Does the target change cars?
    9. What does the security detail do if a motorcycle or another car approaches his car?

C. Information about the house and its site (the exact address, the part of town, the block where the house is, the house or the building itself, the floor, the apartment, the room). After that, there are some important questions related to the complex or the site:

    1. Does the site have walls or not?
    2. Are these walls high?
    3. How high are they? Are the guards inside or outside in relation to the site?
    4. Are there security cameras?
    5. Is there barbed wire and is it electrified?
    6. How many guards are there, how are they armed, and what types of weapons do they have?
    7. Do the guards have a high sense of security awareness?
    8. Do the guards patrol the grounds?
    9. How do the guards deal with passersby?
    10. How do the guards deal with visitors?
    11. Do the guards search those entering and leaving?

    12. How densely populated is the area around the site?

    13. How densely populated is the area around the site [*sic*]?[42]

    14. Where are the police stations near the site? Determine where the danger points are in order to neutralize them.

    15. What are the routes from the house to the office, or for the return home?

D. Information about the route: The distance between home and the workplace or wherever he goes—the routes leading home and to work, determining the times of departure and return, side streets, even those which the target does not use, because the hit squad may use them in approaching or leaving, whether the streets are closed off when he is traveling or not, how completely they are closed off, what bridges he crosses. Note the places where the cars stop, deserted areas, construction sites, traffic jams, and rush hour. Note everything in the area and consider this as raw information that the leadership or the hit squad may find useful in drafting a plan.

Phase Three

Determine the mode of killing or the method of implementation, selecting the mode of liquidation or assassination based on the intelligence collected by the reconnaissance group. This may be by means of explosives, "silent killing," a sharpshooter, poison, small arms, etc.

Phase Four

Drafting a plan by the leadership and briefing it to the rank-and-file. During this phase, it is vital that the leadership explain in simple terms and brief the plan to the personnel of the squad; they must go over it with them until the leadership is satisfied that the squad's personnel have learned the plan thoroughly. In drafting the plan, the assault personnel's limitations and physical ability to carry out such operations must be kept in mind.

Phase Five

Rehearsing the execution of the plan. During this phase, the leadership must also provide the atmosphere, conditions, and appropriate locale replicating those where the operation is to be carried out, so that those mounting the operation can get used to the building or the spot where it has been decided to liquidate the enemy.

Phase Six

Executing the mission. Attention must be paid during this step to anything unexpected that might happen and to executing well. Care must also be taken for a smooth execution, as well as for speed and accuracy in carrying out the mission.

Phase Seven

The withdrawal operation. It is vital to have determined the withdrawal route beforehand and to have rehearsed on it.

METHODS OF ASSASSINATION

1. Sniper.
2. Explosives.
3. Short-range weapons (cutting weapons).
4. Pistol.
5. Machine-gun (submachine gun).

THE BEST TIMES FOR AN ASSASSINATION

1. One of the best times to liquidate and assassinate the enemy is when the latter is alone and far from surveillance.
2. Those times when he is at home or in his office, given his vulnerability in such venues.
3. The times when he exercises.
4. When the target leaves his office or his house (Farag Foda was leaving his office when he was assassinated; the assassination of the enemy of God Nizar Al-Halabi took place near his house).
5. When he gets out of the car; the vulnerability at this point is clear.
6. When the target makes public his daily or weekly movements (his routine); for example, the schedule of his visit to installations or his inaugurating new establishments or where he parties at night.
7. When the target does not abide by the security assigned to him.

OPERATIONAL SECURITY FOR AN ASSASSINATION OPERATION

1. Selecting those individuals who have the aptitude that will enable them to carry out the tasks assigned to them.
2. Breaking down the operation into several phases, and assigning those responsible for each phase.
3. Providing cover for each phase (cover for the intelligence collection group, cover for the assault group). "Cover" in urban warfare means security cover appropriate for an individual, which provides him the excuse to be in a particular place.
4. Realistic, serious, rehearsal for every phase of the operation. The rule to be followed here is: information on a need-to-know basis.
5. Identifying the avenues of approach and the assembly points, identifying the withdrawal routes, and getting the "mission accomplished" confirmation. "Mission accomplished" confirmation means that the leadership, after the members of the operation complete the mission, must reassure itself that everyone is safe and sound, and it does so by getting a specified signal from the members of the operation, which may be visual or aural or by another means. What is important is that this must be agreed upon by the members of the group and the leadership

before the operation is executed. Its utility to the leadership is that it will know the fate of everyone after the operation is complete.

6. Consider all potential and existing factors and rely on God (may He be praised and exalted). "Against them make ready your strength to the utmost of your power, including steeds of war, to strike terror into (the hearts of) the enemies, of Allah and your enemies."[43]

Important Notes:

1. We noted that some of the best times for an assassination were: when the target does not have his security guards with him or when they are few in number. We know that the target may be by himself at certain times, which the reconnaissance element will determine. For that reason, the assault element must always be prepared and at the highest state of readiness.

2. If the target does not have any guards and is not armed, it is recommended that the assault element finish him off immediately.

3. With the execution of any operation, including assassination operations, one must hit the strongest and most dangerous of the enemy's forces, which represent a threat to the assault element. For example, some of the target's guards might be near to the assault element and may prevent the mission from being carried out; therefore, we begin with the [guards] who are closest because they are the greatest threat.

4. It is vital to ensure that the target is finished off (by firing multiple shots to the head).

5. If a car was used in the operation, stop and get out of your car only after the target's car has been blocked and stopped; the individuals carrying out the operation do not get out of the car until the target's car has been blocked.

6. Precautions must be taken in stopping the target's car, putting at least five meters' distance between you and the car because when you kill the driver or hit the tires, the car will go out of control and might crash into your own car or motorcycle.

7. One must refrain from shooting until the assault element is completely in place (so that there is no friendly crossfire).

EXAMPLES OF PAST ASSASSINATION OPERATIONS

The Sadat Assassination Operation

Among the mistakes that occurred in this operation:

a. Not engaging the security forces at the scene. That led to Khalid and 'Ata's being hit.

b. Not preparing a withdrawal plan. Husayn 'Abbas was able to leave and get away; however, the rest of the brothers were hit and were not able to escape.

The Kahane Assassination Operation

Sayyid Nusayr carried this out. Among the mistakes that occurred in this operation:

a. The failure to make alternate plans for the getaway. One of the brothers was outside in a taxi waiting for the operation to be over in order to make the getaway in it. However, a traffic policeman ordered it to move from in front of the hotel entrance. Another taxi came by and Sayyid took that one. However, it broke down a short while later and he had to walk, and a policeman confronted him, whereupon the two exchanged shots. Then, the second mistake occurred.

b. The failure to finish off the policeman. The policeman had been hit by the first shot and had fallen. When Sayyid went by, the policeman returned fire and hit him in the back, and Sayyid fell and was captured. He remains in prison to this day.

The Egyptian Journalist Farag Foda Assassination Operation

Among the mistakes that occurred:

Farag Foda came out when one of the brothers had gone to have breakfast, and the one who went away to have breakfast was the one who was the trigger man according to the plan. However, God made it possible for the other brother to assassinate Foda.

The Attempted Assassination of the Enemy of God Husni Mubarak in Addis Ababa

Among the mistakes that led to its failure (all is according to God's will) were:

a. The owner of the Volvo that had been tasked with blocking the motorcade had turned off the engine and was not able to restart it.

b. The RPG that was to be fired at the car had a faulty trigger mechanism and did not fire, may God help us.

Therefore, let us profit from that:

a. It is vital to have a good new car, or at least that it be in good working order.

b. It is vital to set up alternatives to the RPG, for example setting five kilograms aside in reserve. If the RPG does not go off, then the explosives should be set under or on top of the car.

The Assassination of the Enemy of God, the Lebanese Nizar Al-Halabi

The lions of Islam—Ahmad Al-Hasam, Munir 'Abbud, Abu 'Ubayda, and another brother—assassinated him [i.e., Nizar Al-Halabi].[44] They collected intelligence about the target, and took advantage of the vulnerability when he went out of the house and was getting into his car and opened fire on him. They had a motorcycle as backup. We do not have any information as to why they were arrested and then killed (may God have mercy on them).

The Ahmad Shah Masud Assassination Operation

The intelligence collection process was completed and the appropriate cover—that of foreign journalists—was adopted. Two Tunisian brothers who spoke French well carried out the operation, using Belgian identity documents. They photographed some of the Afghan tribal chiefs before going to Masud, and those chiefs vouched for the two with Masud. They met with him in Panshir the first time, but there was nothing in their camera the first time in order that he would come to trust them and reduce his security measures the next time he dealt with them. The following day, they blew him up with their camera, along with some of his followers.

The *Mujahid* Shaykh Anwar Sha'ban Assassination Operation

Along with the commanders who were with him—Abu Al-Harith Al-Layli, Abu Ziyad Al-Hajiri Amir Al-'Arab, Abu Humam Al-Najjashi (Amir of the Front), and Abu Hamza Al-Jaza'iri, who was Shaykh Anwar's bodyguard (may God have mercy on all of them).

Among the mistakes that the brothers made were:

a. Putting four commanders in a single car with only a single bodyguard who, moreover, was the driver of the car.
b. No backup security cars.
c. Entering enemy territory without having direct communications with the rest of the brothers.

The Assassination Operation against Boudiaf, the Damned Algerian President

One of the brothers who was part of the security detail in the hall in which the enemy of God was going to give a speech was the one who assassinated him. This guard was one of the *mujahidin* brothers and this was a major case of penetration, since he was very close to the president, following right behind him. While Boudiaf was giving his speech, he was standing directly behind him, with only a curtain between them. The brother threw a hand grenade under the curtain, which rolled before stopping in the middle of those present. When they all turned their attention to that, he fired two shots at [Boudiaf's] head, with all that happening in a matter of only a few seconds.[45]

9

OFFICIAL PERSONAL MOTORCADES
FOR IMPORTANT PERSONAGES

Motorcades vary, depending on their importance. If the motorcade is not official (that is, it is not carrying a head of state or his representative or someone who is not an important figure in the regime) the motorcade will usually be made up of the following:

1. Two cars, with the car carrying the target leading the way and his escorts in the car following; sometimes, it is the other way around.
2. There are motorcades composed of three cars, in which case the car carrying the target will be in the middle, with the one before it and after it serving as escorts. This was frequently the case with the Al Sa'ud before events blew up.
3. There are motorcades composed of four cars, with the first leading the way, the second car carrying the target, the third the security car, and the last one bringing up the rear of the motorcade.

If the motorcade is an official one:

1. At the front are the police cars, preceding the motorcade at a sufficient distance (there is no set number of police cars, but ten or more). Their task is to lead the way, at a distance of several kilometers in front of the car carrying the target. If the target is someone important, a radio detection and jamming vehicle will precede the police cars, with the task of setting off any devices it finds, unless the [vehicle's] frequencies are jammed. The escort cars will come next, which will block off the approaches and exits leading to the target's route.
2. After the patrols, the motorcycles usually follow. In the Arabian Peninsula, however, personal escort vehicles are used instead of motorcycles. Then come the cars in which the target is riding, which are usually the same color and model and have the same license plate numbers. Perhaps they may not have any license plate numbers at all.

3. Following the enemy's cars there will be escort cars or motorcycles, then patrols, which bring up the rear of the motorcade.

Note: Sometimes, you may find that a motorcade is traveling without the target on board! The intent is deception, and the target may be traveling instead in a small motorcade along side streets.

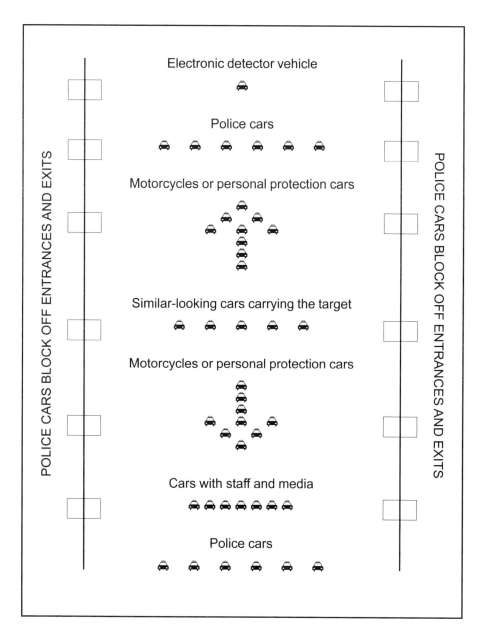

SPECIAL INSTRUCTIONS GIVEN TO DRIVERS IN MOTORCADES

1. The driver of a vehicle in a motorcade must keep his eyes on the road in front and not be distracted by anything else, and he must remain alert to any threats that might appear.
2. He must use his turn signals and brake lights so that his fellow-drivers know how he will maneuver.
3. The drivers of the lead cars must pay attention to the cars that follow and must always be suspicious of any car that tries to pass the motorcade.
4. The security element, which sets the route, must vary the route on a continuous basis.
5. It is vital to prepare the means for defense and attack. In case there is any sudden attack, it is vital that you have a weapon nearby and within reach, because the split second that separates you from your weapon may be fatal for you (barring God's will otherwise).
6. No car is allowed to pass or to maneuver in between the security and escort cars and [the rest of] the motorcade.
7. Rehearse and learn the techniques and methods of assassination in order to avoid them.

SOME TECHNIQUES FOR ATTACKING AND BLOCKING MOTORCADES

First Technique: Using two cars. The first car carries a complete team (four *mujahidin*), while the second car has half a team, whose task is only to block. We will illustrate this technique for blocking by means of this drawing.

Phase One: Lying in ambush and waiting for the target.

Blocking car

The target

Phase Two: Blocking.

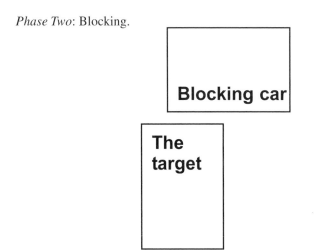

Phase Three: The attack car enters (the team).

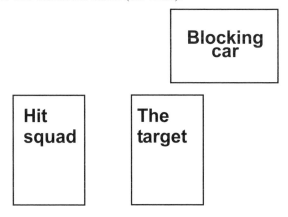

Explanatory illustration of the car carrying the hit squad.

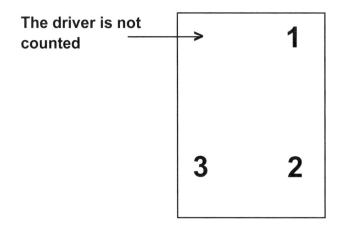

Phase Four: The attack.

Number 1 and number 2 get out of the car immediately (because they are on the same side as the target), while number 3 comes up from behind, since the attack car will not be stopping and the brother might get run over if he comes around from the front.

Note: If we reverse the order of the cars, then the car with the hit team would come from the right of the target, in which case there are some risks:

      1. Brother number 1 and brother number 2 will be coming from behind the
         car, which will slow them down.

      2. Brother number 3 will be in their line of fire.

      3. The brother driving the car must keep at a necessary safe distance of at
         least five meters from the target.

Second Technique: Also using two cars (half a team in the blocking car, a whole team in the attack car).

Phase One: The blocking car comes up on the left of the target car. When it is parallel to the latter, brother number 2 fires at the driver and at the front tires.

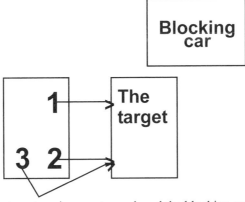

Phase Two: The target car is now stopped, and the blocking car moves up to make room for the attack car. The attack car advances and comes up behind the target, with the brothers getting out and shooting.

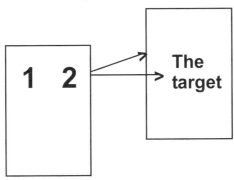

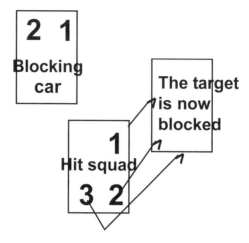

The brothers executing the mission get out and do so.

Third Technique: Using one car (a single team of four *mujahidin*).

The task of this group is twofold (blocking and killing). The members of the team in this mission do not get out of the car.

Phase One: All of them lean out the window.

Phase Two: Brother number 1 shoots the driver and the front tires.

Phase Three: Brothers number 2 and 3 liquidate the enemy.

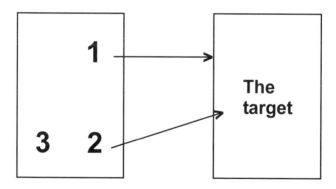

Fourth Technique: Using a car and a motorcycle.

The technique: The motorcycle blocks the target car and the rear rider fires at the driver and at the front tires. The car then comes from the left and attacks.

Note: With the third and fourth techniques, the *mujahidin* do not get out of the car, and they have a specific technique for firing. Number 1 and number 2 fire; the car keeps going a little until it passes the target, whereupon number 3 also fires at the target car, which will now be behind him. The intent in using this technique is to avoid number 3's firing crossing that of numbers 1 and 2. See the explanatory illustration:

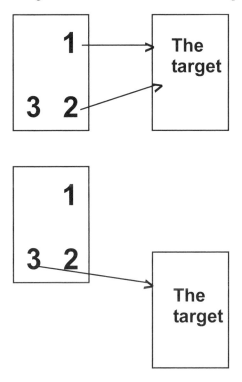

All the brothers who drive the cars and motorcycles must always take into account a sufficient distance necessary for their safety and that of their passengers. The attack teams must stay within the guidelines and orders in executing a mission, and keep speed and accuracy in mind in an attack.

These are some of the techniques from which one can benefit, and we promise the brothers (God willing) that we will do our utmost to provide special exercises at the end of this course.

10

HOSTAGE-TAKING

Definition: [Hostage-taking is] seizing one or more individuals from the enemy, with the following objectives:

1. Forcing the government or the enemy to accede to some demands.
2. Placing the government in a dilemma and causing it political embarrassment with the countries where the hostages are from.
3. Acquiring important information from the one kidnapped.
4. Getting money (ransom) as happened in the case of the brothers in the Philippines, Chechnya, and Algeria, and as our brothers in the Army of Muhammad did in Kashmir, where they got $2 million in ransom money. This will be financial support for the organization.
5. To shine the light on a specific cause, as was the case at the beginning of the issue in Chechnya and Algeria, when the brothers in Algeria hijacked a French airliner. The Chechen brothers also carried out kidnapping operations, and there was the taking of hostages in the Philippines.

NECESSARY CHARACTERISTICS THAT A HOSTAGE-TAKING TEAM OR GROUP MUST HAVE

1. The ability to withstand psychological pressures and harsh conditions. The reason for this is that they will be subjected to severe pressures if the kidnapping is overt.
2. Intelligence and quick-thinking, as anything unexpected may confront the group. A brother must be able deal with that (God willing).
3. The ability to overcome an adversary. What is wanted here is for the brother to be good at hand-to-hand combat so that he can immobilize an adversary quickly and overcome him.
4. A high level of physical fitness and combat skills.
5. A highly developed sense of security awareness, before, during, and after an operation.

6. Proficiency in the use of all types of small arms used in hostage-taking.

TYPES OF HOSTAGE-TAKING

Covert Hostage-Taking

The target is kidnapped and moved to a secure location without the authorities being aware of that. This is the less risky of the two types, as was the case with Daniel Perl, the American Jewish journalist, who was kidnapped from a public place and then transferred to another location. Likewise our brothers in Chechnya kidnap Jews from Moscow and there are the kidnappings of tourists in Yemen.

Overt Hostage-Taking

The kidnappers hold hostages openly in a known location. The government surrounds the location and negotiations follow. Usually, the authorities attempt to trick and attack the hostage-holders, as was the case in the Moscow theater, and with the kidnapping of the Russian officers by Shamil Basayev and the brother *mujahidin*.

According to a military man who conducts special courses on counterterrorism, who quotes another officer: "There has never been a successful hostage-taking operation." His intent was to deter those whom they call terrorists from any thought of conducting a hostage-taking operation in the future. Of course, what he said is dead wrong, because history is replete with facts that prove the contrary. Past operations have shown the success of such operations, whether done by the Mafia or by the *mujahidin*. For example, there was an operation by the Army of Muhammad, Shamil's operation in Moscow, and many others. Some objectives, even if not all, were achieved, as was the case with the operation by the leader Shamil Basayev in Moscow, which succeeded 100 percent because it returned the issue to the limelight of world events. Also, the *mujahidin* returned with money and booty (by God's will).

PHASES OF AN OVERT HOSTAGE-TAKING

1. Selecting the target. It is vital that the appropriate target be selected, one who will force the government to fulfill your objectives for his sake. That is, those kidnapped must be important and have an impact.
2. Collecting sufficient intelligence about the venue (theater of operations), and the individuals present. For example:

Inside a Building:

1. It is vital to do a study of the type and height of the walls, and of the guards and security measures inside.
2. The interior layout: it is vital to know where the rooms are and how many, so

that you know every entrance and exit during the kidnapping operation. It might happen that as you are entering they are exiting by another door, and you will end up being the one trapped inside.

3. The exterior and interior security, the number of guards, how they are armed, and where they are located.
4. The relief system for the guards (night shift).
5. The guards' procedures with those entering and the level of security awareness they have.
6. What vehicles enter without being searched (knowing their type, license plate numbers, model, color, and the times they enter). The guards know that vehicles of such and such a description pass without inspection, and the kidnap team can use such a vehicle. The kidnap team can bring in all its equipment using this vehicle.
7. Knowing which ones of those working inside the place do not get searched.
8. Are there predesignated signals between the guards and the entering vehicles?
9. The parking spots for these vehicles outside these buildings. It is possible to carjack a bus while it is stopped, for example, or to seize people when they are getting on. Also, you can bring in some items using this vehicle.
10. Locations dominating the site (at a higher elevation). These might be useful in setting up an external security perimeter or for snipers, or just to booby-trap so that the enemy cannot make use of them.

On a Bus

1. Knowing the nationality of the passengers, because the operation's violence and impact will depend on what nationality is involved.
2. Where the bus comes from and where it stops (the route).
3. Rest and refueling stops, because the bus may be traveling to a distant city, and the operation can take place at one of the rest stops.
4. Designated guards. In some countries, such as Egypt, one finds units tasked with providing security, and it is necessary to know how many there are, how they are armed, where they are deployed, how they operate, and their level of security awareness.
5. What security precautions does the driver follow? Does he stop at check-points?
6. What is the tourist group's itinerary, or what agency is responsible for this group? Agencies compete with each other and one finds that their itineraries are available publicly to tourists back in their own countries, to include the exact times. Thus, I can select the area with the weakest security precautions and have a greater chance of seizing control of the group easily.

If the Target Is on an Aircraft

1. Determining the route of the aircraft. It is best when it is at a transit stop. Usually, transit terminals in some countries are less well searched and there are more vulnerabilities. The brothers took advantage of that in Nepal, when they smuggled weapons [on board an aircraft] in Nepal and hijacked an Indian aircraft.
2. Knowing what the search procedures are at an airport.
3. The possibility of smuggling weapons or explosives on board an aircraft; ingenuity is important with respect to this.

If the Target Is in a Motorcade

One can refer back to what was said about motorcades. There are also points in common with buses.

After noting phase one, which is that of selecting a target, and phase two, which is that of collecting sufficient intelligence on the target, we come now to phase three, which is that of:[46]

3. Drafting a suitable plan and rehearsing it. We already discussed planning with regard to assassination operations. One should note that the commander or the planner should take into consideration the weakest elements that he has to work with. As they say, "A caravan moves only as fast as the slowest member."
4. The attack (with prayers to God, the goal clear in one's mind, and trust in God). The role of those executing the attack varies according to where the kidnapping operation is carried out. In general, these roles consist of three elements.

    First: The covering force, whose task is to protect those carrying out the attack and to provide early warning to them about any attempt to storm the place (defense and blocking off streets).

    Second: The security and control element. The task of this key element is to control the hostages, to consolidate the control of those who were kidnapped, and to eliminate them in case the operation fails (if they are able to do so). Know for a fact that most governments will not meet your demands as a *mujahid*. If they do acquiesce to any of your demands outwardly, that will usually be only a trick and deception.

    Third: The negotiating team or the negotiator. This is at the same time a very important and crucial player. His task is to negotiate with the individual designated to negotiate with the *mujahidin* and to communicate to him the *mujahidin's* demands. This [negotiator] will usually be the commander of the team. Among the qualities he must possess are that he be intelligent, resolute, and decisive.
5. *Negotiations*: It is imperative to monitor the enemy's negotiator, who is an important and crucial individual. One will always find that the negotiator is the

most capable member of the counterterrorism teams (as they call them). He will be versed in psychology and will be a master of cunning and be very intelligent. Usually, he will be the commander of the operation because he is the one who can give the order to the assault team to go in without jeopardizing the safety of the hostages who you are holding. He is able to sow fear or frustration in the hearts of the kidnappers, relying on his knowledge of the human character and of the kidnappers' psychological state and morale. He will try to gain time and draw things out so that the security forces can prepare an attack plan and carry out the assault operation. He knows whether you are frustrated or are determined and resolved to carry out your threats. Therefore, it is imperative that your negotiator have a calm nature and have a resolute personality. He should not show any signs of tension and must be able to articulate his demands and explain the issue that generated this action. Prolonging the period of captivity is to be rejected because the capability of teams declines and tension increases, as does the effort needed to stay on guard. Likewise, the security and control team's handling of the hostages will become more difficult. This was one of the mistakes that happened in Lima, Peru's capital, when some elements of the Red Army seized a number of officials in the Japanese embassy, in which there were also many diplomats present. The hostage holders prolonged the detention for more than a month. During that time, the assault team was able to dig tunnels underneath the embassy which they used to set the hostages free and to end their detention. It is imperative from the very first that one execute hostages—of course only those whose blood can be shed legitimately—in case the situations drags on so that the authorities know that the hostage-takers are serious. When you carry out another operation they will know that you will do what you say you will do, that you are serious, and that you are credible.

6. *Exchange and Handover Operation*: This is a very important phase. If the enemy gives in and fulfills your demands, it is imperative to confirm the mutual exchange operation for our brothers who are prisoners, if the intent of the operation was to exchange the prisoners they held for the hostages. It is imperative to make sure that our brothers are all right and that they are in good health. This is what happened in the Glimpse of Hope Operation in Bosnia when the [Bosnian] Croats kidnapped and held our brothers.[47] Our brothers then seized the [Bosnian] Croatian Defense Minister, thereby obtaining freedom for their brothers, who were found to be in good health and doing fine. It is imperative to confirm their number and state of health. Likewise, it is imperative to check that the money [i.e., paid out as ransom] is genuine and not counterfeit and not brand new. Also, one has to check for listening or homing devices. It is also necessary to check for surveillance. In Bosnia, the Atheist Nations [i.e., the United Nations] set an ambush for the brothers after they had taken delivery of their brothers. However, the brothers caught on in time and set their own counterambush to the first am-

bush! When the enemy saw the brothers' readiness and their elevated state of security all they could do was to let the brothers pass by unhindered.

We have become convinced thanks to the experience of the *jihadi* operations that the security forces are not able to exercise complete control within cities, so that brothers can help in specific ways to transport the liberated brothers, while exercising extreme security, until they leave the zone of observation. It is best to take the hostages to a secure area, far from search operations.

7. *Evacuation Operation*: The brothers must be careful not to hand over any one of the hostages until our own people are handed over. It is necessary to keep your promises, as our pure religion demands of us. I do not kill hostages once the enemy has accepted my demands and has fulfilled them.

8. When it is time to withdraw, it is necessary to hold on to some of the hostages, preferably those who are the most important, so that the withdrawal can be accomplished safely. The enemy can attack suddenly at any phase.

Security Considerations in Overt Hostage-Taking

1. Do not extend the period of detention.
2. Begin to execute the hostages if the situation drags on, so that the enemy understands that we are serious about what we are saying. This will also enable you to gain credibility for the group in the enemy's eyes.
3. Be careful if freeing some hostages, such as women and children, because they may give some information that can be of use to the enemy.
4. Be careful about the food that is delivered. It is imperative that those delivering it, and then the hostages, eat from it in order to be sure that it is safe to eat. It is best if it is brought in by old people and by children, because combat-age individuals can take advantage of bringing in the food.
5. Be wary of negotiators.
6. If the enemy drags out the process that means that the latter is planning an assault operation.
7. Be careful of surprise attacks, because during the attack they may use stun grenades, which can cause you to lose your balance. Or, they may use sound grenades, or other similar devices. Or, they may use helicopters or set a fire or set off an explosion. The intent of all of that is to divert your attention sufficiently for them to take control of the place.
8. The assault team ordinarily uses two attacks: a supporting attack to draw attention to that and a main attack coming from another direction.
9. In case your demands are met, release the hostages, but only in a location that is safe for you.
10. Be careful of air conditioning vents, or any other vents. It is possible to plant listening and photographic devices there in order to find out how many hostage-

takers there are and where they are located. Or, it is possible to use [such vents] to introduce gasses. Therefore, they should be plugged up well.

11. Be careful not to have pity, and not to pay attention to sighs and tears.
12. Follow the laws of the *shari'a*, because your action can also be a form of propaganda.
13. Do not look at the women.

PHASES OF COVERT HOSTAGE-TAKING

The beginning is the same as for overt hostage-taking. In every case, what is imperative is:

1. Selecting the target. It is imperative that it be a target commensurate with the size of the operation that you want to conduct.
2. Collection of sufficient intelligence on the target: the same as for an assassination.
3. Drafting a plan and rehearsing it.
4. The execution. The team executing the operation should be composed as follows:
   a. The screening force: it informs the hostage-taking team of the target's movements or of the latter's presence at the desired location.
   b. The covering force: its role is to protect the hostage-takers from any external intervention or any support and to secure their backs.
   c. The kidnapping team: its role is to seize the hostage and to deliver him to the holding and safekeeping team.
   d. The holding and safekeeping team: its role is to hold on to a hostage until the latter is exchanged or disposed of. No other team knows the location where the hostage is being held.
   e. The counterpursuit force: its essential mission is to provide security for the holding and safekeeping team from anyone trying to pursue or to tail them.
5. Transferring the target to a secure location. It is imperative that several conditions be present at the location to which he is being transferred:
   a. The surrounding area must be secure. There must not be a lot of the regime's spies around. It must also be far away from the country's vital targets.
   b. The house must be far from neighborhoods or areas that have a bad reputation, such as neighborhoods known for drugs and prostitution, because the police presence in such areas is dense.
   c. It must be far from working-class neighborhoods, where an outsider stands out, because the people all know each other.
   d. It must not attract attention, it must blend in with those living there, and the hideout must fit in with the locale.
   e. This safe house must be difficult to keep under constant surveillance.
   f. The house and the neighborhood must have several ways out.

    g. It must be easy to maneuver there and to fight from there.

    h. It is imperative that the transfer operation not draw attention or raise any suspicions from the neighbors.

6. Freeing the target after achieving the objective: this is to be done by transferring him from the secure location to a place from where he can go easily to wherever he wants, ensuring that the hostage is misled about the location from where he was brought.

Security Measures for Covert Hostage-Taking

1. The location to which the hostage is moved must be secure.

2. When the hostage is being moved, one must be on the lookout for roving security patrols in the area and know where the police are, so that you will not find yourself subjected to a surprise search.

3. Be aware of listening and homing devices being placed on people or with the money that the *mujahidin* get. Often, some important people have watches or similar devices that provide their location. Important figures in the West have an earpiece by means of which they are in contact with their security detail and with their advisers.

4. It is recommended that you place in a metal container anything you receive from the enemy and that it not be opened except in a location that is far from the holding and safekeeping team.

5. There will be no communications from the location where the hostage and the teams are, including telephone conversations.

6. There must be appropriate cover to move a hostage to a secure location, or to take him away from there. Hizballah at times would drug the hostage and would move him using an ambulance.[48]

7. One must confuse the hostage so that he does not know where he is being held, and it is best under such circumstances to administer an anesthetic injection or to hit him so that he loses consciousness.

HOW TO DEAL WITH HOSTAGES (BOTH IN COVERT AND OVERT HOSTAGE-TAKING)

1. Hostages are to be searched, and any weapon or anything that can contain a listening or homing device is to be taken from them.

2. Measures are to be taken to single out and eliminate the security personnel and to separate the young from the old and the women and children, because the young are usually the ones who may resist, and one must be on guard against them. Killing the security personnel immediately will deter others from resisting.

3. Deal with the hostages according to legal guidelines.

4. Do not get close to the hostages unless absolutely necessary, and be accompanied

by a guard whenever you approach them. The distance between you and the hostages should not be less than one and a half meters.

5. Speak in a language or dialect that is not the hostage-takers' native language, so that they cannot be identified after they get rid of the hostages.

6. Cover the hostages' eyes so that they do not recognize the hostage-takers. Also, the hostage-takers' faces should be covered.

7. Booby-trap the location where the hostages are being held, because of the possibility of an assault by the enemy.

11

PLANNING FOR OPERATIONS

This lesson is extremely important. Indeed, it is to be considered the heart of the subject, and it is exactly what a brother should take away from this course. It is the practical application of all the military and security matters that have been dealt with up to now. May God grant that everything we have written be honest and sincere and that He make it a beacon and light that the *Ummah* of Muhammad (God bless him and grant him salvation) can use as a guide.

Planning is defined as the drafting of an appropriate, complete plan to execute any order and the dividing of an operation into several phases, assigning what individuals are to do in each phase, designating the hideouts for each phase (hideouts for the intelligence collection team, and hideouts for the execution team), and setting stages for each phase. For example, the assault phase will consist of plans for the approach, the attack, the retrograde, and for operation termination. As a reminder, the phases of the operation are as follow:

A. *Phase one*: Designating the target precisely.

B. *Phase two*: Collecting sufficient intelligence on the target, diagrams and photos of the target and of the general area as well as of the surrounding areas, a complete diagram of the roads leading to the location and the roads on which the security forces travel (or on which they may drive when coming to reinforce) in order to place the blocking forces, the best avenue of approach for the *mujahidin* forces to the target's location, designating what the nearest safe house is where our forces can assemble and from which we can deploy, and the raw intelligence about the target's area.

C. *Phase three*: Deciding on the means of killing and the best time for executing the mission, deciding the course of action, and selecting the method of eliminating and assassinating, which will be based on the intelligence that the intelligence collection team provides.

D. *Phase four*: Drafting the plan by the leadership and briefing it to the rank-and-file.

E. *Phase five*: Rehearsing the execution of the plan. During this phase, the leadership must recreate the surroundings and conditions, and provide an appropriate place similar to the actual place where the mission will be carried out so that the personnel executing the mission familiarize themselves with the building or the location that has been decided on for the enemy's liquidation. The brothers taking part in the operation can rehearse more than once. At the same time, the intent is to run through the mission so that they can experience the same conditions as those in which they will execute the mission and so that the commander can assess how long executing the mission will take. A thorough and serious rehearsal is to be done for each and every phase. Here, the rule of "the need to know" is to be observed.

F. *Phase six*: Executing the mission. One must be on the lookout for anything unforeseen, and one must be careful to work well and quickly while being precise in executing the mission. Selecting individuals who have those capabilities that will enable them to carry out missions assigned to them is also another factor for success (God willing).

G. *Phase seven*: The retrograde movement. It is imperative to determine the route for the getaway and to have rehearsed on it. During these preceding phases, the leadership must explain and brief the plan to the members of the team in simple terms, and the leadership must go over it with them until they are convinced that the individual members have absorbed the plan completely. In the planning process, it is also necessary to take into account the ability and the physical capabilities of the executing personnel to carry out such an operation. The getaway routes must also be determined, as well as the method of reporting when the mission has been accomplished. "Mission accomplished," as we noted in the preceding lessons, means that after the personnel have executed the mission the leadership must assure itself that everyone is safe, and this is to be done by means of a specific signal from the executing personnel, which may be visual or aural or by another means. What is important is that it be something agreed upon between the members of the team and the leadership before the mission is carried out. The utility of this for the leadership is that that latter will know after the operation is over what happened to the personnel.

Important Note: *The best times for an attack*: When attacking, be careful that the idea of a getaway does not become the overriding concern in your mind so that it prevents you from accomplishing the mission with which you were entrusted. The leadership must therefore be sure to select the best time for an attack and the best cover so that none of the enemy's forces are able to pursue or obstruct the attack teams. The selection of times is done as follows:

PLAN FOR DETERMINING THE TOTAL TIME NECESSARY TO EXECUTE THE OPERATION

It is imperative that before executing any operation the time necessary to execute every phase of that operation be calculated. If there are four phases in the operation—the approach to the closest hideout, then the attack, then the execution of the assigned mission by the designated personnel (whether one of killing, hostage-taking, or freeing someone), then the withdrawal—it is vital to calculate exactly the amount of time necessary to complete each phase. The amount of time will be determined as a result of the necessary rehearsals for each phase, along with numerous other factors. Time can be calculated as follows (just as an example):

Phase one: 20 minutes
Phase two: 30 minutes
Phase three: 30 minutes
Phase four: 10 minutes

Therefore, the total time for this operation is 1½ hours. Training and rehearsals will be carried out in order to adhere to this amount of time when executing. Every phase has an impact on the phase that follows and the latter depends on the preceding one.

PLANNING PROBLEM

After this checklist of the main requirements for planning operations we will address here our reply to a contribution sent in by e-mail from a group of brothers eager for action in God's cause. However, for security purposes, we have changed the particulars that came to us, while retaining the essence as much as possible.

As we noted in the preceding lessons and as we requested from our brothers who are interested in this course, at the end of the course we will offer some planning problems that can be the subject of discussion and further study so that the greatest utility can be extracted from the course and so that the information can be shared with everyone.

The Terms of Reference [for This Planning Problem] Are As Follows

The Target: Nayif bin 'Abd Al-'Aziz, who will be meeting a foreign dignitary in the security arena, arriving on a secret visit to the Kingdom [of Saudi Arabia], specifically at King Khalid International Airport.

Designating the Target: Nayif bin 'Abd Al-'Aziz Al Sa'ud.

Personal Information: [blank in the original].

Name: Nayif bin 'Abd Al-'Aziz Al Sa'ud.

Age: 71 years old, born in 1933.

Position: Saudi Minister of the Interior.

Residential Address: Riyadh, several palaces (among which the palace in 'Irqa, as well as the palace in Umm Al-Hamam; he also has numerous other places where he stays).

Daily Routine: He sleeps from just before dawn until the afternoon. On some days, he leaves for the ministry between 7 and 8:30 p.m. The rest of the day is spent at soirees, parties, and private gatherings.

Number of Guards: Eight trained individuals.

Type of Armament: Small arms. When the target gets out of the car, the guards stand near him without surrounding him tightly.

The Motorcade's Route: The streets are closed off and the target's car travels in the middle of the motorcade, accompanied by similar-looking cars, and they may send more than one similar motorcade as a ruse. The guard detail prevents anyone from following, and sometimes varies the route taken. The number of escort vehicles in the motorcade is not less than ten, and their role is to clear the way. In the front is a radio detector and jamming vehicle, which is followed by the personal protection vehicles, then by the vehicles carrying the target; the vehicles will usually be of the same color and model, and without any license plate numbers or with numbers that are all the same. Then come the security vehicles, then the patrol, which concludes the motorcade. Sometimes, the motorcade travels without the target, who instead takes side streets in a small motorcade. The target varies the car in which he travels. Usually, no other car gets close to him because the roads are blocked off.

Information About the Route: The distance from the palace to the airport is forty kilometers.

Description of the Route. 'Irqa to the Western Ring Road to the Northern Ring Road to the Airport Road. It is possible that he may take another route ('Irqa to Kharis Road to the Eastern Ring Road to the Airport Road or 'Irqa to Al-Dar'iyya to Al-'Ammariya Junction, then to the East and return by way of Takhassusi Road to the Airport Road).

Date Going to the Meeting: 15/4/1425 a. h. [AD May 24, 2005]

Time of Departure: 6 p.m.

Time of Expected Arrival: 6:25 p.m.

Side Streets: There are many side streets, including the exits on the Ring Road (Exits 4, 5, 6, 7), the western gate of King Sa'ud University, and Amir 'Abd Allah Road.

Bridges: The square connecting the Northern Ring Road and the extension of the Eastern Ring Road to the Airport Road.

Places Where the Vehicles Stop and Isolated Locations: None.

Turns: There are numerous turns, including where the Western Ring Road meets the Northern Ring Road, and where the Northern and Eastern Ring Roads meet. There are mid-density growths of trees, gardens, and ball courts. There is a tall multistory building belonging to SABIC, the buildings belonging to the Imam [Muhammad bin Sa'ud Islamic] University, and trees in the area dividing the two streets, which are good for hiding and for setting ambushes or for setting timed explosive devices.[49] At the entrance to the Airport Road there is a gate that can be closed.

After the target had been identified and the operation had been organized into several phases, the leadership issued orders to the appropriate elements. The phases were:

Phase one: Selection of the target. This phase was completed.

Phase two: Collecting intelligence. This phase was also completed.

Phase three: Method of killing—explosives. This was to be done by blowing up his motorcade at the end of the bridge connecting the Northern and the Eastern Ring Roads and at both sides of the street at the start of the curve. The team tasked with making sure of finishing off is to make sure that [the target] has been killed; in case this has not happened, the team will fire at the motorcade with antitank weapons. This phase is the domain of the assault group or squad. The method of killing was selected based on the intelligence that the intelligence collection team obtained.

Phase four: Drafting the plan. The leadership is in charge of this phase and drafts the plan in our case study based on the intelligence that it receives, such as the intelligence listed above.

This ends our brothers' communication (may God preserve them).

We say (God the Exalted, the High help us), in drafting the plan bear in mind the actual conditions and the likelihood of success that can be expected. Usually, the leadership can prepare more than one course of action and then decide which one is the most likely to succeed, and one should build a plan based on a worst-case scenario. Also, alternate plans should be prepared in case the original plan runs into difficulties. We do not believe that it would be appropriate for us to suggest a school solution (*khutta mu'ayyana*) [for this planning problem] at this time. Instead, we welcome anyone undergoing military training to participate by mail and propose their own plan based on the instruction provided in the preceding lessons. Of course, plans are different for different types of operations; assassination operations, for example, differ from hostage-taking operations and both of the latter differ from an operation to assault a prison. What is important is that the drafting of a plan be the result of [experience gleaned from] missions that the operational groups have carried out. This phase provides ample scope for creativity and originality, which are factors that will greatly enhance the likelihood of the operation's success, since creativity and innovation scatter and scramble the enemy's cards and his calculations, unhinge his security preparations, and paralyze his power thanks to the element of surprise. Plans do not have fixed templates that cannot be modified.

It is in this phase during which the succeeding phases are determined, and that will set the substance of the [subsequent] phases and how to carry them out. The subsequent phases are:

Phase five: Rehearsing the plan that has been drafted.

Phase six: The execution.

Phase seven: Retrograde and the mission accomplished check.

Therefore, the noble brothers who submitted this information and drafted this plan should pay careful attention to an important issue, namely that [in their plan] the leadership did not specify the number of individuals to be included in the assault element (the security team, the team to block the road, the hit team) and did not specify precisely where the teams should be positioned. Nor did they mention the number of cars used in the operation or the appropriate cover for the teams to make their approach, or even the safe havens necessary for the retrograde. There are also other issues that need to be considered in a plan. The personnel must rehearse its execution, and we will seek in succeeding issues [of the magazine] to discuss similar planning problems, and hope that future contributions [by the readers] will include some variety, such as a hostage-taking operation, for example, or a hostage-freeing operation, or an attack on a prison (May God grant success and guidance to the right path).

12

OPERATIONAL TECHNIQUES
WITHIN CITIES

Today, we have an important lesson with which we will complete our reply to some queries we received about some important issues, namely a discussion about planning and covert activity within a city. However, as we noted at the very beginning, in deference to operational security, we find ourselves obliged to pass over some questions until the success or completion of some special operations, which some of our brothers are planning to carry out. For that reason, we alert everyone up front that this lesson will be handled within those limitations and that we will discuss what we can. We will postpone [discussing] until another time anything that might compromise current operations.

Let us deal with a question that several youths have raised, specifically, how to operate and fight within cities and how to break an encirclement and withdraw with the least number of casualties. Here, we will refer to Shaykh Yusuf Al-'Ayyiri's valuable observation on combat and operations within a city, which we will quote with some modification. Al-Battar (may God have mercy on him) said, "The dangers surrounding a *mujahid* within cities are many times greater than the dangers in the mountains and in the bush." In our answer below, we will draw attention to several urban skills that will highlight the scope of difficulty of this battlefield. The skills of urban combat differ from those for mountains and the bush and, as is known, the skills for urban combat operations are the most difficult.

It is vital that the *mujahid* know that unit maneuver during urban combat operations will consist of hopping point-to-point, so that a unit or individual can get to cover while being covered [by fire] during the unit's or individual's movement. The moving unit or individual then takes cover and in turn provides covering fire to the previous covering unit. This process will be done in turns. A *mujahid* must be proficient at shooting from either the right or left shoulder because the corner of a building may force him to shoot from either shoulder. He also must be careful not to expose himself or have his shadow show when firing.

PROCEDURES FOR MOVEMENT IN BUILT-UP AREAS

In order to minimize exposure to enemy fire during movement in built-up areas, a *mujahid* must not expose himself as a target. He must do everything he can to conceal himself and take cover. He must avoid crossing open areas such as streets, parks, or blind alleys. If he is forced to move, he must move only under covering fire (covering fire by his brothers or his own fire) or under the concealment of smoke, or zig-zagging, or by crawling. He must choose with the naked eye his next position, which will provide him the appropriate cover, before leaving his current position. He must use every means to conceal himself, and move from one spot to another quickly and carefully. If he expects to be exposed to fire while moving from one spot to the next, he must cover his movements by his own fire against the positions from where he expects someone to appear. If he wants to climb over walls, he must reconnoiter the other side to which he plans to move. Before doing so, he must determine the easiest spot on the wall to climb over and must move quickly toward the wall. When he climbs over, he must keep his body down and cling to the wall when he jumps, and he should descend quickly to the other side. If the *mujahid* wishes to carry out observation of a street, he must not expose his body or head around a corner or outside a door. Instead, he should lie prostrate and only expose a small part of his head, enough for him to see the street. He can also use a mirror to get a reverse image of the street without having to expose his head at all.

WINDOWS IN CITIES

One of the greatest dangers that a *mujahid* faces in a city is that of moving in front of windows, which is usually where the enemy has his positions. Windows are of two types: windows on the ground floor and cellar windows. A *mujahid* must be careful with these windows and must be good at crossing in front of them. To cross in front of windows on the ground floor, one has to move below the window sill and move along the walls, quickly and quietly. In order to cross cellars, a *mujahid* must jump above the level of the windows without exposing his legs to danger when he passes by the window. If it is a wide window, it is hard to jump above it to get by, and instead he will have to take some cover between himself and the window in order to pass by.

A *mujahid* must be cautious and avoid using doors to enter and exit. Often, the enemy has covered such doors with fire or has planted booby traps and mines in order to kill anyone who tries to use these doors. Instead, a *mujahid* must use windows to enter and exit [a building]. If a brother can do all this, all the better. Otherwise, a brother should throw a hand grenade or smoke grenade or two to prevent his being spotted by the enemy so that he can reach the nearest suitable cover. Or, he can open new entrances for himself, or try to enter buildings by climbing from above or to exit buildings by lowering himself down. He must not cross open areas without covering fire or smoke concealment or without points of cover. If he is forced to cross open ground, he must not move in a straight line, but rather as fast as he can zig-zagging. When moving within a building, he must avoid standing next to doors and windows in order to avoid getting shot by the enemy either from outside or inside the building, which is usually where [the enemy] aims. Individual personnel must leave a distance of three to five meters between each other when moving within a city.

HOW TO CLEAR BUILDINGS AND ROOMS

A *mujahid* must select his entry point before moving toward a building. He must avoid entering through windows and doors and must use smoke or fires to cover his movement toward the building. He must create his own entrances to a building by using explosives or rockets in order to avoid having to use windows and doors. He must also use hand grenades in entering any courtyard in a building, and it is vital that he enter immediately after the hand grenade explodes so as not to give the enemy the opportunity to catch his breath. He must also get support from one of his comrades while entering and clearing a room. The best way to clear buildings is to begin from the top and move down. Getting to the top of a building has to be done by any means possible, whether by climbing up using ropes, through the water pipes, by ladder, from trees, across the roofs of neighboring buildings, or by any other means possible. The fighter must master climbing using ropes and carabiners. He has to practice making knots in ropes and throwing them onto roofs of buildings and then climbing by that means. It is best to tie knots about a meter apart to help make the climb. The fighter also has to practice rappelling by rope from the top of buildings using special climbing gear, that is a harness. Using these ropes makes it possible to descend from the top of a building and to then sweep the outer rooms very easily.

HOW TO USE HAND GRENADES IN BUILT-UP AREAS AND IN ROOMS

A *mujahid* must master the use of hand grenades because they are used frequently in urban combat, and a *mujahid* must use hand grenades in clearing every room, breach, or staircase. He must know how to throw a grenade in every situation and, through training, master how to aim and throw a grenade at the desired spot accurately. He must also train to time the explosion of the grenade and when to throw it in order to prevent giving the enemy a chance to throw it back [at the *mujahid*] before it explodes. He must know how to yank the pull ring from the grenade while carrying a weapon in his other hand, to do so if he is prone, and in all positions. He must know how to hold on to the safety pin after throwing the grenade so that his fingerprints cannot be taken or the type of grenade determined, which could provide information of use to the enemy. A *mujahid* must know the impact range of the grenade's fragmentation and its destructive power so that he can take precautions and take cover when clearing buildings.

HOW TO SELECT FIRING POSITIONS FOR ANY WEAPON

The success of operations inside buildings is dependent on the individual's mastery of combat skills. However, these skills will not achieve the objective either on the defense or the offense, whether withdrawing or advancing, either for the individual or the collective, unless the fighter is proficient in directing his fire against the enemy and in suppressing him. A fighter's firepower in cities is his capital and it is a mistake for him to underrate it or waste it. He must know how to fire. And, when to fire. And, why he should fire. And, to fire with what. And, from where to fire.

All these are urgent requirements for a *mujahid*. He must be intelligent, able to react quickly, resolute, and brave so that he can deal with these requirements extremely quickly in combat. Among these requirements are: Where should he fire from? He must always be on the lookout for a suitable place from which to fire, where he will not be exposed to enemy fire and where he can take advantage of his own fire completely while trying to avoid dead zones, which the enemy can take advantage of in maneuvering. He should choose the corners of buildings, or shoot from behind walls, from the sides of windows, from rooftops, from small openings that the shooter prepares, from behind sand bags prepared beforehand, from inside manholes in the middle of the street, or from behind concrete planters on the sidewalks. In case he uses antitank weapons, [a *mujahid*] must move away from the rear wall so that the backblast does not engulf him. He must select locations overlooking the main streets and he must know that when tanks approach a building they cannot elevate their gun above a 45° angle in order to fire at the roof of a building. This permits a gunman to make use of the roofs of houses overlooking the main streets to hit vehicles. A *mujahid* must keep in mind that the glass in windows presents a danger to him so that before he uses windows as a firing position he must remove all of the glass to prevent being hit by it in case there is an explosion nearby. He must also cover a window with a fine-mesh metal screen to prevent hand grenades from coming in, which enemy personnel can throw from outside the building.

HOW TO MANEUVER, USE CAMOUFLAGE AND CONCEALMENT, AND TAKE COVER

In order to exhaust the enemy and enhance security for our personnel, it is necessary to make skillful use of camouflage, concealment, and cover. The first necessary step for camouflage is a careful assessment of the area, so that one can set up equipment, weapons, personnel, and vehicles to have the same natural appearance as the area. Do not make openings for firing in buildings if there has been no destruction and structural damage to buildings caused by war. Do not try to exaggerate the camouflage, which, on the contrary, will give the position away. Do not use bright shiny material in your position, which will betray your position and expose it to shelling as a target of opportunity. Darkness provides wonderful natural cover for concealment and maneuver; the shadows provided by walls and buildings are suitable to hide vehicles and equipment because someone far away cannot distinguish who is in the shadows except by coming closer. Try to mask the shine of your body, gear, and weapons by using charcoal, mud, or burnt cork. Put wet clothes under the muzzles of any type of gun while firing in order to prevent raising up dust. Try to fire from inside rooms at night. If the nearby buildings and other rooms in the building are lit up, try to shoot while the lights are on, in order mask the muzzle flash of your rifle. You must hide the muzzle of your rifle when firing so that its flash is does not show as you shoot and give away your position. It is useful to create false targets for the enemy in order to exhaust him, disperse his focus, and undermine his trust in his intelligence.

When *mujahidin* are encircled and attempts are made to flush them out to then liquidate them, the *mujahidin* under such circumstances must break out of the encirclement into which they have fallen by attacking at a single point to create a breakthrough. Or, they must scatter into several groups and then exfiltrate in different directions, taking care to concentrate their attack against the enemy's weakest points in order to create breaches. It is important during the attack and the penetration of the forces surrounding the *mujahidin* that firing be intense and include the launching of grenades and the use of antitank weapons. If these two methods fail, the *mujahidin* should try to blend in with the people so that they can exfiltrate from the area. The use of maneuver and movement in open areas and in populated areas is discussed above (may God grant guidance to the right path).

NOTES TO PART 2

1. "Al-Battar," which means the sharp sword, was the nom-de-guerre of Shaykh Yusuf Al-'Ayyiri, founder and leader of Al-Qa'ida in Saudi Arabia until his death at the hands of Saudi security in 2003. *Mu'askar Al-Battar* is the military journal of Al-Qa'ida in Saudi Arabia, and appeared twice a month on the Internet from December 2003 to October 2004.

2. According to Islamic tradition, those who die as martyrs are assured seventy-two virgins in paradise, as well as the right to intercede for others' sins. In popular culture today, the families of "martyrs" killed in battle or in suicide bombings normally organize a posthumous wedding ceremony to celebrate the joining of their relative to the *hur* in paradise. For all cultural matters related to the Islamic world, the standard reference work is Bernard Lewis, Charles Pellat, and Joseph Schacht, eds., *The Encyclopaedia of Islam*, 2nd edition.

3. Abu Barza Al-Aslami was one of Muhammad's Companions and a source of many *hadith*. Abu 'Isa Muhammad Al-Tirmidhi (209/824-279/892) was the compiler of one of the leading collections of *hadith*, the *Sahih*. A *hadith* is a narration about Muhammad's life (although this is sometimes also extended to his Companions), reporting what he said or did, and documented by a source and chain of transmission. The *hadith* were compiled in a number of authoritative collections and have served as a source of guidance and doctrine. The *Sunnah* is similar, but more specifically a set of practices reputedly established by Muhammad during his life. The *Sunnah* and the *Qur'an* are two of the principal sources of Islamic law, or *shari'a*.

4. The *Ummah* is a community or nation and, specifically, the Muslim community.

5. John Garang, former Sudanese army officer and academic, led a two decades-long rebellion in the largely Christian and animist South, which sought independence from the Muslim and Arab-dominated Northern government. He was killed in an airplane crash in August 2005, shortly after having been appointed Vice President in a new Sudanese Government of National Unity as part of an agreement ending the war. See Gray Phombeah, "Obituary: John Garang," *BBC News*

(August 3, 2005). Retrieved from http://news.bbc.co.uk/2/hi/africa/2134220.stm.

6. Yahya Al-Mashadd, an Egyptian-born nuclear scientist working on the French-Iraqi nuclear program, was found dead in a Paris hotel in 1980, with suspicion for the crime directed largely at the Mossad, Israel's intelligence service. See Victor Ostrovsky and Claire Hoy, *By Way of Deception*, 23.

7. Khattab refers to Samir bin Salih Al-Suwaylim, a Saudi-born *mujahid* commander with experience in Afghanistan and Tajikistan before he became active in Chechnya in 1995, where he was the commander of the foreign *mujahidin* until his death in 2002. His biography can be found in the series "Heroes of Islam in Our Day," *Mu'askar Al-Battar*, no. 14 (June–July 2004), 22–30.

8. *The Holy Qur'an* (Medina: King Fahd Holy Qur'an Printing Complex, 1410/1989–1990), IX, 32. All *Qur'an* quotes in English are taken from this edition.

9. Safar Al-Hawali was one of a group of radical clerics imprisoned by the Saudi government who, upon their release, apparently became more accommodating. In his case, he reportedly served later as a go-between for the government with militants wishing to surrender. See International Crisis Group, *Saudi Arabian Backgrounder: Who Are the Islamists?* 16. Muhsin Al-'Awaji was also imprisoned on more than one occasion by the Saudi authorities for his religious-based opposition.

10. Prince Turki Al-Faisal, Saudi Arabia's long-time intelligence chief, became his country's ambassador to the UK in 2003 and, subsequently, to the United States from 2005 to early 2007.

11. Muhammad Najibullah was installed by the Soviets as Afghanistan's president in 1987, remaining in that position until the *mujahidin* overthrew his regime in 1992. When the Taliban took Kabul in 1996, they hanged Najibullah. Actually, it was his predecessor, Babrak Karmal, who had requested Soviet help in 1979, resulting in the Soviet invasion of that year.

12. The reference here is to the agreement signed in January 2005 in Nairobi between the Sudanese People's Liberation Movement and the Sudanese government, ending the two-decades-long civil war.

13. *Hadith* originated by 'Abd Al-Rahman Al-Dawsi (Abu Hurayrah), one of Muhammad's Companions, and reported by Abu Al-Husayn Muslim (210/816–261/873), a noted compiler of *hadith* in his *Sahih*.

14. *Qur'an* IV, 140.

15. The explosion at Al-'Ulya refers to the bomb attack against the Saudi Arabian National Guard training center in Riyadh. "Al Sallul" is a highly derogatory term used by Islamists for the Saudi royal family, the house of Al Sa'ud. The term is derived from 'Abd Allah bin Ubayy bin Sallul Al-'Awfi, considered in Islamic tradition to have been a leading slanderer of Muhammad.

16. *Hadith* from Muhammad, reported in Muslim's *Sahih*.

17. *Qur'an* VIII, 60.

18. *Qur'an* V, 54.
19. *Qur'an* II, 44.
20. The PK is a Soviet-made 7.62mm machine gun.
21. The text has the English "overalls" written phonetically in Arabic, but that is probably intended to mean "track suit."
22. Point number 3 is missing in the text.
23. The image is that of an organizational pattern similar to a rosary or set of "worry beads," with elements linked only to the ones adjacent to them, but all eventually linked together by the head-piece, representing the letter "A" of "Allah," where the two strands of the rosary are joined.
24. There is apparently some missing text in the original.
25. 'Uthman ibn 'Affan was an early supporter of Muhammad, who provided financial support to the latter, including equipping Muhammad's "Army of Hardship" (*'Usra*) for its first battle, the Battle of Badr. 'Uthman eventually became the third Caliph to succeed Muhammad after the latter's death.
26. The reference is to the car bomb set off at a Saudi Arabian National Guard facility on November 13, 1995. The alleged perpetrators were executed in May 1996. The foreign victims included American advisers, apparently working for a U.S. contractor, the Vinnell Corporation, one of whose facilities, as noted in the text, was targeted again in May 2003. See "Explosions Rock Western Enclaves in Saudi Capital," *New York Times (*May 13, 2003), A1.
27. The reference is to a suicide car bombing on November 9, 2003 of Al-Muhayya compound in Riyadh, housing foreign workers. See Robin Wright, "Car Bomb Explodes At Saudi Complex; Deadly Blast Injures Dozens At Riyadh Housing Compound," *Washington Post* (November 9, 2003), A1.
28. In December 2002, a local gunman killed three American missionaries and wounded a fourth working at a Baptist missionary hospital in Jibla, Yemen. See Neil MacFarquhar, "Threats and Responses: Terror; 3 U.S. Citizens Slain in Yemen in Rifle Attack," *New York Times* (December 31, 2002), A1.
29. Rabbi Meir Kahane was an American-Israeli political activist known for his extremist views on Arabs and Muslims, who called for a "Greater Israel," including the deportation of the Palestinians. Kahane was assassinated in New York City in 1990, with Egyptian immigrant Sayyid Nusayr convicted of the crime. See John T. McQuiston, "Kahane Is Killed after Giving Talk in New York Hotel, *New York Times* (November 6, 1990), A1, and Ronald Sullivan, "Judge Gives Maximum Term in Kahane Case," *New York Times* (January 30, 1992), A1.
30. This incident appears to refer to the attack on October 6, 2002 against the French oil tanker *Limburg* in Yemeni waters. See Karl Vick, "Boat Pieces Found on Damaged Tanker; Debris Is Seen as Evidence of Attack," *Washington Post* (October 11, 2002), A30.

31. *Qur'an* XVI, 126. Significantly, the author does not complete the verse, which urges patience: "But if ye show patience, that is indeed the best (course) for those who are patient."

32. Originally a name for the crypto-Manicheans in the early centuries of the Islamic state, *zindiq* later became a general term for atheists and heretics. Considered to have abandoned the *Ummah*, those proven to be *zindiq* are guilty of an offense punishable by death.

33. *Qur'an* VIII, 60.

34. *Qur'an* XVI, 126.

35. The text erroneously has "After" instead of the correct "Before."

36. *Qur'an* III, 200.

37. *Tafhit*, or "drifting," is the practice of driving at high speeds and then suddenly applying the brakes to cause a controlled skid, and is a dangerous activity popular with thrill-seeking Saudi youth. It has achieved something of a cult status, with its own websites and posted videos, and has become the subject of recent government crackdowns, Raid Qusti, "Riyadh Cracking Down on 'Drifting Shababs,'" *Arab News* (May 2, 2007).

38. Abu Al-Rafi' Ibn Abu Al-Huqayq was a chief of the Jewish tribes in the Khaybar region after their banishment from Medina. According to tradition, Muhammad had him assassinated because the latter had written satirical poetry at his expense.

39. Ka'b bin al-Ashraf, was a Medinan Jew who supported Muhammad's enemies, the Meccans, and wrote satirical poetry critical of Muhammad, calling the latter's prophetic mission into question.

40. According to tradition, Muhammad sent 'Abd Allah bin Unays to kill Khalid Al-Hudhali upon reports the latter was gathering forces to attack Madina. As part of the mission, Muhammad gave 'Abd Allah bin Unays permission to tell lies, and to commit an act of deception in order to get close to the target. Abu Da'ud Sulayman ibn Ash'ath Al-Azadi Al-Sijistani (817/202–888/275) was a noted compiler of *hadith*, as in his compendium, the *Sunan*.

41. Farag Foda was an Egyptian secularist human rights activist and journalist who wrote extensively criticizing Islamist extremists. The Islamic establishment in Egypt declared him an apostate, and a local terrorist group, Al-Gama'a Al-Islamiya, assassinated him on June 8, 1992. See Raymond William Baker, *Islam without Fear: Egypt and the New Islamists*, 5–10, 190–191; and Milton Viorst, *In the Shadow of the Prophet: The Struggle for the Soul of Islam*, "The Murder of Farag Foda," 31–77.

42. Both phrases say the same thing using synonyms.

43. *Qur'an* VIII, 60.

44. Nizar Al-Halabi was a *shaykh* who headed the Association of Islamic Philanthropic Projects, a Syrian-sponsored Lebanese political and welfare organiza-

tion of the heterodox Ahbash sect, which combines Sunni and Shi'a beliefs and opposes extremist Islamic movements. In August 1995, Islamic radicals assassinated Al-Halabi. See Daniel Nassif, "Al-Ahbash," *Middle East Intelligence Bulletin*, vol. 3, no. 4 (April 2001). Retrieved from http://www.meib.org/articles/0104_ld1.htm.

45. Mohamed Boudiaf was a significant figure in Algeria's War of Independence. Absent from Algeria for almost thirty years in exile as a result of political rivalries, he was able to return home in 1992 to become Algeria's president, but was assassinated in June 1992 in the city of Annaba.

46. Points number 1 and 2 are missing in the text.

47. It is not clear to which operation the author is referring here, that is whether the code name is garbled or whether the reference is to some internal operation. In any case, the reference to the Croatians here is assuredly to the Bosnian Croats who set up their own para-state of Herceg-Bosna during the Bosnian War and who, apparently, clashed in this instance with the international *mujahidin* fighting on the Bosnian government's side.

48. A typographical error in the text has "Al-Lat," the pre-Islamic goddess of Mecca, instead of "Allah," the Arabic word for God in "Hizballah."

49. The largely government-owned SABIC (Saudi Arabian Basic Industries Corporation) is a diversified conglomerate engaged in chemicals, fertilizers, and metals, and has its headquarters in Riyadh. On November 13, 1995, an explosion in the parking lot killed six, four of whom were Americans. The Imam Muhammad Bin Sa'ud Islamic University, with over twenty thousand students, is the country's largest religious institution of higher learning.

SELECTED BIBLIOGRAPHY

BOOKS AND ARTICLES

Aboul-Enein, Youssef H., and Sherifa Zuhur. *Islamic Rulings on Warfare*. Carlisle Barracks, PA: Strategic Studies Institute, 2004.

Abukhalil, As'ad. *The Battle for Saudi Arabia: Royalty, Fundamentalism, and Global Power*. New York: Seven Stories, 2004.

'Anazi, 'Abd Al-'Aziz bin Rashid Al-. *Hukm istihdaf al-masalih al-naftiya* [Judgment on the Targeting of Oil Assets]. n.p.: Markaz al-dirasat wa-l-buhuth al-islamiya, [2005].

'Atiyat Allah, Luways. "Al-Fitna" [Discord]. In *Al-Kathir yas'al hal al-mujahidun fi Jazirat Al-'Arab qad akmalu tajhizathum wa-a'addu al-'udda?* [*Many Ask Whether the Mujahidin in the Arabian Peninsula Completed Their Preparations and Prepared Their Arms*], in the series *Tasa'ulat wa-shubuhat hawl al-mujahidin wa-'amaliyathim* [*Second-guessing and Specious Arguments Surrounding the Mujahidin and Their Operations*]. http://qa3edoon.com/KotobWaBayanatWEB/Shobohat—11.htm.

Azadi, Abu Jandal Al-. [Faris Bin Ahmad Al Shuwayl Al-Zahrani], *Al-Bahith 'an hukm qatl afrad wa-dhubbat al-mabahith* [The Researcher and the Judgment on the Killing of Mabahith Personnel and Officers]. www.qa3edoon.com.

Baker, Raymond William. *Islam without Fear: Egypt and the New Islamists*. Cambridge, MA: Harvard University Press, 2003.

Bar, Shmuel. *Jihad Ideology in Light of Contemporary Fatwas*. "Research Monographs on the Muslim World," 1, Paper no. 1. Washington, DC: Hudson Institute, 2006.

Bill, James A., and Robert Springborg. *Politics and the Middle East*, 5th edition. New York: Longman, 2000.

Bin Laden, Usama. "Al-Risala ila al-muslimin fi Bilad Al-Haramayn khassatan wa-ila al-muslimin fi ghayrha 'ammatan" [Letter to the Muslims in the Land of the Two Shrines in Particular and to Muslims Elsewhere in General]. December 15, 2004. www.paldf.net/forum/showthread.php?t=23632.

Brachman, Jarret M., and William F. McCants. CTC Report, *Stealing Al-Qa'ida's Playbook*. West Point, NY: Combating Terrorism Center, 2006.

Bradley, John R. "Al Qaeda and the House of Saud: Eternal Enemies or Secret Bedfellows?" *The Washington Quarterly* 28, no. 4 (Fall 2005): 139–152.

———. *Saudi Arabia Exposed: Inside a Kingdom in Crisis*. New York: Palgrave MacMillan, 2005.

Callwell, C. E. *Small Wars: Their Principles and Practice*, 3rd edition. Lincoln: University of Nebraska Press, 1996.

Clausewitz, Carl von. *On War*. Edited and Translated by Michael Howard and Peter Paret. Princeton, NJ: Princeton University Press, 1989.

Copulos, Milton. Testimony before the House Resources Subcommittee on Energy and Mineral Resources. *The Economic Impacts of Import Dependence on Mineral and Energy Commodities*. 108th Cong., 2nd sess., March 4, 2004. www.nma.org/pdf/cong_test/copulos_030404.pdf.

Corbin, Jane. *Al-Qaeda: The Terror Network That Threatens the World*. New York: Thunder's Mouth Press, 2002.

Cordesman, Anthony H. *Saudi Arabia Enters the 21st Century: Main Report*. Washington, DC: Center for Strategic and International Studies, 2002.

———. *Saudi Arabia Enters the 21st Century: Military and Internal Security Issues, IX, Saudi Paramilitary and Internal Security Forces*. Washington, DC: Center for Strategic and International Studies, 2002. http://www.csis.org/media/csis/pubs/s21_01.pdf.

———. *Saudi Counter Terrorism Efforts: The Changing Paramilitary and Domestic Security Apparatus*. Washington, DC: Center for Strategic and International Studies, 2005.

Cordesman, Anthony H., and Nawaf Obaid. "Al-Qaeda in Saudi Arabia: Asymmetric Threats and Islamic Extremists." Working draft. Washington, DC: Center for Strategic and International Studies, 2005.

Department of State, Office of the Coordinator for Counterterrorism. *Country Reports on Terrorism 2005*. Washington, DC: U.S. Department of State, 2006.

Doran, Michael Scott. "The Saudi Paradox." *Foreign Affairs* 83, no. 1 (January–February 2004): 35–51.

Echeverria, Antulio J., II. *Fourth-Generation War and Other Myths*. Carlisle Barracks, PA: Strategic Studies Institute, 2005.

Esposito, John L. *Unholy War: Terror in the Name of Islam*. New York: Oxford University Press, 2002.

Fandy, Mamoun. *Saudi Arabia and the Politics of Dissent*. New York: Palgrave Macmillan, 2001.

Gerges, Fawaz A. *Journey of the Jihadist: Inside Muslim Militancy*. Orlando, FL: Harcourt, 2006.

Gunaratna, Rohan. *Inside Al Qaeda: Global Network of Terror*. New York: Columbia University Press, 2002.

Hashim, Ahmed S. *Insurgency and Counter-insurgency in Iraq*. Ithaca, NY: Cornell University Press, 2006.

———. "The World According to Usama Bin Laden." *Naval War College Review* (Fall 2001): 11–35.

Henzel, Christopher. "The Origins of al Qaeda's Ideology: Implications for U.S. Strategy." *Parameters* (Spring 2005): 69–80.

Hilsman, Roger. "Guerrilla Warfare." *Military Review* (March 1993): 51–60.

Hoffman, Bruce. *Inside Terrorism*. New York: Columbia University Press, 1998.

Hofheinz, Roy, Jr. "The Autumn Harvest Insurrection." *The China Quarterly*, no. 32 (October–December 1967): 37–87.

Holy Qur'an, The. Medina: King Fahd Holy Qur'an Printing Complex, 1410/1989–1990.

Hutchinson, Martha Crenshaw. "The Concept of Revolutionary Terrorism." *Journal of Conflict Resolution* 16, no. 3 (September 1972): 383–396.

International Crisis Group. *Saudi Arabia Backgrounder: Who Are the Islamists?* ICG Middle East Report No. 31. Amman: ICG, September 2004.

Johnson, Chalmers. "The Third Generation of Guerrilla Warfare." *Asian Survey* 8, no. 6 (June 1968): 435–447.

Johnson, James Turner. *The Holy War Idea in Western and Islamic Traditions*. University Park: Pennsylvania State University Press, 1997.

Johnson, Jennie L. "Exploiting Weakness in the Far Enemy Ideology." *Strategic Insights* 4, no. 6 (June 2005). www.ccc.nps.navy.mil/si/archiveDate.asp#vol4issue6.

Johnson, Wray R. "War, Culture, and the Interpretation of History: The Vietnam War Reconsidered." *Small Wars and Insurgencies* 9, no. 2 (Fall 1998): 83–113.

Jones, Toby. "Seeking a Social Contract for Saudi Arabia." *Middle East Report*, no. 228 (Fall 2003): 42–48.

Katzenbach, E. L., Jr., "Time, Space, and Will: The Political-Military Views of Mao Tse-tung." Originally published in *Marine Corps Gazette*, January 1962. Reprinted in U.S. Marine Corps, *The Guerrilla and How to Fight Him*, FMFRP 12–25. Washington, DC: Headquarters United States Marine Corps, 1990: 11–21.

Kechichian, Joseph A. "The Role of the Ulama in the Politics of an Islamic State: The Case of Saudi Arabia." *International Journal of Middle East Studies* 18, no. 1 (February 1986): 53–71.

Kepel, Gilles. *The War for Muslim Minds: Islam and the West*. Cambridge: Belknap Press, 2004.

Lewis, Bernard, Charles Pellat, and Joseph Schacht, eds. *The Encyclopaedia of Islam*, 2nd edition. London: Brill, Luzac, 2005.

Liang, Qiao, and Wang Biangsui. *Unrestricted Warfare*. Translated by the Foreign Broadcast Information Service. Beijing: PLA Literature and Arts Publishing House, 1999. http://www.terrorism.com/documents/TRC-Analysis/unrestricted.pdf.

Lind, William S., John F. Schmitt, and Gary I. Wilson. "Fourth Generation Warfare: Another Look." *Marine Corps Gazette* (December 1994): 34–37.

Lind, William S., Keith Nightengale, John F. Schmitt, Joseph W. Sutton, and G. I.

Wilson. "The Changing Face of War into the Fourth Generation." *Military Review* (October 1989): 2–11.

Lippman, Thomas W. *Inside the Mirage: America's Fragile Partnership with Saudi Arabia*. Boulder, CO: Westview Press, 2004.

Lowther, Adam. "Asymmetric Warfare and Military Thought." *London Security Policy Study* 3. London: Glen Segell, 2006.

Mao Tse-tung. *Mao Tse-tung on Guerrilla Warfare*. Translated by Samuel B. Griffith, 1961. Reprinted as U.S. Marine Corps FMFRP 12–18. Washington, DC: Headquarters USMC, 1989.

McCants, William, ed. *Militant Ideology Atlas*. West Point, NY: Combating Terrorism Center, 2006.

McDermott, Terry. *Perfect Soldiers: The Hijackers: Who They Were, Why They Did It*. New York: HarperCollins, 2005.

Muqrin, 'Abd Al-'Aziz Al-. "Bayan li-l-umma" [Communique to the Ummah]. N.d., printed text from the video entitled *Ayyuha Al-Amrikan* [Oh, You Americans!]. www.qa3edoon.com/KotobWaBayanatWEB/BayanLelOmah.htm.

———. "Risala ila man tarak al-silah" [Letter to Those who Have Abandoned the Fight]. Undated audio tape transcribed by the *Sawt al-jihad* staff. www.qa3edoon .com/KotobWaBayanatWEB/ElaMnTrkAlsela7.htm.

"Mustaqbal al-'amal al-'askari fi Jazirat Al-'Arab" [The Future of Military Activity in the Arabian Peninsula]. Posted on the Mubashir Jihadi Forum (January 2007). http://mobasher.110.com/vb/showthread.php?t=251.

Nasa'ih wa-tawjihat 'askariya li-l-mujahidin fi Ardh Al-Rafidayn [Advice and Instructions to the Mujahidin in Mesopotamia]. N.p.: Markaz al-dirasat wa-l-buhuth al-islamiya, 1424/March 2003–February 2004.

Nasiri, Omar. *Inside the Jihad: My Life With Al Qaeda: A Spy's Story*. New York: Basic Books, 2006.

Nevo, Joseph. "Religion and National Identity in Saudi Arabia." *Middle Eastern Studies* 34 (July 1998): 34–53.

Obaid, Nawaf E. "The Power of Saudi Arabia's Islamic Leaders." *Middle East Quarterly* (September 1999). www.meforum.org/article/482.

Obaid, Nawaf E., and Anthony H. Cordesman. *Saudi Militants in Iraq: Assessment and Kingdom's Response*. Washington, DC: Center for Strategic and International Studies, 2005.

Odom, William E. "Soviet Military Doctrine." *Foreign Affairs* 67 (Winter 1998–1999): 114–133.

O'Neill, Bard E. *Insurgency and Terrorism*, 2nd edition. Washington, DC: Potomac Books, 2005.

Ostrovsky, Victor, and Claire Hoy. *By Way of Deception*. New York: St Martin's Press, 1990.

Palmer, Monte, and Princess Palmer. *At the Heart of Terror: Islam, Jihadists, and*

America's War on Terrorism. Lanham, MD: Rowman & Littlefield, 2004.

Peters, Rudolph. *Jihad in Classical and Modern Islam*. Princeton, NJ: Markus Wiener, 1996.

Pike, Douglas. *PAVN: People's Army of Vietnam*. Novato, CA: Presidio Press, 1986.

Pomeroy, William J. *Guerrilla Warfare and Marxism*. New York: International Publishers, 1968.

Poole, H. John. *Tactics of the Crescent Moon: Militant Muslim Combat Methods*. Emerald Isle, NC: Posterity Press, 2004.

Post, Jerrold M. "Killing in the Name of God: Osama Bin Laden and Al Qaeda." In *Know Thy Enemy; Profiles of Adversary Leaders and Their Strategic Cultures*. Edited by Barry R. Schneider and Jerrold M. Post. Maxwell Air Force Base: USAF Counterproliferation Center, July 2003: 17–39.

Qaeda Training Manual, Al. www.usdoj.gov.ag/trainingmanual.htm.

Rasheed, Madawi Al-. *Contesting the Saudi State: Islamic Voices from a New Generation*. Cambridge: Cambridge University Press, 2006.

Richards, Alan. *Socio-economic Roots of Radicalism? Towards Explaining the Appeal of Islamic Radicals*. Carlisle Barracks, PA: Strategic Studies Institute, 2003.

Roy, Olivier. *Globalized Islam: The Search for a New Ummah*. New York: Columbia University Press, 2004.

Royal Embassy of Saudi Arabia, Information Office. *Initiatives and Actions Taken by the Government of Saudi Arabia to Combat Terrorism*. Washington, DC: Royal Embassy of Saudi Arabia, 2006. http://www.saudiembassy.net/ReportLink/KSA%20WOT%20Report%20Dec06.pdf.

Sageman, Marc. *Understanding Terrorist Networks*. Philadelphia: University of Pennsylvania Press, 2004.

Schanzer, Jonathan. *Al-Qaeda's Armies: Middle East Affiliate Groups and the Next Generation of Terror*. Washington, DC: Washington Institute for Near East Policy, 2005.

Scott, William F., and Harriet Fast Scott. *Soviet Military Doctrine: Continuity, Formulation, and Dissemination*. Boulder, CO: Westview Press, 1988.

Shavit, Uriya. "Islamist Ideology: Al-Qaeda's Saudi Origins." *Middle East Quarterly* (Fall 2006): 3–13.

Shultz, Richard H., Jr., and Andrea J. Dew. *Insurgents, Terrorists, and Militias: The Warriors of Contemporary Combat*. New York: Columbia University Press, 2006.

Shy, John, and Thomas W. Collier. "Revolutionary War." In *Makers of Modern Strategy: From Machiavelli to the Nuclear Age*. Edited by Peter Paret. Princeton, NJ: Princeton University Press, 1986: 815–862.

Simon, Steven. "The New Terrorism: Securing the Nation against a Messianic Foe." *Brookings Review* 21 (Winter 2003): 18–26.

Strange, Joe. *Centers of Gravity and Critical Vulnerabilities*. Quantico, VA: Command and Staff College Foundation, 1996.

Streusand, Douglas. "What Does Jihad Mean?" *Middle East Quarterly* (September 1997). www.meforum.org/pf.php?id=357.

Sun Tzu. *The Art of War*. Translated by Samuel B. Griffith. Oxford: Oxford University Press, 1971.

Suskind, Ron. *The One Percent Doctrine: Deep Inside America's Pursuit of Its Enemies Since 9/11*. New York: Simon & Schuster, 2006.

Taber, Robert. *War of the Flea: The Classic Study of Guerrilla Warfare*. Washington, DC: Brassey's, 2002.

Teitelbaum, Joshua. "Terrorist Challenges to Saudi Arabian Internal Security." *Middle East Review of International Affairs* 9, no. 3 (September 2005): 1–11.

Tenet, George. *At the Center of the Storm: My Years at the CIA*. New York: HarperCollins, 2007.

Terrill, W. Andrew. *Regional Fears of Western Primacy and the Future of U.S. Middle Eastern Basing Policy*. Carlisle Barracks, PA: Strategic Studies Institute, 2006.

Trinquier, Roger. *Modern Warfare: A French View of Counterinsurgency*. Ft. Leavenworth, KS: U.S. Army Command and General Staff College, 1985.

Tyan, E [mile]. "Djihad." In *Encyclopaedia of Islam*, Vol. 2 (1965): 538–540

U.S. Marine Corps. *Small Wars Manual, 1940*. Washington, DC: Government Printing Office, 1940. Reprint: Washington, DC: Headquarters USMC, December 1990.

———. *A Tentative Manual for Countering Irregular Threats: An Updated Approach to Counterinsurgency*. Quantico, VA: Marine Corps Combat Development Command, 2006.

Vego, Milan. "On Doctrine." Unpublished draft, October 30, 2006.

———. "The Problem of Common Terminology." *Joint Forces Quarterly*, no. 43 (4th Quarter 2006): 44–49.

Villacres, Edward J., and Christopher Bassford. "Reclaiming the Clausewitzian Trinity." *Parameters* (Fall 1995): 9–19.

Viorst, Milton. *In the Shadow of the Prophet: The Struggle for the Soul of Islam*. Boulder, CO: Westview Press, 2001.

Ward, Blake D. *Osama's Wake: The Second Generation of Al Qaeda*. Maxwell Air Force Base, AL: Air University Press, 2005.

Wiktorowicz, Quintan. "The New Global Threat: Transnational Salafis and Jihad." *Middle East Policy* (December 2001): 18–38.

Zayyat, Montasser Al-. *The Road to Al-Qaeda: The Story of Bin Laden's Right-Hand Man*. Translated by Ahmed Fekry. London: Pluto Press, 2004.

Zuhur, Sherifa. *Saudi Arabia: Islamic Threat, Political Reform, and the Global War on Terror*. Carlisle Barracks, PA: Strategic Studies Institute, 2005.

MEDIA SOURCES

Al-'Arabiya TV, www.alarabiya.net (Abu Dhabi, United Arab Emirates)

Arab News, www.arabnews.com (Jeddah, Saudi Arabia)

Al-Haras al-watani, www.ngm.gov.sa (Riyadh, Saudi Arabia)

Al-Hayat, www.daralhayat.com (London)

Al-Jazira TV, www.aljazeera.net (Doha, Qatar)

Al-Jazira, www.al-jazirah.com (Jeddah, Saudi Arabia)

Al-Madina, www.almadinapress.com (Medina, Saudi Arabia)

Al-Quds, www.alquds.co.uk (London)

Al-Riyadh, www.alriyadh.com (Riyadh, Saudi Arabia)

Al-Sharq Al-Awsat, www.asharqalawsat.com

'Ukaz, www.okaz.com.sa (Jeddah, Saudi Arabia)

Al-Watan, www.alwatan.com.sa (Abha, Saudi Arabia)

Al-Wifaq, www.alwifaq.net (Saudi Arabia). This electronic newspaper was shut down by the Saudi government in March 2006.

Al-Yawm, www.alyaum.com.sa (Dammam, Saudi Arabia)

INDEX

ABOUT THE AUTHOR

Normal Cigar is a Research Fellow at the Marine Corps University, Quantico, Virginia. Before retiring, he taught at the Marine Corps Command and Staff College and the Marine Corps School of Advanced Warfighting. Previously, he was a senior political-military analyst in the Pentagon, where he was responsible for the Middle East in the Office of the Army's Deputy Chief of Staff for Intelligence, and supported the secretary of the army, U.S. Army chief of staff, and congressmen with intelligence. He also represented the Army on national-level intelligence issues with the interagency intelligence community. During the Gulf War, he was the Army's senior political-military intelligence staff officer on the Desert Shield/Desert Storm Task Force.

He is the author of numerous works on politics and security issues dealing with the Middle East and the Balkans, and has been a consultant at the International Criminal Tribunal for the former Yugoslavia at the Hague. He has also taught at the National Defense Intelligence College, was a visiting fellow at the Institute for Conflict Analysis and Resolution, George Mason University, and is a senior associate with the Public International Law and Policy Group. He is now focusing on the strategic and military aspects of radical Islamic movements and on proliferation issues.

Dr. Cigar holds a D.Phil. from Oxford (St Antony's College) in Middle East History and Arabic, an M.I.A. from the School of International and Public Affairs, Columbia University, and an M.S.S.I. from the National Defense Intelligence College. He has studied and traveled widely in the Middle East. He lives in the Washington, D.C., area.